# Qualitative Inquiry and the Politics of Advocacy

# INTERNATIONAL CONGRESS OF QUALITATIVE INQUIRY

The International Congress of Qualitative Inquiry has been hosted each May since 2005 by the International Center for Qualitative Inquiry at the University of Illinois, Urbana-Champaign. This volume, as well as five preceding volumes, are products of plenary sessions from these international congresses. All of these volumes are edited by Norman K. Denzin and Michael D. Giardina and are available from Left Coast Press, Inc.

**Qualitative Inquiry and the Politics of Advocacy**
2012, based on the 2011 Congress
ISBN 978-1-61132-162-3 hardcover 978-1-61132-163-0 paperback
**Qualitative Inquiry and Global Crises**
2011, based on the 2010 Congress
ISBN 978-1-61132-021-3 hardcover 978-1-61132-022-0 paperback
**Qualitative Inquiry and Human Rights**
2010, based on the 2009 Congress
ISBN 978-1-59874-537-5 hardcover, 978-1-59874-538-2 paperback
**Qualitative Inquiry and Social Justice**
2009, based on the 2008 Congress
ISBN 978-1-59874-422-4 hardcover, 978-1-59874-423-1 paperback
**Qualitative Inquiry and the Politics of Evidence**
2008, based on the 2007 Congress
ISBN 978-1-59874-321-0 hardcover, 978-1-59874-322-7 paperback
**Ethical Futures in Qualitative Research**
2007, based on the 2006 Congress
ISBN 978-1-59874-140-7 hardcover, 978-1-59874-141-4 paperback
**Qualitative Inquiry and the Conservative Challenge**
2006, based on the 2005 Congress
ISBN 978-1-59874-045-5 hardcover, 978-1-59874-046-2 paperback

Another product of the Congress is the quarterly refereed journal of the Institute. INTERNATIONAL REVIEW OF QUALITATIVE RESEARCH is a peer-reviewed journal that encourages the use of critical, experimental, and traditional forms of qualitative inquiry in the interests of social justice. We seek works that are both academically sound and partisan and works that offer knowledge-based radical critiques of social settings and institutions while promoting human dignity, human rights, and just societies around the globe. Submissions to the journal are judged by the effective use of critical qualitative research methodologies and practices for understanding and advocacy in policy arenas, as well as clarity of writing and willingness to experiment with new and traditional forms of presentation. Linked to the annual Congress for Qualitative Inquiry, much of the journal's content will be drawn from presentations and themes developed from these international meetings. The journal is also published by Left Coast Press, Inc.

**INTERNATIONAL REVIEW OF QUALITATIVE RESEARCH**
Editor: Norman K. Denzin
Quarterly in May, August, November, February
ISSN 1940-8447
For more information on these publications, or to order, go to
www.LCoastPress.com

# Qualitative Inquiry and the Politics of Advocacy

Norman K. Denzin
Michael D. Giardina
Editors

Left
Coast
Press
Inc.

Walnut Creek, California

LEFT COAST PRESS, INC.
1630 North Main Street, #400
Walnut Creek, CA 94596
www.LCoastPress.com

ISBN 978-1-61132-162-3 hardback
ISBN 978-1-61132-163-0 paperback
ISBN 978-1-61132-164-7 institutional eBook
ISBN 978-1-61132-598-0 consumer eBook

Library of Congress Cataloging-in-Publication Data:

Qualitative inquiry and the politics of advocacy / Norman K. Denzin, Michael D. Giardina, editors.
    p. cm. — (International congress of qualitative inquiry ; v. 7)
Includes bibliographical references.
 ISBN 978-1-61132-162-3 (hardback : alk. paper) — ISBN 978-1-61132-163-0 (pbk. : alk. paper) — ISBN 978-1-61132-164-7 (institutional ebook) — ISBN 978-1-61132-598-0 (consumer ebook)
 1. Qualitative research. 2. Evidence. I. Denzin, Norman K., 1941- II. Giardina, Michael D., 1976-
H62.Q347 2012
001.4'2—dc23
                        2012007027

Printed in the United States of America

⊗™ The paper used in this publication meets the minimum requirements of American National Standard for Information Sciences—Permanence of Paper for Printed Library Materials, ANSI/NISO Z39.48–1992.

**green press**
INITIATIVE

Left Coast Press, Inc. is committed to preserving ancient forests and natural resources. We elected to print this title on 30% post consumer recycled paper, processed chlorine free. As a result, for this printing, we have saved:

7 Trees (40' tall and 6-8" diameter)
3 Million BTUs of Total Energy
630 Pounds of Greenhouse Gases
2,840 Gallons of Wastewater
180 Pounds of Solid Waste

Left Coast Press, Inc. made this paper choice because our printer, Thomson-Shore, Inc., is a member of Green Press Initiative, a nonprofit program dedicated to supporting authors, publishers, and suppliers in their efforts to reduce their use of fiber obtained from endangered forests.

For more information, visit www.greenpressinitiative.org

Environmental impact estimates were made using the Environmental Defense Paper Calculator. For more information visit: www.papercalculator.org.

# Contents

## Acknowledgments

We thank our publisher of all publishers, Mitch Allen, for his continued support and guidance throughout the years. We also thank Carole Bernard for expert copyediting, Hannah Jennings for superb production design, and Katie Flanagan for assistance in gathering the index. Many of the chapters contained in this book were presented as plenary or keynote addresses at the Seventh International Congress of Qualitative Inquiry, held at the University of Illinois, Urbana-Champaign, in May 2011. We thank the Institute of Communications Research, the College of Media, and the International Institute for Qualitative Inquiry for continued support of the congress as well as those campus units that contributed time, funds, and/or volunteers to the effort.

The congress, and by extension this book, would not have materialized without the tireless efforts of Katia Curbelo, Ted Faust, Bryce Henson, Melba Vélez, Li Xiong, Yiye Liu, Robin Price, Mary Blair, and James Salvo (the glue who continues to hold the whole thing together). For information on future congresses, please visit http://www.icqi.org.

Norman K. Denzin
Michael D. Giardina
December 2011

# Introduction

## Qualitative Inquiry and the Politics of Advocacy

### Norman K. Denzin and Michael D. Giardina

*With the advance of corporate and financial power, violence now comes in the form of corrupt legislation and a political ideology that strips government of its universal social protections; removes government oversight; builds on fear; decimates the power of unions; defunds public institutions; and expands the culture of cruelty, fraud and avarice through policies that perpetuate a crushing inequality.*

— Henry A. Giroux (2011, para. 7)

*In a world already moving in certain directions, where wealth and power are already distributed in certain ways, neutrality means accepting the way things are now. It is a world of clashing interests—war against peace, nationalism against internationalism, equality against greed, and democracy against elitism—and it seems to me both impossible and undesirable to be neutral in those conflicts.*

— Howard Zinn (1990, p. 7)

*Qualitative Inquiry and the Politics of Advocacy,* edited by Norman K. Denzin and Michael D. Giardina, 9–38. © 2012 Left Coast Press, Inc. All rights reserved.

*Advocacy and ethics require that the "I" of my personal responsibility ... be explicitly stated in order to address for me a fundamental question, "What do I do now?"*
—D. Soyini Madison (2012, p. 97)

## Proem

The December 26, 2011 issue of *Time* magazine said it all: Its famed "Person of the Year" cover featured not presidents, prime ministers, captains of industry, entrepreneurs, musicians, actors, or athletes—or even Steve Jobs.[1] Rather, it was "The Protester" who received top billing, underscored by a headline stating "From the Arab Spring to Athens, From Occupy Wall Street to Moscow." Indeed, it seemed as if every new month of 2011 brought with it another uprising, protest, walk-out, call to action, or flashpoint event unseen to this collective degree in years.

One might say the "Year in Protest" began a few weeks early, with Mohamed Bouazizi's December 18, 2010 self-immolation in Tunisia in protest of police corruption and ill-treatment. This singular act—brought about by the "stifling bureaucracy and an impenetrable and intimidating security apparatus" of Tunisia— would later be recorded as an act of martyrdom, with the *New York Times* going so far as to call him the "revolution's icon" (Fahim, 2011, para. 4). As Andrew Sullivan (2011) notes, it "was an act of civil disobedience that became the spark for the democratic wave in the place we never expected it: the Arab Middle East. He was one man, with no power but his own conviction" (para. 8). And what a spark it was, both in Tunisia and, later, throughout the region: The waves of largely peaceful protest throughout Tunisia resulted in its president, Zine el-Abidine Ben Ali (who had seized power through a bloodless coup in 1987), fleeing the country less than a month later.

From there, the seeds of revolution spread, most notably to Egypt, where hundreds of thousands (if not millions) of citizens took to the streets protesting a myriad of legal and political issues, including "torture, poverty, corruption, and unemployment" (*The Daily Star*, 2011, para. 3). Utilizing advances in social media (Twitter, Facebook, etc.) to aid in facilitating on-the-ground demonstrations, marches, rallies, labor strikes, and other forms of civil disobedience, the protesters made themselves heard as they demanded "the downfall of the regime of President Hosni Mubarak and his ministers," "the cessation of the Emergency Law," "freedom," "justice," "the formation of a new, non-military government with the interests of the Egyptian people at heart," and "the constructive administration of all of Egypt's resources" (see Madrigal, 2011).[2] Tahrir Square in Cairo became a particular focal point of the protesters, with upward of 250,000 people occupying it throughout the early days of the pro-democracy demonstrations; this public spectacle helped draw global media attention that cemented the struggle as the whole world looked on.

Libya, too, experienced a similar popular uprising, which exploded into civil war and ultimately involved international military intervention; in the end, its ruler of forty-one years, Muammar Gaddafi, was captured and killed by the National Liberation Army[3] after months of fighting throughout 2011. Moreover, countries such as Algeria, Jordan, Morocco, Sudan, and Lebanon experienced their own versions of uprising or revolt (to varying degrees of success and intensity).[4] Importantly, as the president of the American University in Cairo, Lisa Anderson (2011), wrote in *Foreign Affairs*:

> The patterns and demographics of protests varied widely. The demonstrations in Tunisia spiraled toward the capital from the neglected rural areas, finding common cause with a once powerful but much repressed labor movement. In Egypt, by contrast, urbane and cosmopolitan young people in the major cities organized the uprisings. Meanwhile, in Libya, ragtag bands of armed rebels in the eastern provinces ignited the protests, revealing the tribal and regional cleavages that have beset the country for decades. Although they shared a common call for personal dignity and responsive government, the revolutions across these three countries reflected divergent economic grievances and social dynamics—legacies of their diverse encounters with modern Europe and decades under unique regimes.

Which is to say, the voice of protest was not generated from a singular entity or formation, or even organized around similar principles; rather, it was contextually specific to the respective historical present of the countries in question.

Despite the powerful events of the Middle East, however, the story of "The Protester" does not end there. Rather, we can identify (at least) two additional coordinates of major protest—and resultant forms of advocacy therein—that moved to the forefront of the popular imagination in the last year: the assault on unions and public workers, especially those in education (see Giroux, this volume; Goodall, this volume; Stronach & Clarke, this volume); and the assault on economic justice and equality, which led to the Occupy Wall Street (OWS) protests and its various outgrowths across the United States and elsewhere. In each of these examples, to borrow from Dylan Thomas, the voices of opposition did not go gently into the good night.

Let's start with the assault on unions and public workers, which had been steadily gaining traction throughout the last decade but which burst forth with some widespread success following the 2010 midterm elections in the United States that resulted in the election of right-wing politicians such as Scott Walker (R-WI), Rick Scott (R-FL), and John Kasich (R-OH), among others. Most notable of this trio was Walker (a close ally of the free-market fundamentalist billionaire Koch brothers), who introduced a bill to "kill collective bargaining rights for public-sector workers" in Wisconsin, one that was met with widespread outrage among state employees and generated a firestorm of debate across the nation (see Kroll, 2011, para. 2). Importantly for us, as *The Nation*'s Chris Hayes (2011) forcefully states, those impacted most directly by Walker's bill would be teachers[5] (and, by extension, the imperatives of civic education):

> Teachers unions are the stewards of preserving public education, which is the core element of our civic life, of the collective democratic enterprise that is these United States. Conservatives have wanted to abolish public education in its current form for a while, and getting rid of the teachers unions is a necessary first step. (TV broadcast)

In their neoliberal vision of education, critical discourse and the free exchange of ideas stands as impediments to the dictates of the market. Or, as Jason Del Gandio (2010) explains:

> While most colleges are still nonprofit institutions, their primary function is to serve the neoliberal enterprise. This happens in at least three ways—by targeting student-consumers, channeling students into corporate careers and contributing to rather than reducing social stratifications. (para. 8)

Such dictates were effectively endorsed by the National Governor's Association, whose Center for Best Practices suggested that "colleges need to do a better job of aligning their programs with the economic needs of their states" by moving "beyond their traditional emphasis on a broad liberal-arts education to thinking more about skills for specific jobs" through the use of "'rigorous labor-market data' to set goals and get more input from local businesses on the skills students need" (*The Chronicle of Higher Education*, 2011, para. 1). Which is to say, as Ryan King-White, Joshua I. Newman, and Michael D. Giardina (2011) argue in their essay on the money politics of body knowledge,

> *knowledge is treated like a commodity* generated for the purpose of capital accumulation; students are marketed to and socially-engaged as "consumers"; pedagogues are managed to be more productive (and less expensive) laborers (whose labor is increasingly de-skilled, rationalized, and made more efficient); and the institutional spaces themselves have become more commercialized and spectacularized. (p. 12; emphasis in the original)

This growing institutional acceptance of what Giroux (2007) and others have condemned as the rise of the "corporate university" (see also Johnson, 2008; Rutherford, 2005; Shumar, 1997) has not gone unnoticed. From movements such as Occupy Cal[6] in California, to the tireless efforts of unions such as the Graduate Employees' Organization (GEO) at the University of Illinois, to the recent Southern Illinois University-Carbondale faculty strike over collective bargaining agreement talks (not to mention major student protests throughout England during late 2010 against draconian budget cuts in the educational system [see Davis et al.,

2010]), students and faculty alike have increasingly stood up to show that the status quo is untenable and must be changed.

University administrators have, to varying degrees, come forward to speak out against the austere plans of Walker, Scott, and others, as when Arizona State University President Michael M. Crow (2011) wrote in response to Gov. Scott's call for reductions in state appropriations for specific disciplines (i.e., the humanities) so that public universities in his state (Florida) could focus resources on science, technology, engineering, and math fields:

> The notion that we must strip away academic programs not seemingly relevant to workforce development reflects a simplistic and retrograde view of the role of higher education in the American economy. ... Curricula expressly tailored in response to the demands of the workforce must be balanced with opportunities for students to develop their capacity for critical thinking, analytical reasoning, creativity, and leadership—all of which we learn from the full spectrum of disciplines associated with a liberal arts education. (para. 2–4).

At the same time, Naomi Klein (2011) points us to the further economic modalities of the attack on public sector employees: The issue at hand is not a matter of unions versus taxpayers, as Govs. Walker, Scott, Kasich, and their acolytes would have it; rather, it serves as a proxy "fight about who is going to pay for the [economic] crisis created by the wealthiest elite in this country. ... Is it going to be regular working people? Or is it going to be the people who created this crisis?" (TV broadcast).

This notion directly links us to OWS, which dominated headlines throughout the last quarter of the year. Encouraged by such armatures as *Adbusters* (a Canadian-based not-for-profit, anti-consumerist magazine), the Internet group Anonymous, and ordinary citizens through social media organization conducted via Facebook, Twitter, and YouTube, the inaugural protest occupied Zuccotti Park in New York City beginning September 17, 2011. Embracing the peaceful principles of nonviolence that guided Martin Luther King, Jr.,[7] the gathered mass of humanity was not simply a pampered bunch of disorganized, upper-class, white, anti-American hippie-socialists (as many in the mainstream media would uncritically have it [see Boykin, 2011]), but a representative sample of everyday Americans standing up to be heard on matters of social and economic inequality (including rising unemployment, corporate greed, and political corruption).[8] Notably, as Michael Hardt and Antonio Negri (2011) point out:

> The political face of the Occupy Wall Street protests comes into view when we situate it alongside the other "encampments" of the past year. Together, they form an emerging cycle of struggles. In many cases, the lines of influence are explicit. Occupy Wall Street takes inspiration from the encampments of central squares in Spain, which began on May 15 and followed the occupation of Cairo's Tahrir Square earlier last spring. (para. 5)[9]

Predictably, the OWS movement became a focal point of (largely) incoherent (corporate) media coverage and uninformed debate, not to mention a regular talking point for many of the candidates vying for the Republican presidential nomination. The usual propaganda from Fox News was readily apparent: For example, *Hannity* show contributor Kimberly Guilfoyle referred to OWS as "Woodstock meets Burning Man meets people with absolutely no purpose" (on a segment titled "Lunatics of the Left," no less); reporter Jesse Watters characterized it by saying "I think if you put every single left-wing cause into a blender and hit power, this is the sludge you'd get"; business news anchor Charles Gasparino intoned that "they are some of the most uninformed people if you listen to them. ... I think the only thing [they are] affecting is traffic"; and everyone's favorite demagogue on the Right, Ann Coulter, noted that such protest is "always the beginning of totalitarianism" (see Hartmann, 2011). Yet, it should come as no surprise to us that almost *every other traditional media outlet*—from CNN to NBC—also characterized OWS in a similar—if not necessarily so unhinged—manner throughout the latter portion of 2011.

Elected politicians fared no better in their misguided, condescending, and/or patronizing view of OWS: To give but a random sample, Rep. Peter King (R-NY) referred to those participating in OWS as "anarchists" who "have no sense of purpose other than a basically anti-American tone and anti-capitalist—it's a ragtag mob, basically" (quoted in Amato, 2011); New York City mayor, billionaire Michael Bloomberg, accused OWS protesters of trying to "take jobs away from people working in [New York]," while likewise maintaining that the protests "[weren't] productive," and were bad for tourism (*Reuters*, 2011); Republican presidential hopeful Newt Gingrich stated that protesters should, "Go get a job right after you take your bath" (quoted in Oremus, 2011), while another, Rick Santorum,[10] criticized the idea of redistribution of wealth by playing the race card when he stated, "I don't want to make black people's lives better by giving them somebody else's money" (quoted in Madison, 2012); and 2008 GOP vice-presidential candidate, Sarah Palin, bizarrely compared OWS to billionaires wanting a bailout (see Nelson, 2011).

Despite such rhetoric, public polling data suggests that the views of OWS are squarely in the mainstream, recording quite favorable levels of support. In October 2011, for example, a CBS News/*New York Times* poll found that 46% of Americans agreed that OWS "represents the views of most Americans" (as compared to 34% who said it did not); the same poll found that 66% of respondents were in favor of money and wealth being more fairly distributed (compared with 26% who did not) (Montopoll, 2011). Two months later, in December 2011, public support for OWS registered at similar levels: a Pew Research Center (2011) poll found that 44% of respondents supported the movement, compared with 35% opposed and 22% "other/don't know"; 48% of respondents agreed with "concerns the protesters raised." This should not (necessarily) surprise us. According to a 2011 report by the Organization for Economic Cooperation and Development (OECD), income inequality in the United States is rising, and is now "greater than in all developed countries other than Chile, Mexico, and Turkey" (*The Los Angeles Times*, 2011). Or, to put the U.S. case into more stark relief, consider that the "top 1%" of U.S. citizens have seen their income gains rise 277% since 1979, while the "middle 60%" has seen a parallel rise of only 38%, and the "bottom 20%" a rise of only 18% (Sherman & Stone, 2010).

Such inequality is compounded by the decided lack of economic mobility in the United States relative to Canada and much of Western Europe. This is in stark contrast to the mythical yet still widely believed view of the United States as a beacon of class mobility based simply on hard work and rugged individualism rather than on education, class privilege, and so forth (see, e.g., DeParle, 2012; Fletcher, 2011; Jäntii et al., 2006).

At the same time, and while it can be said that an economic conservatism (or, at least, an economic imperative) is woven throughout the public discourse of the above examples, we should not lose sight of the various regressive cultural politics that lie beneath the surface—and that are deeply stitched into the fabric of such struggle. In the United States, the last few years have seen a dramatic public resurgence of the so-called culture wars that have been ongoing since at least the 1960s.[11] Put differently, the open hostility and disdain held by those on the Right for public workers, teachers, union members, and those protesting economic injustice from New York to Berkeley extends beyond the economic into and through debates over gay rights, abortion, racial politics, science, and religion: *They are two sides of the same coin* (see, e.g., Newman & Giardina, 2011; Skocpol & Williamson, 2011).

Perhaps nowhere was this made clearer over the last year than in the race for the Republican presidential nomination. As Frank Bruni (2011), Peter Beaumont (2012), Steve Benen (2012), and a host of others explain, the leading contenders were individuals who: Trumpeted the endorsement of a pastor who has endorsed executing homosexuals (Ron Paul); pledged to send military predator drones to the U.S.-Mexico border so as to keep out "every last illegal immigrant" (Rick Perry); stated he was a "Jesus candidate" (his words) who wanted to ban same-sex marriage, overturn *Roe v. Wade*, and gut the 10th Amendment because it is incompatible with moral law (Rick Santorum); and apparently believe there is no right to privacy (Mitt Romney).[2] And these were the *leading* contenders! At the same time, we've had to contend with shootings at abortion clinics, the racial denigration of President Obama, local school boards rewriting curricular requirements so as to oppose the teaching of evolution and sex education, and an upswing in nationalist ideological positioning, among other things.

From where is this hateful agenda coming? One might argue that the increased volatility, if not outright absurdity of such candidate positions, was the result of significant *gains* made throughout the last several years against such regressive agendas. Here we can point to policy advances made by the Obama administration that repealed "Don't Ask, Don't Tell," which had banned gay, lesbian, and bisexual persons from openly serving in the military, and the decision to stop defending the Defense of Marriage Act (DOMA) in court; state-level advances that led to the legalization of same-sex marriage in Connecticut, Iowa, California, Massachusetts, New York, and Vermont as well as growing acceptance toward such an eventuality in other states; and, perhaps most importantly, the growing collective majority of under-thirty-year-old Americans who are in favor of affirmative action, gay rights, racial and ethnic diversity, and the right of women to choose their own reproductive health care.[13] Thus, and while we may be in the midst of a "long revolution," to borrow from Raymond Williams (1961), the cracks and fissures are becoming ever more readily apparent. And although the public face of such protests is not always marches in the streets or occupations of state capitols, or rewarded with quick and definitive change, "those who stand up for justice are always on the right side of history" (Obama, quoted in Ackerman, 2009, para.6).[14]

•  •  •

Together and in isolation, the major developments discussed above reveal the transformative power of protest, "that the struggle for justice should never be abandoned because of the apparent overwhelming power of those who have the guns and the money and who seem invincible in their determination to hold on to it" (Zinn, 1997, p. 642). At every turn, change was brought about by getting one's hands dirty, by inserting oneself into the material conditions and realities of the historical present. Translated to the scholarly arena, it is not enough to simply endeavor to *understand* any given reality. There is a need to *transform* it, to *advance the cause of social protest, action, and change*. Educators, as transformative intellectuals, must actively participate in this project. *This volume is one step in this direction.*

## Acts of Activism ↔ Politics of Possibility: On Advocacy and Pedagogy[15]

Book after book has expertly chronicled the rise of right-wing ideologies, neoliberal economics, technologies of surveillance, the politics of culture undermining democratic institutions, and so forth (see, e.g., Alterman, 2004, 2009; Alterman & Greem, 2004; Bageant, 2007; Dean, 2007; Frank, 2005, 2008; Goldberg, 2007, 2009; Hedges, 2008; Isikoff & Corn, 2007; Kaplan, 2005; Klein, 2008; Palast, 2007; Phillips, 2007, 2008; Rich, 2007; Ricks, 2006; Suskind, 2007, 2008). They line our respective bookshelves, contribute significantly to unraveling the "Great Moving Right Show" (see Hall, 1979) of the historical present, and give us counsel that we aren't alone in seeing our way through the tumultuousness of the last decade.

Yet, lost in these pages is a way to move *forward*, to imagine our way to a place that "is not yet" (see Weems, 2002). To such an end, and over the course of our previous seven volumes on qualitative inquiry and interpretive research,[16] one of the chief aims has been the advocacy of a *new performative cultural politics*, a radical democratic imagination that redefines the concept of civic participation and public citizenship (especially within the academy). Such a critical imagination is pedagogical and interventionist, requiring a commitment to a progressive democratic politics, an ethics and aesthetics of performance (Pollock, 1998) that moves from critical theory to the radical pedagogical formulations of Paulo Freire (1998, 1999 [1992], 2011) and those who have reformulated and reinvented his work (see, e.g., Darder, 2002; Fischman & McLaren, 2005; Giroux, 2001, 2003, 2004; Giroux & Giroux, 2005; Kincheloe & McLaren, 2005). Building on Freire (1998, p. 91) and James Carey (1997a, p. 115), this imagination dialogically inserts itself into the world, provoking conflict, curiosity, criticism, and reflection, and contributes to a public conversation—a dialogue that puts the very notions of democracy and freedom, citizen and patriot, into play (Carey, 1997b, pp. 208, 216).

Within the above, the performative and the political intersect on the terrain of a praxis-based ethic. This is the space of

Critical Pedagogical Theatre, which draws its inspirations from Augusto Boal's major works: *Theatre of the Oppressed* (1979 [1974]), *The Rainbow of Desire* (1995), and *Legislative Theatre* (1998). This ethic performs pedagogies that resist oppression. It enacts a politics of possibility (Madison, 1998) grounded in performative practices that embody love, hope, care, and compassion. Viewed as struggles and interventions, performances and performance events become gendered transgressive achievements, political accomplishments that break through "sedimented meanings and normative traditions" (Conquergood, 1998, p. 32).[17]

As an *interventionist* project, then, the critical imagination is hopeful of change, *but is not blind to the contours of history standing in its way* (see Dimitriadis, 2011). It seeks and promotes an ideology of hope that challenges and confronts hopelessness (Freire, 1999 [1992], p. 8). It understands that hope, like freedom, is "an ontological need" (Freire, 1999 [1992], p. 8). Hope is the desire to dream, the desire to change, the desire to improve human existence. Hopelessness is "but hope that has lost its bearings" (Freire, 1999 [1992], p. 8).

Hope is ethical.

Hope is moral.

Hope is peaceful and nonviolent.

Hope seeks the truth of life's sufferings.

Hope gives meaning to the struggles to change the world.

Hope is grounded in concrete performative practices, in struggles and interventions that espouse the sacred values of love, care, community, trust, and well-being (Freire, 1999 [1992], p. 9).

Hope, as a form of pedagogy, confronts and interrogates cynicism, the belief that change is not possible or is too costly.

Hope works from rage to love (see Bratich, 2011).

Hope articulates a progressive politics that rejects "conservative, neoliberal postmodernity" (Freire, 1999 [1992], p. 10).

Hope rejects terrorism.

Hope rejects the claim that peace comes at any cost.

Furthermore, this critical imagination is *pedagogical* in at least four ways. First, as a form of instruction, it helps persons think critically, historically, and sociologically. Second, as critical pedagogy, it exposes the pedagogies of oppression that produce and reproduce oppression and injustice (see Freire, 2001, p. 54). Third, it contributes to an ethical self-consciousness that is critical and reflexive, giving people a language and a set of pedagogical practices that endeavors to turn oppression into freedom, despair into hope, hatred into love, doubt into trust. Fourth, in turn, this self-consciousness shapes a critical racial self-awareness that contributes to utopian dreams of racial equality and racial justice.

Enacted as *radical democratic pedagogy* (see Denzin, 2009), citizens and citizen-scholars alike must be committed to taking risks, to taking sides, to be willing to act in situations where the outcome cannot be guaranteed in advance. They are anchored in a specific community of progressive moral discourse. The moral researcher-as-performer takes sides, working always on the side of those who seek a genuine grassroots democracy (Hartnett, 1998, p. 288). This business of taking sides is a complex process (Becker, 1967), involving the following steps: Researchers must make their own positions clear, including the so-called facts and ideological assumptions that they attach to these positions. Scholars must identify and analyze the values and claims to objective knowledge that organize positions that are contrary to their own. In so doing, they will show how these appeals to ideology and objective knowledge reflect a particular moral and historical standpoint, revealing how this standpoint disadvantages, and disempowers, members of a specific group.[18] Let us not forget, as the radical historian Howard Zinn (1997) reminds us, "We find that so much of what is called "intellectual history is the aimless dredging up of what is and was, *rather than a creative recollection of experience pointed toward the betterment of human life*" (p. 622, emphasis added). For as Karl Marx once wrote, "The philosophers have only interpreted the world in various ways; the point however is to *change* it."

Clearly, this view challenges the idea of positivist social science currently practiced and taught throughout much of the corporate university curriculum. In his essay "The Uses of Scholarship," Zinn (1997, pp. 502–507) notes the following five rules "that sustain the wasting of knowledge":

1. carry on "disinterested scholarship"
2. be objective
3. stick to your discipline

4. to be "scientific" requires neutrality
5. a scholar must, in order to be "rational," avoid "emotionalism"

With Zinn, we reject this narrow view of the scholarly profession, or what Edward Said (1996) has called "intellectual professionalism"; that is, the organization of a scholarly life in which an academic does not rock the boat, does not stray outside the "accepted paradigms or limits," explicitly works to make oneself marketable, and above all else makes oneself "uncontroversial and unpolitical and 'objective'" (p. 55). Framing Said's point for the present tense, Michael L. Silk, Anthony Bush, and David L. Andrews (2010) contend: "*Proper* professional academic behavior—and in our present moment we have to equate *proper* with that which holds the centre, the *gold standard*, EBR [Evidence-Based Research]—represents a threat to our *critical sense*, our ability to be prepared to be self-reflexive to relations of power" (p. 120)." And it cannot be allowed to stand. As academics, we have a moral and professional obligation to speak the truth, to expose lies, and see events in their historical perspective (see Chomsky, 1967).

## The Chapters

*Qualitative Inquiry and the Politics of Advocacy* is comprised of three sections: Theory, Method, and Politics. Robert E. Stake and Luisa-Maria Rosu ("Energizing and Constraining Advocacy") begin our volume by outlining various theoretical and philosophical dynamics of advocacy, arguing that "advocacy within research is rooted in the origins of qualitative inquiry and the emergence of new forms of qualitative inquiry," including critical theory and autoethnography. Specifically, they discuss advocacy within research, intermittent advocacy, values rationality, researcher responsibility, multiperspectivalism, and the middle ground between encouraging advocacy and constraining it so as to remain true to ethical commitments of the research endeavor. Importantly, they ask us to remember that while advocacy will at times enhance inquiry, there are many times it will, in fact, interfere with the research act.

In their chapter "Back to the Educational Future, Again: A 'Double-Dip' in the Long Recession," Ian Stronach and John

Clarke tackle head-on the economic imperatives and implications of the so-called credit crunch for the knowledge economy. Building on their previous work (see, e.g., Stronach & Clarke, 2010), they address four particular contentions: (1) that "scientific capitalism" in the West and "scientific socialism" in the East became hegemonic ways of thinking about all sorts of social knowledge; (2) that blame for such an economic collapse has been successfully deflected from its economic and capitalist origins to more palatable bogey-men in the public sector and the "national memory"; (3) that the capitalist crisis, far from undermining its simulacrum, the "knowledge economy," will intensify the drive toward making education serve capitalism; and (4) that the current crises of both the economy and the role within it of knowledge insist on new analyses of possibility, which include the renaissance of forms of qualitative inquiry, from the anthropology and history of the global to the kinds of educational processes and outcomes that count for a post-global education. Stronach and Clarke conclude by imploring us that "Education cannot go on mimicking a failure-prone capitalism by way of whatever 'knowledge economy.'"

Mirka Koro-Ljungberg and Tim Barko's chapter ("'Answers,' Assemblages, and Qualitative Research") follows, serving as a companion piece to Stronach and Clarke. Writing against what they call "corporative science," Koro-Ljungberg and Barko interrogate "simplicity" and "technical professionalism" in the pursuit of "truth." In so doing, they put forth the idea of "answers as assemblages"; that is, "an anti-structural concept that permits the researcher to speak of emergence, heterogeneity, the decentered and the ephemeral in nonetheless ordered social life." They expand on this notion through a considered discussion of the "jar assemblage," drawing on theorists such as Gilles Deleuze, Jacques Derrida, and Friedrich Nietzsche to explicate their point. They conclude with the radical assertion that by "staying confused and uncertain we may be able to get to know ourselves better and make our lives and education more meaningful."

John H. Stanfield II's chapter ("Turning the Next Wide 21st Century Corner: Holistic Restorative Justice as Science in Qualitative Inquiry") concludes Section I and focuses on the theme of holistic restorative justice, or the "process of authenticity and transparency to get to the bottom of the horrible en-masse episode or institutionalized system and to reestablish accountability human beings have to each other in institution, community, or society." Drawing on examples ranging in scope from the South African Truth and Reconciliation Commission to desegregation in the United States, and especially to the 2008 presidential election campaign of Barack Obama and what he calls the "Obama Phenomenon," Stanfield argues that qualitative inquiry should turn "to our humanity and that of those we research and walk out and live out together in unity as we tackle quality-of-life problems that cannot be addressed through the mandates of 19th- and 20th-century research protocols requiring sciences—which fail to heal—and restore the researcher and the researched as a gesture of rehumanization of all of us."

Section II focuses attention on methodological concerns, especially related to multi- or mixed-method research. Kathy Charmaz ("Mixing or Adding Methods? An Exploration and Critique") opens the section, addressing three interrelated questions. (1) What are mixed methods? (2) Where do the discussions of mixed methods take us? (3) How do varied qualitative analytic approaches shape the research process and product? Additionally, and informed by constructivist grounded theory, Charmaz reflects on a demonstration project in which she and four psychologists analyzed the same data and draws out "potentials and problems in assessing mixed methods research."

Nigel Fielding's chapter ("Pulling Together: Postmodernism and Multiple Methods") argues that there is common ground between the contemporary practice of mixed methods research and the theoretical position of postmodernism. To this end, he elaborates on several different forms of postmodernism and iterations of mixed method analysis, suggesting, contrary to simplistic views of each, that "neither postmodernism nor mixed methods are as inflexible as their critics claim."

The section concludes with Uwe Flick's chapter ("Vulnerability and the Politics of Advocacy: Challenges for Qualitative Inquiry Using Multiple Methods"), which discusses triangulation within the context of research on/with vulnerable populations. Utilizing examples drawn from research on unemployment as a collective experience, sleeping disorders in nursing homes, and chronic illness in the context of homelessness, Flick illustrates how particular methods were selected for different projects. At the same time, he asserts that we need to move beyond the often-cited view of triangulation as simply a "combination of methods" that seek confirmation of findings to one of integrated social research that "allow setting up mosaics of research issues."

Section III opens with Michal Krumer-Nevo's chapter ("Writing against Othering"), which examines the differences between "battling Othering and enhancing it" within the research act of a social change agenda, one that is a decidedly political activity. Building on Michael Pickering's (2001) understanding of Othering as the translation of difference to inferiority, Krumer-Nevo delves into the oppressive power of Othering and its implication in structures of inequality. From there, she provides examples from her own research with immigrant Kavkazi[19] groups in Israel and explains how such groups contend with harsh stereotypes. She concludes by discussing ways of resisting Othering through partnership, interpretation, and writing.

Susan Finley's chapter ("Ecoaesthetics: Critical Arts-Based Research and Environmental Advocacy") continues the focus on politically grounded and activist minded scholarship. In it, she outlines a programmatic implementation of what she calls an "ecoaesthetic pedagogy," or the use of "arts-based research that is committed to democratic, ethical, and just problem solving to arrive at creative solutions to local ecological problems." To this end, Finley engages in an exploration of self-and-nature and self-and-others as it relates to community-based projects and the idea of "green art." At the same time, she unmasks the profitability of ecological destruction within globalization and points us toward developments in ecojustice.

Jean Halley's chapter ("The Production of Girl Life") shines as a lyrical exploration of gender, violence, and trauma and its normalizing effects on (her) childhood. At the same time, Halley examines the ways that (her) childhood experiences reflect "the larger normative culture as described by the radical feminist movement of the 1970s … which had brought the reality of gendered violence into mainstream consciousness." Weaving together personal vignettes with feminist theory, Halley brings us face to face with the stark violence of the world, while simultaneously allowing for a healing, recuperative way forward.

The section concludes with H. L. (Bud) Goodall, Jr.'s chapter ("'I Read the News Today, Oh Boy. ...' The War on Public Workers"), which serves as a stunning rebuke to the assault on public education in the United States (and elsewhere), especially in terms of funding, tenure, and the myth of the current professoriate as the "cultural elite." At the same time, Goodall challenges academics to quit "hiding behind the very traditions that are under attack" and remember that we are "working-class intellectuals" whose very existence is at stake.

The volume concludes with Henry Giroux's passionate Coda ("Why Faculty Should Join Occupy Movement Protesters on College Campuses"), which, in line with Goodall (this volume), challenges faculty to stand up and make "a choice about what kind of society we all want to live in, and how the urgency of that question at the current historical moment demands that academics take that question seriously and act as quickly as possible, with passion and conviction."

## Coda

It has become a kind of rallying call, in our previous work, to conclude by invoking the phrase, "We have a job to do. Let's get to it." We do so to reinforce our belief that we—those of us privileged to be in the academic professions—have a moral and professional obligation to our communities and ourselves to actively, consciously, and politically insert ourselves to debates such as those outlined in this Introduction and throughout the course of this volume. For, as Zinn (1994) once said, "You can't be neutral on a moving train."

*History is on the move; we should do all that we can to bend that arc toward a more perfect union.*

## Notes

1. *Time* names its "Person of the Year" on the basis of the person, group, idea, or object that, "for better or worse ... has done the most to influence the events of the year." In the last decade, honorees have included individuals such as U.S. Presidents Barack Obama (2008) and George W. Bush (2004), Facebook creator Mark Zuckerberg (2010), and U.S. Federal Reserve Chairman Ben Bernanke (2009), and groups such as "The American Soldier" (2003) and "Good Samaritans" (2005, represented by Bono, Bill Gates, and Melinda Gates).

2. Circulated primarily through emails and photocopies, the translated pamphlet from which Madrigal (2011) draws was titled "How to Protest Intelligently: Important Information and Tactics." It included not only the demands of the Egyptian people, but also sections titled "The Strategic Goals of Civil Disobedience" and "How to Publish and Disseminate This Information." For more, see news coverage by Siddique, Owen, and Gabbat (2011).

3. Libya's National Liberation Army is a military organization formed during the civil war by former military members and civilian volunteers.

4. This is but a simplistic snapshot of the Jasmine Revolution in Tunisia, the Egyptian Revolution, and the Libyan Civil War, though it will suffice for our purposes here. For more detailed ruminations, see Aswany (2011), Erdbrink and Sly (2011), Fahim (2011), Mackey (2011), Noueihed (2011), Osman (2011), Pollack (2011), and St. John (2011).

5. Walker's bill exempted public safety workers (i.e., police and firefighters).

6. An outgrowth/ally of Occupy Wall Street, Occupy Cal is an ongoing series of demonstrations that began on November 9, 2011, on the campus of the University of California, Berkeley, and has since grown to other campuses through the University of California system. The most public of these demonstrations resulted in the violent pepper-spraying of nonviolent student protesters by law enforcement officials at the University of California, Davis.

7. The six principles of Kingian nonviolence are: Nonviolence is a way of life for courageous people; the beloved community is the goal; attack forces of evil, not persons doing evil; accept suffering without retaliation for the sake of the cause to achieve the goal; avoid internal violence of the spirit as well as external physical violence; and the universe is on the side of justice (see Boykin, 2011).

8. Bill Maher (2011) captured it perfectly when he said of the OWS participants: "These people down there, they're not the counter culture, they're the culture" (n.p.).

9. Within the United States, adds Sonia K. Katyal and Eduardo M. Peñalver:

   A straight line runs from the 1930s sit-down strikes in Flint, Michigan, to the 1960 lunch-counter sit-ins to the occupation of Alcatraz by Native

American activists in 1969 to Occupy Wall Street. Occupations employ physical possession to communicate intense dissent, exhibited by a willingness to break the law and to suffer the—occasionally violent—consequences. (2011, para. 3)

10. Santorum won the Iowa caucus by a mere 34 votes over Romney. Clearly, his incendiary rhetoric resonates with a sizable segment of Republican voters as of this writing.

11. In this chapter, we will focus primarily on the context of the United States. For a look at the way in which cultural politics was embedded in the Arab Spring, see Creswell (2011) and Mehrez (2010, 2012).

12. This was taken up by Romney in a New Hampshire debate when asked about contraception, and by association, the 1956 ruling in Griswold v. Connecticut, which was later used as the foundation to the Roe ruling in 1973. At the time, Romney pleaded ignorance to the question, though it would be impossible for a Harvard Law School graduate, as Romney is, to not have understood the question. For more, see Benen (2012).

13. While change in these long-contested cultural arenas moves at a glacial pace, it is worth noting that change does remain afoot. To give but one example, sport, long-considered a closed space of hypermasculinity and heteronormativity, has witnessed a growing chorus of fans, athletes, and administrators speaking out in favor of gay rights. Popular athletes such as Steve Nash, Michael Strahan, Grant Hill, Ben Cohen, Hudson Taylor, Sean Avery, Brian Wilson, and Scott Fujita, in particular have been especially vocal, including filming public service announcements for the Human Rights Campaign or Dan Savage's "It Gets Better" project.

14. This was a phrase President Obama used in tangential support of the "Green Revolution" in Iran in 2009.

15. This section is drawn in part from Denzin (2009, pp. 379–380), Denzin and Giardina (2011, pp. 16–17), and Giardina and Denzin (2011, pp. 321–322).

16. See Denzin and Giardina, 2006a, 2006b, 2007, 2008, 2009, 2010, 2011.

17. A postcolonial, indigenous participatory theater is central to this discourse (Balme & Carstensen, 2001; Greenwood, 2001). Indigenous theater nurtures a transnational, yet historically specific, critical race (and class) consciousness. This theater incorporates traditional indigenous and nonindigenous cultural texts into frameworks that disrupt colonial models of race and class relations. This is a utopian theater that addresses issues of equity, healing, and social justice.

18. On the political politics of "taking sides," Arundhati Roy (2001) is worth quoting at length:

I take a position. I have a point of view. What's worse, I make it clear that I think it's right and moral to take that position and what's even worse, use everything in my power to flagrantly solicit support for that position. For a writer of the 21st century, that's considered a pretty uncool, unsophisticated thing to do. It skates uncomfortably close to the territory occupied by political party ideologues—a breed of people that the world has learned (quite rightly) to mistrust. I'm aware of this. I'm all for being circumspect. I'm all for discretion, prudence, tentativeness, subtlety, ambiguity, complexity. … I love the unanswered question, the unresolved story, the unclimbed mountain, the tender shard of an incomplete dream. Most of the time. But is it mandatory for a writer to be ambiguous about everything? Isn't it true that there have been fearful episodes in human history when prudence and discretion would have just been euphemisms for pusillanimity? When caution was actually cowardice? When sophistication was disguised decadence? When circumspection was really a kind of espousal? Isn't it true, or at least theoretically possible, that there are times in the life of a people or a nation when the political climate demands that we—even the most sophisticated of us—overtly take sides? I believe that such times are upon us. And I believe that in the coming years, intellectuals and artists will be called upon to take sides. […]

We will be forced to ask ourselves some very uncomfortable questions about our values and traditions, our vision for the future, our responsibilities as citizens, the legitimacy of our "democratic institutions," the role of the state, the police, the army, the judiciary and the intellectual community. (p. 12)

For more on taking sides within the academy, see Denzin and Giardina, 2011.

19. Kavkazi is the Hebrew word for Caucasus, the region in the southern former Soviet Union where the groups come from.

# References

Ackerman, S. (2009). Those who stand up for justice are always on the right side of history. *The Washington Independent*, June 23. http://washingtonindependent.com/48354/those-who-stand-up-for-justice-are-always-on-the-right-side-of-history (accessed January 8, 2012).

Alterman, E. (2004). *What liberal media? The truth about bias and the news*. New York: Basic Books.

Alterman, E. (2009). *Why we're liberals: A handbook for restoring America's most important ideals*. New York: Penguin.

Alterman, E., & Green, M. J. (2004). *The book on Bush: How George W. Bush (mis)leads America*. New York: Viking

Amato, J. (2011). Rep. Peter King attacks OWS: We must stop those ragtag mobs and anarchists. *Crook and Liars,* October 9. http://crooksandliars.com/taxonomy/term/23776 (accessed December 29, 2011).

Anderson, L. (2011). Demystifying the Arab spring: Parsing the differences between Tunisia, Egpyt, and Libya. *Foreign Affairs, 90,* 3. http://www.foreignaffairs.com/articles/67693/lisa-anderson/demystifying-the-arab-spring (accessed December 28, 2011).

Aswany, A. (2011). *On the state of Egypt: What made the revolution inevitable* (J. Wright, Trans.). New York: Vintage.

Bageant, J. (2007). *Deer hunting with Jesus: Dispatches from America's class war.* New York: Broadway.

Balme, C., & Carstensen, A. (2001). Home fires: Creating a Pacific theatre in the diaspora. *Theatre Research International, 26,* 1, 35–46

Beaumont, P. (2012). Rick Santorum: Bearer of the Christianist mantle. *The Guardian* (London), January 5. http://www.guardian.co.uk/commentisfree/belief/2012/jan/05/ricksantorum-christianist-mantle (accessed January 8, 2012).

Becker, H. (1967). Whose side are we on? *Social Problems, 14,* 3, 234–247.

Benen, S. (2012). It's about privacy, not contraception. *Washington Monthly,* January 8. http://www.washingtonmonthly.com/political-animal/2012_01/its_about_privacy_not_contrace034590.php (accessed January 8, 2012).

Boal, A. (1979). *Theatre of the oppressed.* New York: Urizen Books. (Originally published in Spanish in 1974.)

Boal, A. (1995). *The rainbow of desire: The Boal method of theatre and therapy.* London: Routledge.

Boal, A. (1998). *Legislative theatre.* London: Routledge.

Boykin, K. (2011). Everything the media told you about Occupy Wall Street is wrong. *The Huffington Post,* October 19. http://www.huffingtonpost.com/keith-boykin/occupy-wall-street-media_b_1019707.htm (accessed December 29, 2011).

Bratich, J. (2011). Pox populi: Network populism, network sovereigns, and experiments in power-powers. *Cultural Studies⇔Critical Methodologies, 11,* 4, 341–345.

Bruni, F. (2011). Iowa's harvest. *New York Times,* December 31. http://www.nytimes.com/2012/01/01/opinion/sunday/bruni-the-iowa-caucuses-bitter-harvest.html (accessed January 8, 2012).

Carey, J. (1997a). "Putting the world at peril": A conversation with James W. Carey. In E. Munson & C. Warren (Eds.), *James Carey: A critical reader* (pp. 95–116). Minneapolis: University of Minnesota Press.

Carey, J. (1997b). "A republic, if you can keep it": Liberty and public life in the age of Glasnost. In E. Munson & C. Warren (Eds.), *James Carey: A critical reader* (pp. 207–227). Minneapolis: University of Minnesota Press.

Chomsky, N. (1967). The responsibility of intellectuals. *The New York Review of Books*. http://www.nybooks.com/articles/archives/1967/feb/23/a-special-supplement-the-responsibility-of-intelle/ (accessed January 2, 2012).

*Chronicle of Higher Education, The.* (2011). Colleges should serve the job market, governors say (2011). March 23. http://chronicle.com/blogs/ticker/colleges-should-serve-the-job-market-governors-say/31530 (accessed December 20, 2011).

Conquergood, D. (1998). Beyond the text: Toward a performative cultural politics. In S. J. Dailey (Ed.), *The future of performance studies: Visions and revisions* (pp. 25–36). Annadale, VA: National Communication.

Creswell, R. (2011). Egypt: The cultural revolution. *New York Times*, February 4. http://www.nytimes.com/2011/02/20/books/review/Creswell-t.html (accessed December 30, 2011).

Crow, M. M. (2011). America needs broadly educated citizens, even anthropologists. *Slate*, October 21. http://www.slate.com/articles/news_and_politics/politics/2011/10/michael_m_crow_president_of_arizona_state_university_explains_wh.html (accessed December 20, 2011).

*Daily Star, The.* (2011). Egypt braces for nationwide protests. Bangladesh newspaper, January 26. http://www.thedailystar.net/newDesign/news-details.php?nid=171577 (accessed December 28, 2011).

Darder, A. (2002). *Reinventing Paulo Freire: A pedagogy of love.* Boulder, CO: Westview.

Davis, A., Cecil, N., Murphy, J., & Davenport, J. (2010). Thousands of students storm Tory HQ in protest at tuition fees rise. *Evening Standard* (London), November 10. http://www.thisislondon.co.uk/standard/article-23896267-thousands-join-london-march-in-protest-at-soaring-tuition-fees.do (accessed December 28, 2011).

Dean, J. (2007). *Conservatives without conscience.* New York: Penguin.

Del Gandio, J. (2010). Neoliberalism and the academic-industrial complex. *Truthout.* http://archive.truthout.org/neoliberalism-and-academic-industrial-complex62189 (accessed December 20, 2011).

Denzin, N. K. (2009). Critical pedagogy and democratic life, or, a radical democratic pedagogy. *Cultural Studies ⇔ Critical Methodologies, 9,* 3, 379–397.

Denzin, N. K., & Giardina, M. D. (2006a). Introduction: Cultural studies after 9/11/01. In N. K. Denzin and M. D. Giardina (Eds.), *Contesting empire/globalizing dissent: Cultural Studies after 9/11* (pp. 1–21). Boulder, CO: Paradigm.

Denzin, N. K, & Giardina, M. D. (Eds.). (2006b). *Qualitative inquiry and the conservative challenge: Confronting methodological fundamentalism.* Walnut Creek, CA: Left Coast Press, Inc.

Denzin, N K., & Giardina, M. D. (2007). Introduction: Ethical futures in qualitative research. In N. K. Denzin and M. D. Giardina (Eds.), *Ethical futures in qualitative research: Decolonizing the politics of knowledge* (pp. 9–44). Walnut Creek, CA: Left Coast Press, Inc.

Denzin, N. K., & Giardina, M. D. (2008). Introduction: The elephant in the living room, OR advancing the conversation about the politics of evidence. In N. K. Denzin and M. D. Giardina (Eds.), *Qualitative inquiry and the politics of evidence* (pp. 9–52). Walnut Creek, CA: Left Coast Press, Inc.

Denzin, N. K., & Giardina, M. D. (2009). Introduction: Qualitative inquiry and social justice: Toward a politics of hope. In N. K. Denzin and M. D. Giardina (Eds.), *Qualitative inquiry and social justice* (pp. 11–50). Walnut Creek, CA: Left Coast Press, Inc.

Denzin, N. K., & Giardina, M. D. (Eds.). (2010). *Qualitative inquiry and human rights.* Walnut Creek, CA: Left Coast Press, Inc.

Denzin, N. K., & Giardina, M. D. (Eds.). (2011). *Qualitative inquiry and global crises.* Walnut Creek, CA: Left Coast Press, Inc.

DeParle, J. (2012). Harder for Americans to rise from lower runs. *New York Times*, January 5. www.nytimes.com/2012/01/05/us/harder-for-americans-to-rise-from-lower-rungs.html (accessed January 5, 2012).

Dimitriadis, G. (2011). The political paranoid in contemporary politics. *Cultural Studies ⇔ Critical Methodologies, 11*, 4, 3901–3391.

Erdbrink, T., & Sly, L. (2011). In Libya, Moammar Gaddafi's rule crumbling as rebels enter heart of Tripoli. *The Washington Post*, August 21. http://www.washingtonpost.com/world/middle-east/libyan-rebels-converging-on-tripoli/2011/08/21/gIQAbF3RUJ_story.html (accessed December 28, 2011).

Fahim, K. (2011). Slap to man's pride set off tumult in Tunisia. *New York Times*, January 21. http://www.nytimes.com/2011/01/22/world/africa/22sidi.html (accessed December 27, 2011).

Fischman, G. E., & McLaren, P. (2005). Rethinking critical pedagogy and the Gramscian legacy: From organic to committed intellectuals. *Cultural Studies ⇔ Critical Methodologies, 5*, 4, 425–447.

Fletcher, M. A. (2011). Many in U.S. slip from middle class, study finds. *The Washington Post*, September 6. http://www.washingtonpost.com/business/economy/many-in-us-slip-from-middle-class-study-finds/2011/09/06/gIQA76ut7J_story.html (accessed December 30, 2011).

Frank, T. (2005). *What's the matter with Kansas? How conservatives won the heart of America.* New York: Holt.

Frank, T. (2008). *The wrecking crew: How conservatives rule.* New York: Metropolitan.

Freire, P. (1998). *Pedagogy of freedom: Ethics, democracy, and civic courage* (translated by P. Clarke, foreword by D. Macedo, introduction by S. Aronowitz). Boulder, CO: Roman & Littlefield.

Freire, P. (1999 [1992]). *Pedagogy of hope.* New York: Continuum.

Freire, P. (2001). *Pedagogy of the oppressed* (30th anniversary edition, with an introduction by Donaldo Macedo). New York: Continuum.

Giardina, M. D., & Denzin, N. K. (2011). Acts of activismóPolitics of possibility: Toward a new performative cultural politics. *Cultural Studies⇔Critical Methodologies, 11,* 4, 392–402.

Giroux, H. (2001). Cultural studies as performative politics. *Cultural Studies⇔Critical Methodologies, 1,* 1, 5–23.

Giroux, H. (2003). *The abandoned generation: Democracy beyond the culture of fear.* New York: Palgrave.

Giroux, H. (2004). *The terror of neoliberalism: Authoritarianism and the eclipse of democracy.* Boulder, CO: Paradigm Publishers.

Giroux, H. (2007). *The university in chains: Confronting the military–industrial complex.* Boulder, CO: Paradigm Press.

Giroux, H. (2011). Got class warfare? Occupy Wall Street now! *Truthout,* October 6. http://www.truth-out.org/got-class-warfare-occupy-wall-street-now/1317760461 (accessed December 5, 2011).

Giroux, H., & Giroux, S. S. (2005). Challenging neoliberalism's new world order: The promise of critical pedagogy. *Cultural Studies⇔Critical Methodologies, 6,* 1, 21–32.

Goldberg, M. (2007). *Kingdom coming: The rise of Christian nationalism.* New York: W. W. Norton & Co.

Goldberg, M. (2009). *The means of reproduction: Sex, power, and the future of the world.* New York: Penguin.

Greenwood, J. (2001). Within a third space. *Research in Drama Education, 6,* 2, 193–205.

Hall, S. (1979). The great moving right show. *Marxism Today,* January, pp. 14–20.

Hardt, M., & Negri, A. (2011). The fight for "real democracy" at the heart of the Occupy Wall Street: The encampment in Lower Manhattan speaks to a failure of representation. *Foreign Affairs*, October 11. http://www.foreignaffairs.com/articles/136399/michael-hardt-and-antonio-negri/the-fight-for-real-democracy-at-the-heart-of-occupy-wall-street (accessed December 29, 2011).

Hartmann, T. (2011). The big picture: How the 1% is reacting to the 99%. *The Thom Hartmann Show* (transcript), October 19. http://www.thomhartmann.com/blog/2011/11/transcript-thom-hartmann-big-picture-how-1-reacting-99-19-october-11 (accessed December 29, 2011).

Hartnett, S. J. (1998). "Democracy is difficult": Poetry, prison, and performative citizenship. In S. J. Dailey (Ed.), *The future of performance studies: Visions and revisions* (pp. 287–297). Washington, DC: National Communications Association.

Hayes, C. (Guest Host) (2011). *MSNBC Live at 6 p.m.* MSNBC, February 18. New York.

Hedges, C. (2008). *American fascists: The Christian right and the war on America.* New York: Free Press.

Isikoff, M. & Corn, D. (2007). *Hubris: The inside story of spin, scandal, and the selling of the Iraq War.* New York: Three Rivers Press.

Jäntii, M., Bratsberg, B., Røed, Raaum, O., Naylor, R., Österbacka, E., Björklund, A., & Ericksson, T. (2006). *American exceptionalism in a new light: A comparison of intergenerational earnings mobility in the Nordic countries, the United Kingdom, and the United States.* Bonn, Germany: Institute for the Study of Labor.

Johnson, R. (2008). Afterword: University challenge: Neoliberal abstraction and being more concrete. In J. E. Canaan & W. Shumar (Eds.), *Structure and agency in the neoliberal university* (pp. 278–298). New York: Routledge

Kaplan, E. (2005). *With God on their side: George W. Bush and the Christian Right.* New York: New Press.

Katyal, S. K., & Peñalver, E. M. (2011). Occupy's new tactic has a powerful past. *CNN*, December 16. http://edition.cnn.com/2011/12/16/opinion/katyal-penalver-occupy/index.html (accessed December 29, 2011).

Kincheloe, J. L., & McLaren, P. (2005). Rethinking critical theory and qualitative research. In N. K. Denzin & Y. S. Lincoln (Eds.), *Handbook of qualitative research*, 3rd ed. (pp. 303–342). Thousand Oaks, CA: Sage.

King-White, R., Newman, J. I., & Giardina, M. D. (2011). Articulating fatness: Obesity and the scientific tautologies of bodily accumulation in neoliberal times. Unpublished manuscript.

Klein, N. (2008). *The shock doctrine: The rise of disaster capitalism.* New York: Picador.

Klein, N. (2011). *Interview with Chris Hayes on MSNBC Live at 6 p.m.* MSNBC, February 18. New York.

Kroll, A. (2011). Wisconsin Gov. Scott Walker: Funded by the Koch Bros. *MotherJones*, February 18. http://motherjones.com/mojo/2011/02/wisconsin-scott-walker-koch-brothers (accessed December 29, 2011).

*Los Angeles Times, The.* (2011). OECD report cites increasing income inequality in U.S. December 5. http://latimesblogs.latimes.com/money_co/2011/12/income-inequality-rising-faster-in-us-than-other-developed-countries.html (accessed December 30, 2011).

Mackey, R. (2011). Video that set off Tunisia's uprising. *New York Times*, January 22. http://thelede.blogs.nytimes.com/2011/01/22/video-that-triggered-tunisias-uprising/ (accessed December 27, 2011).

Madrigal, A. (2011). Egyptian activists' action plan: Translated. *The Atlantic*, January 27. http://www.theatlantic.com/international/archive/2011/01/egyptian-activists-action-plan-translated/70388/ (accessed December 28, 2011).

Madison, D. S. (1998). Performance, personal narratives, and the politics of possibility. In S. J. Dailey (Ed.), *The future of performance studies: Visions and revisions* (pp. 276–286). Washington, DC: National Communication Association.

Madison, D. S. (2012). *Critical ethnography: Method, ethics, and performance* (2nd Ed. ). Thousand Oaks, CA: Sage.

Madison, L. (2012). Santorum targets Blacks in entitlement reform. *CBS News*, January 2. http://www.cbsnews.com/8301-503544_162-57350990-503544/santorum-targets-blacks-in-entitlement-reform/ (accessed January 3, 2012).

Maher, B. (2011). *Real Time with Bill Maher.* HBO, October 21. HBO Productions.

Mehrez, S. (2010). *Egypt's culture wars: Politics and practice.* Cairo: American University in Cairo Press.

Mehrez, S. (Ed.). (2012). *Translating Egypt's revolution: The language of Tahrir.* Cairo: The American University in Cairo Press.

Montopoll, B. (2011). Poll: 43 percent agree with the views of "Occupy Wall Street." *CBS News*, October 25. http://www.cbsnews.com/8301-503544_162-20125515-503544/poll-43-percent-agree-with-views-of-occupy-wall-street/ (accessed December 29, 2011).

Nelson, S. (2011). Palin opens up about "Occupy" movement, says Obama gives "the fat cats" their "cat nip." *The Daily Caller*, November 4. http://dailycaller.com/2011/11/04/palin-obama-the-antithesis-of-occupy-movement/ (accessed December 30, 2011).

Newman, J. I., & Giardina, M. D. (2011). *Sport, spectacle, and NASCAR nation: Consumption and the cultural politics of neoliberalism.* New York: PalgraveMacmillan.

Noueihed, L. (2011). Peddler's martyrdom launched Tunisia's revolution. *Reuters,* January 19. http://uk.reuters.com/article/2011/01/19/uk-tunisia-protests-bouazizi-idUKTRE70I7TV20110119 (accessed December 27, 2011).

Oremus, W. (2011). Gingrich to OWS: Take a bath, get a job. *Slate,* November 21. http://slatest.slate.com/posts/2011/11/21/newt_gingrich_to_occupy_wall_street_take_a_bath_get_a_job.html (accessed December 30, 2011).

Osman, T. (2011). *Egypt on the brink: From Nasser to Mubarek.* New Haven, CT: Yale University Press.

Palast, G. (2007). *Armed madhouse: From Baghdad to New Orleans—Sordid secrets and strange tales of a White House gone wild.* New York: Plume.

Pew Research Center. (2011). Frustration with Congress could hurt Republican incumbents. December 15. http://www.people-press.org/2011/12/15/frustration-with-congress-could-hurt-republican-incumbents/ (accessed December 29, 2011).

Phillips, K. (2007). *American theocracy: The peril and politics of radical religion, oil, and borrowed money in the 21ˢᵗ century.* New York: Penguin

Phillips, K. (2008). *Bad money: Reckless finance, failed politics, and the global crisis of American capitalism.* New York: Viking.

Pickering, M. (2001). *Stereotyping: The politics of representation.* London: PalgraveMacmillan.

Pollack, K. (Ed.). (2011). *The Arab awakening: America and the transformation of the Middle East.* Washington, DC: Brookings Institute Press.

Pollock, D. (1998). A response to Dwight Conquergood's essay: "Beyond the text: Towards a performative cultural politics." In S. J. Dailey (Ed.), *The future of performance studies: Visions and revisions* (pp. 37–46). Washington, DC: National Communication Association.

*Reuters.* (2011). New York's Bloomberg says protestors trying to destroy jobs. October 7. http://www.reuters.com/article/2011/10/08/us-usa-wallstreet-bloomberg-idUSTRE79704W20111008 (accessed December 29, 2011).

Rich, F. (2007). *The greatest story ever sold: The decline and fall of truth in Bush's America.* New York: Penguin.

Ricks, T. (2006). *Fiasco: The American military adventure in Iraq.* New York: Penguin.

Roy, A. (2001). *Power politics.* Cambridge, MA: South End Press.

Rutherford, J. (2005). Cultural studies in the corporate university. *Cultural Studies, 19,* 3, 297–317.

Said, E. (1996). *Representations of the intellectual.* New York: Pantheon.

Sherman, A., & Stone, C. (2010). Income gaps between very rich and everyone else more than tripled in last three decades, new data show. *Center on Budget and Policy Priorities.* http://www.cbpp.org/cms/?fa=view&id=3220 (accessed January 20, 2012).

Shumar, W. (1997). *College for sale: A critique of the commodification of higher education.* London: The Falmer Press.

Siddique, H., Owen, P., & Gabbatt, A. (2011). Protests in Egypt and unrest in Middle East—as it happened. *The Guardian* (UK), January 25. http://www.guardian.co.uk/global/blog/2011/jan/25/middleeast-tunisia#block-32 (accessed December 28, 2011).

Silk, M. L., Bush, A., & Andrews, D. L. (2010). Contingent intellectual amateurism, or, the problem with evidence-based research. *Journal of Sport & Social Issues, 34*, 1, 105–128.

Skocpol, T., & Williamson, V. (2011). *The Tea Party and the remaking of Republican conservatism.* New York: Oxford University Press.

St. John, R. B. (2011). *Libya: Continuity and change.* London: Routledge.

Stronach, I. & Clarke, J. 2010. Bring back *Das Kapital* punishment. The credit crunch and the fall of the knowledge economy. *Forum, 52*, 1, 119–123.

Sullivan, A. (2011). The ides of 2011. *The Daily Dish.* http://andrewsullivan.thedailybeast.com/2011/12/the-ides-of-2011.html (accessed January 2, 2012.

Suskind, R. (2007). *The one percent doctrine: Deep inside America's pursuit of its enemies since 9/11.* New York: Simon & Schuster.

Suskind, R. (2008). *The way of the world: A story of truth and hope in an age of extremism.* New York: Harper.

Weems, M. (2002). *I speak from the wound in my mouth: Public education and the imagination-intellect.* New York: Peter Lang.

Williams, R. (1961). *The long revolution.* London: Chatto and Windus.

Zinn, H. (1990). *Passionate declarations: Essays on war and justice.* New York: HarperPerennial.

Zinn, H. (1994). *You can't be neutral on a moving train: A personal history of our times.* Boston: Beacon Press.

Zinn, H. (1997). *The Zinn reader.* New York: Seven Stories Press.

# Section I
# Theory

**Chapter 1**

# Energizing and Constraining Advocacy

Robert E. Stake and Luisa-Maria Rosu

## Introduction

Across time, advocacy has pulled at opposite poles of legitimacy. Justifications have been argued, but the constant presence of advocacy cannot be ignored. Advocacy in research is found in various voices and for an assortment of uses. Common are the voices of collectivity, empathy, spirituality, reason, and justice. The venues extend from the kitchen table to the United Nations. The relevance of research to societal responsibility establishes opportunities for advocacy and research to stand together.

Contrasted with the rigor of dispassionate investigation, advocacy has been regularly associated with the effects of bias on the integrity of a study. Bias has been an unmistakable taboo (Scriven, 1997) for respectable research. Ironically, the beliefs and attachments for certain values penetrate data collection, choice of data sources, methods of data collection, fieldwork, and argumentation of findings. These are challenges for the ethical management of research.

*Qualitative Inquiry and the Politics of Advocacy,* edited by Norman K. Denzin and Michael D. Giardina, 39–58. © 2012 Left Coast Press, Inc. All rights reserved.

Researchers are trained to see and foresee the voids in their studies and argumentation and to recognize such attachments. Educated researchers and more experienced audiences know where to look for appropriate evidence to build a consistent and proper argument and make the values engagement less visible. This is true for both quantitative and qualitative researchers and stands at the very beginning of the study when the design takes shape as well as at the very end of the study when findings are assembled to make a good conclusion and argument.

Much of the time, researchers advocate common values and procedures. It is important to acknowledge the diversity as well as the commonality in thinking. Yet researchers have different ways of pursuing their advocacies, sometimes even contradicting those around them. Researchers' advocacies are not a constant pitch, but come intermittently. In its swings, advocacy spreads along a spectrum from more conservative to more liberal views. Researchers learn how and when to energize their advocacy and to push for needed constraints. Supporting good values does not lead to good advocacy, and good advocacy does not imply good values.

Advocacy within research is rooted in the origins of qualitative inquiry and the emergence of new forms of qualitative inquiry. Value-structured forms of qualitative methodology such as critical theory, auto-ethnography, and dialogic analysis exist because they uncover aspects of social reality not found by the more quantitative forms of inquiry (Denzin & Lincoln, 2000). The search for truth and the responsibility inherited with this search has been directed toward the pursuit of more complex representations of reality. Seeing great contrast between the pursuit of social justice and the conduct of objective research, qualitative researchers have set aside their disciplined reluctance to organize research along advocacy lines.

Still, it is simplistic to think of social justice as the legacy and the expertise of qualitative inquiry. Within each camp and within each individual researcher, there are struggles between caring and seeking clarity. To pose the question as a simple contrast is to dismiss the intricacy of qualitative research and the involvedness of advocacy. But values rationality is on the rise almost wherever researchers gather.

Values can be conceptualized as simple vectors, at the cost of ignoring situations, relationships, and syndromes, leading to single-minded perspectives in advocacy. The compounds of advocacy need to be checked for integrity and legitimacy, but especially as to their connection with social reality and in the ways this reality exists for the particular individual and for society in general. As researchers analyze their observations and seek better understanding of the phenomena—with participants being part of the audience—conflicts in terms of value are to be expected. Accepting that advocacy is part of doing research, that it is a needed part of qualitative inquiry, the question becomes one of constraining and encouraging, a matter of refining the quality of advocacy.

## Ethical Management of Research

The title of this chapter is misleading. It implies that there are ways of encouraging and constraining advocacy for the conduct of research as an enterprise. Essentially, there are not. But advocacy and constraint can be steered for the conduct of research by individuals and small groups of researchers. And the enterprise could be changed in the collective action of great numbers of individual researchers. But there are no mechanisms by which the research enterprise can centrally be manipulated.

What about using funding as a mechanism for steering advocacy? Can't the funders of research require or solicit more or less advocacy as a part of the grant? Funded research is provided mostly by governments. Governments fund topics that are aligned with their own advocacies, and applicants express alignment with their advocacies in their proposals. Substantively, research becomes aligned with funder values. But advocacy as a process within research remains the domain of the individual researchers; they show it voluptuously if it suits their purposes and they disguise it if it appears to compromise their inquiries.

In the United States, the most prominent funder of research is the National Science Foundation (NSF). In recent years, with its STEM (Science, Technology, Engineering, and Mathematics) programs, NSF has strongly supported a social and practical value: the increased inclusion of minorities and women in science, technology, engineering, and mathematics. Its encouragement for researchers themselves to be advocates for this position has only been indirect. NSF has maintained a position of following the ethics of the researchers, including their associations, in restraining or endorsing advocacy.

Individuals and their professional associations do take many ethical matters seriously. Many groups publish ethical standards for the conduct of research. Violation of the standards is seldom a simple matter, more often a trade-off between gaining something ethically important by inattention to another, trading off one standard against another. Thus, a constraint on advocacy could be a restraint on providing information to the public.

The largest effort to influence research ethics has been the federal government's requirement that institutions, particularly universities, create Institutional Review Boards (IRBs). According to Trochim (2006), the primary actions of these boards in minimizing risk to human subjects are obtaining voluntary participation, getting informed consent, avoiding risk of harm, guaranteeing participants confidentiality and anonymity, and providing participants a right to service. Management is assumed. The IRBs do not attempt to constrain or encourage advocacy.

The IRBs attempt to guide ethics by monitoring proposals. They depend on the conscience of researchers to recognize departure from intention and to request modification of plans. There are many problems with present practice (Denzin, 2000), but a more supervisory and legalistic approach would probably curtail legitimate research even more than it does now. When people see administrative guidelines formally expressed, there is a tendency to see them in legal and economic terms rather than in ethical terms. (An Israeli preschool attempted to reduce failure to pick up children on time by imposing a charge for late pick-up, instead increasing the parents' lateness—interpreted as parents perceiving the matter as economic rather than social cooperation) (Levitt & Dubner, 2005). IRBs might do better by advocating personal responsibility for risk to human subjects, but such teaching does not have a good track record. Control of advocacy, procedural or punitive, has no easy mechanism.

In research literature and course materials, management of ethics is assumed largely to be an individual researcher matter. The guidelines are for self-compliance. There are no inspectors, no courts, and no penalties. There are no guidelines for ethics that influence funders or social systems. In this chapter, we will not be able to provide suggestions for encouraging or constraining advocacy. Instead, we will discuss how researchers, implicitly or explicitly, exercise energizing and constraining advocacy in their qualitative inquiry.

## What Is Advocacy?

For human beings, advocacy is a default setting. We seek change for the better; we struggle to protect that what we have. Advocacy is a plea for what we want and see needed. Our actions convey our advocacies as much as words. We evolve, we survive, we exist, and we threaten our existence, partly because we are advocates.

The common meaning indicates a speaking out regularly for a condition more than for a commodity. We advocate inquiry and we advocate skepticism. We advocate immediate relief and we advocate for an enduring status. Advocacy rides on bias, pity, reason, love, and hate. We plead with ourselves to mend our ways.

The motivation for advocacy is seldom single minded. We plead a case, we argue our point of view, not only because we see it as worthy but because we anticipate our advocacy casting us in favorable light. We advocate being part of a company of advocates and we advocate being separate from those standing in the way.

For a while, advocacy can be depersonalized. An advocacy can be a movement, a referendum, a call for the change, or resistance to change. It can become larger than the sum of individual advocacies. It can be consuming so that little else is important, only that the battle be fought. Triumph is no satiation, although it changes the vision of the goal.

Advocacy seldom needs large clarification. Fellow travelers will have a different refinement, but welcome the joining of forces. Opponents may have sympathy for the essence, but see too much lost in granting the difference. Whether in court of law, in work, or in family life, the urge to gain ground outplays the urge to understand the contest. Advocacy may take the form of rational argument but is selective in the evidence put forth.

There is at least a patina of advocacy in all that we do. The advocacy-free life might be worth living, but so far remains not ventured.

## Advocacy within Research

Here we concern ourselves with the role of advocacy in social and educational research. Advocacy follows preference, but also affects preference. F. W. Boreham said in the early 20th century, "We make our decisions and then our decisions turn around and make us." We plead for what we value. In research we value understanding and explanation, but we also have preferences for particular outcomes of research, both substantively and for their reactive effects on us. We write the proposal in ways that hide our advocacy and we may be successful in suppressing it, but we cannot know the full effect of our biases.

The usual expectation is that we will reduce the influence of our biases by conducting our research as objectively as we can. Max Weber (1897) said,

> There is no absolutely "objective" scientific analysis of culture. … All knowledge of cultural reality … is always knowledge from particular points of view. … An "objective" analysis of cultural events, which proceeds according to the thesis that the ideal of science is the reduction of empirical reality to "laws," is meaningless … [because] … the knowledge of social laws is not knowledge of social reality but is rather one of the various aids used by our minds for attaining this end.

But Weber sustained the goal of objectivity, seeking objectivity through disciplined interpretation if not through methodological purity. In this way, Weber granted the deeper realization of meaning of social phenomena through relation to subjective experience.

Many researchers claim to make dispassionate searches for quality and dysfunction. Some speak disdainfully of advocacy and promotion. Yet it is clear that most researchers have strong feelings about certain matters that we promote in our work. Here are six advocacies common in research studies:

1. We care about the people being studied. Often they are engaged in care-giving work that we admire: counseling, teaching, nursing. Some studies are internal, studying a part of one's own organization. Occasionally, we have a conflict of interest; more often a *confluence* of interest. We hope to find the program working well. We may be disposed to see evidence of success more quickly than evidence of failure.

2. We care about disciplined inquiry. We want to see others care about it. We want to encourage them to do it. We promote research services, our own and those of our profession. We favor methods that probe well and encourage others to use them. It is an advocacy we flaunt.

3. We advocate rationality. We would like our clients and other stakeholders, our colleagues, and heads of department to explicate, to be logical and even-handed. We often pause in our data gathering or reporting to point out a way that the work we observe could have been more rational.

4. We care to be heard. We are troubled if our studies are not used. We may feel research is more useful if program participants take some ownership in it. Many of us, including ourselves (authors) are strong advocates of self-study and action research. External studies can profitably use value positions from participants—including suggestions for design and interpretation. Many of us, not including ourselves, strongly support participatory studies in which some of the people studied take responsibility for design, data gathering, and resolving questions of merit and shortcoming.

5. We are distressed by underprivilege. We see gaps between privileged patrons and managers and staff and underprivileged participants and communities. We aim some at studying issues of privilege, conceptualizing issues that might illuminate or alleviate underprivilege, and assuring distribution of findings to those often excluded.

6. We are advocates of a democratic society. We see democracies depending on the exchange of good information, which our studies may provide. But we also see democracies needing the exercise of public expression, dialogue, and collective action. Most social and educational researchers try to create reports that warrant action.

These six advocacies are easy to find in research reports. Although we are troubled by the possibility that our advocacies will cause us to search more vigorously for aspiration-based evidence than other evidence, we cling to some advocacies more than to neutrality, believing these well-considered biases to be compatible with the interests of the profession, our clients, and society.

Each of us is more than a researcher. We are complex human beings. Some of the things we do are part of our work and some are outside our work. We have political, spiritual, aesthetic, and other advocacies. Some of the panorama of advocacy cannot help but become part of the research we do, even if we try to confine it to the rest of our lives. Perceptions and values from any part of our lives may influence the interpretations we make.

## Intermittent Advocacy

We do not want to imply that advocacy, researcher personal advocacy, is a static permanent state, rather than, for most of us, an up-and-down within our character. Even the radical is sometimes passive; even the passive is sometimes moved by indignation. Even within a research project or report, most of us preserve a certain detachment most of the time, only occasionally exposing our personal values or calling for redress of wrongs. In this chapter, we are talking about the degree to which we should sharpen or suppress those moments that champion a cause.

Our values are not absent from seeing and saying, but they are never all on display. Even with ourselves, we are not aware of the full panorama of feelings and attachments we have for and against causes, the alliances we have for conquering and convincing and for devastation and refuting. We rationalize, we edit, or we keep a poker face to reserve our protestation and aspiration for another venue. But the coloring of value remains in our response, more sometimes and less in others.

It would be difficult to impossible to try to be equally "advocative" all the time. There are times and places for full effort, and times and places for keeping our partisanship unexpressed. We have multiple advocacies and they cannot all be shouted simultaneously. For physical and political reasons, our advocacies are *intermittent*.

Some of our advocacies are tuned to making ourselves both knowledgeable and effective. There are times to hear what others are saying. There are times for us to improve on what we say. Perfect pitch may have values in music, but sometimes a lower/assonant pitch is the better choice.

In a pairing of music research and qualitative methods, aesthetician Liora Bresler (2011) took a stand for empathetic detachment, posting it between full embrace and dispassionate focus. She said:

I claim that the field of research methodology can greatly benefit from moving beyond the dichotomy of detachment versus connectedness through the concept of non-attachment. A space of heightened observation can, with guidance, allow us to see ourselves and our engagement with more clarity, leading to openness to perceive beyond ourselves. That is where empathetic understanding starts.

Clearly there is a need for both empathy and detachment, but there is not a need for fixing a distance from phenomena. There are times to look closer and times to look broadly. There are times to feel the experience of participating and times to resist the emotion of belonging. Having been too close or too far might possibly damage the ability to know what is happening, but with mechanisms for triangulation and acknowledging multiple realities, recovery is to be expected.

## Constraining and Encouraging Advocacy

Qualitative inquiry is the study of the world from a human perspective, a perspective made meaningful through human experience. Much of that experience is values related, with and without acknowledgment that humans have preferences, rational and irrational, and act to fulfill those preferences. As indicated before, all inquiry is accompanied by advocacy—the yearning, the reaching, the pleading, for something valued. At some point, the yearning will distract inquiry. Some of the view will be blocked. At times advocacy will enhance the inquiry, and much of the time it will interfere. Understanding of the world will be less complete. At times, perhaps generally, it will be important to constrain advocacy.

Much advocacy will take the form of support for worthy causes, showing empathy and partisanship for those engaged in the endeavor. It is natural to avoid speaking ill of those we befriend. It is natural to censor our speech when it might put compatriots at risk. Our duty as friend and citizen is not to speak all the truth. We will review the matter of social honesty in our consideration as to when advocacy needs constraint.

Other advocacies take the form of being quiet when it is time to expose simplistic social narratives (Kushner, 2011) found in causes dear to us. Sometimes good work is in danger of running aground, so we may remain quiet about its narrow perspective and stereotypic representation. Silent advocacies have their place, but their costs as well, depriving the public and the partner of better views of opportunity and responsibility.

The mechanisms for constraint are not clear. Most will be self-constraint, exercised because it is in the best interest of the advocate, the communities of membership, and of the larger society. Some efforts at constraint will take the forms of professional customs and codes of ethics. There will continue to be little enforcement other than that of social pressure and self-constraint.

## Values Rationality

Advocacy is rooted in value commitments, and no matter how urgent the need, narrows the consideration of possibilities. Understanding only grows with the growth of possibilities. Action is not always better by waiting for understanding.

In *Making Social Science Matter*, Bent Flyvbjerg (2004) lamented the long dominance in social research of "instrumental rationality" over "values rationality." He spoke of the teaching, funding, criticizing and practice of research through most of the 20th century as an instrumental rationality, a technical advocacy for isolating the personality of the researchers and their community from the phenomena being studied. Flyvbjerg drew on Aristotle (1976) to point out these tensions, noting the reasoning patterns and events that distinguished science, technical craftwork, and ethics. He said:

> the principal objective of social science with [an ethical] approach is to carry out analyses and interpretations of the status of values and interests in society aimed at social commentary and social action. ... The point of departure for classical research [of this kind] can be summarized in the following value-laden questions:
>
> 1.  Where are we going?
> 2.  Is this desirable?
> 3.  What should be done? (Flyvberg, 2004, p. 60)

These are not the questions of conventional social science.

Flyvbjerg's social values questions might be seen as suggesting that there were no answers before the research and some answers only after completion. But the researcher regularly has hunches, hopes, and preferences, even before the research is contemplated. And as the postulating, designing, and observing come along, those questions are refined and better answers become clear. Some hopes and preferences take the shape of advocacies, whether held tight to the chest or voiced widely. Ethical research is rarely untouched by advocacy.

Values rationality is the heart of research on ethics, where it is generally taken that rights, respect, and privilege should be distributed equally to all. But for various purposes, including survival, legality, and personal preference, the distribution will regularly be unequal. In his theory of justice, John Rawls (1999) recognized that privilege cannot always be distributed equally, or justice equally served, but argued that erring should fall on the side of the least advantaged. There are diverse and competing ways of being rational. To think through a matter deeply is not necessarily a heading toward advocacy of equity.

Strongly influenced by Rawls, philosophers Ernest House and Kenneth Howe (1999) published *Values in Education and Social Research*. They urged that program evaluators promote democratic values even to the point of evoking deliberation on issues developed in their reports. Democratic evaluation had been created earlier by Barry MacDonald (1977) to prioritize issues particularly of public interest in government-funded research. Its designs are attendant to issues put forward by government agencies and other funders of evaluation, but at the same time quietly advocate a public need to know. House and Howe agreed to deliver what the public should know but went on to advocate facilitating dialogue among the various stakeholders. While Rawls (1999) apparently would concentrate on researcher sensitivity during interpretation, more of a silent advocacy, House and Howe would make the advocacies audible.

Michael Scriven (1967) claimed that the major choices in program evaluation are between formative and summative evaluation, but that needs be twisted only a touch to be between searches for quality in the process versus quality in the product. Similarly, advocacy can be for bettering the process or product. It can be less for remedial action and more for comprehension. Advocates can strive to take action or only to turn a point of view. Goodness is not their distinction, change is.

## Researcher Responsibility

Good and bad, advocacies are fundamental to our work. We have few guidelines for examining distinctions between good or bad advocacies. "Lacking the backing of positivist authority, we qualitative researchers are caught in a great web of advocacy and have become unwittingly, sometimes willingly, simply a party to promotionalism" (Stake, 1997, p. 475). Sometimes it seems that the authenticity of qualitative inquiry has been overcome by the power of advocacy.

We claimed in previous sections that advocacy is a fundamental act of human *being*. Advocacy interweaves when taking decisions, rationalizing situations, or just simply extending relationships and dominion. We cannot separate human *being* from human *work*, and human work comes to enclose and be surrounded by advocacies. Researchers acknowledge the impossibility of being separated from who they are, but they advocate for the possibility to place their research work in various positions: separated from, partially immersed, entirely displayed, or fundamentally anchored in advocacy. It has become researchers' responsibility to know how to incorporate advocacy in their work, tempering and refining.

Researchers want to protect the integrity of their work, the respectability it has to serve the common good for society, however the common good is envisioned. Integrity of the work, no matter the differences in the stance for advocacy, is part of the responsibility of the researcher. It could be a limited professional responsibility or a broader social responsibility. The responsibility is valued for the integrity of research and for the influence of researcher's work on the common good.

Some have long argued that advocacy should be pared away from the research process; others, to the contrary, claimed it a main responsibility to advocate the deep concerns inside and outside research. Those who have supported advocacy often have pursued equity, addressing the needs of people underrepresented, while those opposing advocacy have dispassionate inquiry into the social reality. Both positions have attempted to improve how the social order is represented in their research. Still, they differ in their views and differ as to where to place their advocacies: intertwined with their research mechanism or separated. The separation is not a mechanism to ensure research quality, but a matter of persuasion and responsibility.

## Energizing Advocacy

At first, cranking up seems unnecessary. Advocacy has its own energy. We are more often concerned about tapping it down, even exorcizing it. But often the advocacy is too muted, too timid to express what qualitative inquirers need to say. One might say, as House and Howe (1999) have, that, at a minimum, in a democratic society, social researchers have an obligation to prepare findings in a form and medium that facilitates public dialogue. It is to energize by drawing dialogue toward advocacy.

One of the strongest advocates for more transparent advocacy has been evaluation theorist Jennifer Greene. At a presentation she said: "Since advocacy seems to be an inevitable part of evaluative inquiry, the important question then becomes *not* should we or should we not *advocate … but rather what and whom should we advocate for?* (1995; emphasis added)" She implied that by explicating our advocacy, we will channel it more effectively.

Greene argued that "advocacy is best understood as *the absence of value neutrality and that it most importantly implies a value commitment* rather than a partisan stance toward a particular program or … stakeholder group" (1995; emphasis added). She headed a team for NSF, developing a guidebook for program evaluation within a "values-engaged, educative" framework (Greene et al., 2006), noting that: "Values engagement has two main dimensions. First, it signals *purposeful attention to the values* that are intrinsic in the programs … and second it pays special attention to the values of *diversity* and *equity*" (p. 60; emphasis in the original).

Qualitative inquiry advocates empathic understanding, not only for researchers but for those who will come to know what the research has to say. It is conceivable that one might be empathic with a cause or community without ever being its advocate, but a qualitative report is incomplete without express-ing value commitments of the actors and audiences. Even if the advocacy is overshadowed by the impartialities of description and analysis, there are needs for energizing the dispositions and agitations embedded in the data.

## Social Honesty and Utility

In our social affairs we are less than completely honest. We sup-port those we hold dear and withhold support from others. We join in the advocacies of those close to us and mute those we find offensive. We do not see ourselves as dishonest, but we are. We deceive (Bok, 1999) to put others and ourselves in a better light. David Nyberg (1993) called it "the varnished truth."

It is the same with advocacy. We try to avoid diminishing the good work of others. One of us (Stake, 1997) sweetened a negative conclusion in a draft evaluation report of a good works program when the director said that her enemies "would use it to kill us." Implicitly we advocate. The values of our society hold that complete honesty is hurtful.

We feel the tension between complete honesty and utility. We live by social practice more than by truth. Advocacy is an instrument of utility and usefulness. Just as our descriptions are incomplete, our honesty is selective. It is not only intentionally selective; it is unconsciously selective (Postman, 1962). We do not suddenly become honest when we do research. We advocate. We sometimes say what we need to say to enhance the research. Final paragraphs of research reports veer into partiality beyond the impartial data of the chapters preceding. Just as in social sit-uations, we varnish the truth. Advocacy is part of the language.

We experience a tension between honesty and utility. They are at odds. Our honesty is selective. As Greene, Boyce, and Ahn say in their guidebook (2011), we cannot report the entire truth. What we do not say influences the meaning of the research.

Social reality asks for action. The ideas of research inquiry and advocacy are related. The mechanisms of reporting make them both functional. The fact that ideas are good does not ensure that we have good mechanisms, and the fact that the mechanisms work does not validate the ideas.

Research studies are financially supported by organizations advocating and supporting specific ideological principles. To be able carry out research, the proposal of the study may or may not make clear its intent to work toward understanding of those issues and questions that eventually may promote their ideological principles.

## Advocacy for Multiple Perspectives

The benefit of pondering social honesty with the practical implications of that research is visible within the existence of multiple realities. And for it, empathy pushes the limits and facets of advocacy, especially of the values rationality. In his presentation "Shake up your story" at TED, K. K. Raghava (2011) talked about the possibility and the implications of giving children the chance of learning not only about their own cultural family values, but also about the cultural values of their friends and enemies. Similarly, qualitative researchers need to be trained to see and need to show empathy for the different realities they encounter.

One would believe that if we share the same values we will also see the reality with the same lens. That's not the reality, and when researchers dig for their questions and for understanding, they learn the multiple facets of reality. They discover that their values may be good and solid, however, compatible with only one version of social reality. Some of these researchers start changing the reality, while others start adapting their values.

The individual researcher is constantly sharing understanding of a reality and enlarging perceptions. Qualitative inquiry refines understanding of social realities. As the qualitative researcher moves to change reality or modify our values, he or she moves toward empathy. The concept of empathy may reflect simplistic understandings:

1. Help our people.

2. Help all the people.

3. Understand better the plight of the others.

These empathies lead more to avenging than to the amelioration of problems. Action is important, but action, blind or half-blind, is often mean. Seeing the realities as multiple is at the heart of qualitative inquiry. The realities are unequal and cannot be made equal. Most advocacies push towards Michael Scriven's claim (1997, p. 480): "There are no equal realities, one will be superior; there are preferences, and they too are not equal."

Reaching for the best reality is a problem of the politics of advocacy. Good advocacy prioritizes immediate relief but presumes that better long-term action lies elsewhere. Rhetorical or action forms of advocacy carry negotiations over the perpetuation of certain values, of their resistance or adherence to circumstances, situations, or contexts.

## Conclusion

Advocacy can be seen as the art of persuading others that your aspirations are congruent with theirs. You all could be worlds apart, but you make them seem not. Whether or not they agree on the deeper values or the action you prefer, the aim is to have them endorse your aspiration. There is nothing holy about advocacy, but nothing holy happens without it.

Everyone has multiple aspirations. And somewhere inside, there's an aspiration to make everyone happy. In many people, it's pretty small, most of the time, but it's there. And in a smaller number of people, most of the time there's a large aspiration for improving human well-being. For many qualitative researchers, it's pretty large, but intermittent. So for their research, they select people and issues and methods that seem at the time most likely to do some good. And then they advocate for what they do and urge others to do likewise.

For matters of social benefit, most of us are lukewarm about equity. We have a strong sense of social distance (Bogardus, 1926). We care deeply about benefits for family and friends and we care less for those further away. If we have to pay for others' benefits, the drop is steeper. That is the prospect the advocate faces. The advocate has close to zero chance to make social service more important than social distance. So advocacy regularly means making the pursuit of social service appear to benefit those near at hand. The ethics of values rationality most often will be submerged by yearnings to extend privilege as a function of social distance.

Yet the cost of advocacy is small. Researchers will continue to advocate for obviously good things, including social justice. They will arrange their studies to do so. They will sometimes neglect their responsibilities to do so. They will seldom be deterred from doing so. They should be constrained when straying into deception and putting communities at risk, including the community of researchers. They should be helped to constrain themselves. But the mechanisms of government and organizations for encouraging and constraining advocacy are weak. Social pressure helps. Mostly it is up to the individual researchers and their colleagues to raise the quality of advocacy.

## References

Aristotle. (1976). *The Nicomachean ethics*. Harmondsworth, UK: Penguin.

Bogardus, E. S. (1926). Social distance in the city. *Proceedings and Publications of the American Sociological Society, 20*, 40-46.

Bok, S. (1999). *Lying: moral choice in public and private life* (2nd Ed.). New York: Vintage Books.

Bresler, L. (2011). The spectrum of distance: Emphatic understanding and the pedagogical power of arts. Manuscript in preparation.

Denzin, N. K. (2000). The practices and politics of interpretation. In N. K. Denzin & Y. S. Lincoln (Eds.), *Handbook of qualitative research* (2nd Ed.) (pp. 897–922). Thousand Oaks, CA: Sage.

Denzin, N. K. & Lincoln, Y. S. (Eds.). (2000). *Handbook of qualitative research* (2nd Ed.). Thousand Oaks, CA: Sage.

Flyvbjerg B. (2004). *Making social science matter*. Cambridge: Cambridge University Press.

Greene, J. C. (1995). Evaluators as advocates. Paper presented at the annual meeting of the American Evaluation Association, Vancouver, Canada, November 6.

Greene, J. C., Boyce, A. C., & Ahn, J. (2011). *A values-engaged, educative approach for evaluating education programs. A guidebook for practice.* University of Illinois at Urbana-Champaign. http://comm.eval.org/resources/viewdocument/?DocumentKey=f3c734c0-8166-4ba4-9808-a07e05294583 (accessed February 8, 2012).

Greene, J. C., DeStefano, L., Brugon, H., & Hall, J. (2006). An educative, values-engaged approach to evaluating STEM educational programs. *New Directions for Evaluations, 109*, 53–71, Spring, Wiley Periodicals Inc, DOI: 10.1002/ev178.

House, E. R. (1977). *The logic of evaluative argument.* CSE Monograph Series in Evaluation, No. 7. Los Angeles: Center for the Study of Evaluation, University of California.

House, E. R. & Howe, K. R. (1999). *Values in education and social research.* Thousand Oaks, CA: Sage.

Kushner, S. (2011). Narrative control, the appliance of science and the challenge of independent evaluation. Presented at the meeting of the American Evaluation Association, Anaheim, California, November 5.

Levitt, S. D. & Dubner, S. J. (2005). Freakonomics. *New York Times*, May 15. http://www.nytimes.com/2005/05/15/books/chapters/0515-1st-levitt. html?pagewanted=all (accessed February 8, 2012).

MacDonald, B. (1977). A political classification of evaluation studies. In D. Hamilton, D. Jenkins, C. King, B. MacDonald, & M. Parlett (Eds.), *Beyond the numbers game* (pp. 175–198). London: MacMilllan.

Nyberg, D. (1993). *The varnished truth: Truth telling and deceiving in ordinary life.* Chicago: University of Chicago Press.

Postman, L. (Ed.). (1962). *Psychology in the making: Histories of selected research problems.* New York: Knopf.

Raghava, K. K. (2011). Shake up your story. Presentation at TED (2011), Long Beach, California. http://www.ted.com/talks/raghava_kk_shake_up_ your_story.html (accessed February 6, 2012).

Rawls, J. (1999). *A theory of justice.* Revised ed. Cambridge, MA: The Belknap Press of Harvard University Press.

Scriven, M. (1967). The methodology of evaluation. In R. W. Tyler, R. M. Gagne, & M. Scriven (Eds.), *Perspectives of curriculum evaluation* (pp. 39–83). Chicago: Rand McNally.

Scriven, M. (1997).Truth and Objectivity. In E. Chelmisky & W. R. Shadish (Eds.), *Evaluation for the 21st Century* (pp. 477–501). Thousand Oaks, CA: Sage

Stake, R. E. (1997). Advocacy in evaluation: A necessary evil? In E. Chelmisky & W. R. Shadish (Eds.), *Evaluation for the 21ˢᵗ century* (pp. 470–477). Thousand Oaks, CA: Sage.

Trochim, W. (2006). *Research methods knowledge base.* Web center for social research methods. http://socialresearchmethods.net/kb/ (accessed February 8, 2012).

Weber, M. (1897). *"Objectivity" in social science. http://www.marxists.org/reference/subject/philosophy/works/ge/weber.htm#s2* (accessed February 8, 2012).

Chapter 2

# Back to the Educational Future, Again

## A "Double-Dip" into the Long Recession

Ian Stronach and John Clarke

*The crisis consists precisely in the fact that the old is dying and the new cannot be born; in this interregnum a great variety of morbid symptoms appear.*
—Antonio Gramsci (1971, p. 276)

## Introduction

This chapter is the latest in a series of essays written between 2009 and 2011, all of them seeking to develop and expand our understanding of the "credit crunch" and its implications for the "knowledge economy."[1] We will not repeat our previous arguments, but it would be useful to summarize the first four of our contentions in earlier work. They were:

- that "scientific socialism" went bust in 1989. People noted the socialist defeat but ignored the scientific bit;

- that "scientific capitalism" went bust in 2007. This time, the scientific defeat was noted, and the capitalism bit ignored;

*Qualitative Inquiry and the Politics of Advocacy,* edited by Norman K. Denzin and Michael D. Giardina, 59–78. © 2012 Left Coast Press, Inc. All rights reserved.

- that "green shoot" optimism of imminent recovery is ill founded and addresses none of the underlying crisis of capitalism; and

- that the Twin Towers of scientific socialism and scientific capitalism share a positivistic fallacy.

We intend here to develop and extend what were Contentions 5–8 in earlier writing.

### Contention 5: That scientific capitalism in the West and scientific socialism in the East became hegemonic ways of thinking about all sorts of social knowledge

The kinds of normative statistical modeling that underpinned capitalistic assessments of risk (Jones, 2009; Norman, 2010; Taleb, 2008; Tett, 2009) came to invest many other forms of professional reasoning, from medical decisions (Chang, 2011 [2010]; McCartney, 2009) to education and care decisions (Lather, 2009) via the ideologies of efficiency, effectiveness, quality, improvement, best practice, and evidence-based practice. The "standard economic model" (Norman, 2010, p. 63) became the hegemonic science of the social. This paracapitalist mimicry was accompanied by a swing against qualitative forms of inquiry and a drive toward measuring inputs, outputs, outcomes, targets—often enshrined in planning that ignored processes of change or indeed precedents in the history of the professions (Strathern, 2000). Professionals found themselves distrusted and required to "evidence-base" their judgments. Thus, the work processes of a wide range of professions came to be influenced by a kind of economistic metaphor of efficiency and so-called quality, targeted, measured, recorded, and held publicly accountable via increasing penetration of a league table culture that is still in expansion, despite the underlying crisis in its original onto-metaphorical heartlands. Such a phenomenon is "essentially theological" rather than "scientific" (Lanchester, 2011, p. 3). Chang (2011, p. 95) notes the one-dimensional obsession with efficiency: "If a string quartet trots through a twenty-seven minute piece in nine minutes, would you say its productivity has trebled?"

Indeed, recent higher education reforms in the United Kingdom inaugurate a "quasi-market world" (Mroz, 2011, p. 5; Uvalic-Trumbic, 2011, p. 17), in which the market, vocationally defined, and the customer (formerly student) achieve the nirvana of the "industry-ready" graduate (Price, 2010) whose "World of Work" skills ("WOW," of course) maximize employability (*WOW Star*, 2011). Thus are the young and unemployed insulated by the "career service" from knowledge of the jobless recovery (Webb, 2011). This is an interesting cultural phenomenon in its own right. Individuals are simultaneously encouraged to internalize a general economic crisis as individual responsibility and personal deficit, and externalize their selves as assessable bundles of skills, competencies, and qualities. Self and Other change place in a DIY alienation. The latter "self-trackers" and "self-quantifiers" constitute an embryonic field of knowledge, as indicated by the first international "Quantified Self Conference" in Silicon Valley, California (Dembosky, 2011). Self-surveillance becomes a scientific form of continuous assessment—medically, physically, and dynamically.[2] Thus, a "credit rating culture" (Kettle, 2010) simultaneously addresses the health or otherwise of "bodies without organs" (national economies, eurozones, banks) and "organs without bodies" (pulses, heart rates, stool analysis). Deleuze would be amused. Standard and Poor, thus universalized and personalized in the same moment, address capitalism's last frontier.

Overall, the result was a commodification of most forms of educational knowledge relating to performance, from the crèche to the university. This kind of capitalistic mimicry was expressed within an overall rationale that education—hitherto a philosophical and cultural question of being, becoming, forms of knowledge, tradition, civilization, culture, emancipation, etc.—could and should be reduced to a "paracapitalist" practice (Stronach, 2010), a question of economic instrumentalism, however mythic. Such an expansion of the market into the polity, an educational simulacrum to the credit bubble, has powerful elements of cargo cult about it. It is also deeply ironic in that the United Kingdom once again becomes the "workshop of the world," but this time only with an all-encompassing vocationalist rhetoric. This paradox surfaces in the more intelligent media, with disparaging editorials chiding that "Treating economics as a morality play is one reason the European crisis is not over" (*Financial Times* [FT], 2011a), and in a bizarre appeal by U.K. Prime Minister David Cameron to directly equate national debt to household debt: "The only way out of a debt crisis is to deal with your debts. That means—all of us—paying off the credit card and store card bills" (*Guardian*, 2011b).

It is highly significant that this pre-speech release statement had to be hastily retracted: It would cause a "double-dip" (via the well-known "paradox of thrift") and reflects once again the triumph of populism over policy. As Harford noted, "the metaphor is daft" (2011). Such false analogies between household and national debt were earlier condemned as the work of "economic primitives" (*Observer*, 2011)—cargo cultists indeed. But we should note its political efficacy: If household debt and national debt are equated, and the latter is the sum of the former, then the debt is ours and not theirs [see later, Contention Six]. Not a banker in sight.

So we conclude that the knowledge economy is not some inevitable functional relation between education and the global economy: It is a fragile and somewhat demented extension of an economic model that in itself crashed in 2007 and led to the worst economic crisis of at least sixty years (according to the then U.K. chancellor of the Exchequer, Alistair Darling). We also conclude that the practice of nations "competing-by-proxy" economically with their education systems and measuring quality by global league table position has expanded remarkably in the last fifty years, but it is a metaphorical and rather mythic extrapolation, which has long been mocked as well as advocated (Carrier & Miller, 1998; Chang, 2011; Stronach, 1999; Stronach & Clarke, 2010).

Such an economism was equally apparent in scientific socialism. In reflecting on prerevolutionary Bolshevism, Trotsky commented that "we Marxists were already armed with the scientific method of comprehending historical processes" (Trotsky, 1971 [1907], p. 7). He later argued that our understanding of 'social relations' had until then lagged far behind our understanding of "physio-chemical sciences" (Trotsky, 1967 [1934], p. 322), a belief maintained with equal certainty by scientific capitalism, though its metaphorical model has recently tended to be medical rather than physical science (Hargreaves, 1996). Later Marxists knew to condemn "*all forms of positivism and empiricism*" (Althusser, 1971, p. 52; emphasis in the original), but nevertheless held on to what seem now to be perverse certainties: Marx's *Kapital* was "one of the three great scientific discoveries of the whole of human history" (Althusser, 1971, p. 71). Both sciences had parallel conceptual armories: concrete, objective, correct, and robust targets and plans invested in social thinking and planning. The realm of politics grew increasingly the province of a centralized administration. The shrinkage of political space was remarkable (Rancière, 2010, p. 72). In the 20th century, one size fits all was both a socialist and a capitalist delusion. Jibes that New Labour was a case of "market Stalinism" (Graebner, 2002) have a point beyond casual irony: There was a congruence between the two pseudo-sciences. And both clearly embodied the "idea of historical necessity" (Arendt, 2006 [1963], p. 39) pursued by an elite "according to standards and criteria which are themselves profoundly unpolitical" (Arendt, 2006 [1963], pp. 269–270).

Thus, both scientific socialism and scientific capitalism seem parallel in their declines. Perhaps the following satirical Soviet parable can be populated by the West as well as the erstwhile East:

> The train is speeding into a luminous future. Lenin is at the controls. Suddenly—stop, the tracks come to an end. Lenin calls on the people for additional Saturday work, tracks are laid down, and the train moves on. Now Stalin is driving it. Again the tracks end. Stalin orders half the conductors and passengers shot, and the rest he forces to lay down new tracks. The train starts again. Krushchev replaces Stalin, and when the tracks come to an end, he orders that the ones over which the train has already passed be dismantled and laid down before the locomotive. Brezhnev takes Krushchev's place. When the tracks end again, Brezhnev decides to pull down the window blinds and rock the cars in such a way that the passengers will think the train is still moving forward. (Boriev, *Staliniad*, cited in Kapuscinski, 2007, pp. 307–308)

"Pulling down the blinds and rocking the cars" might also be said to characterize both growth strategies and sovereign debt initiatives in the Long Recession. In addition, Krushchev's strategy could be used to characterize the ripping up of the tracks of an industrial capitalism to make progress through laying a track ahead for financial capitalism (Thatcher, Reagan, Bush, Blair)—the neoliberal fantasy of progress. But perhaps the greatest deception concerned risk analysis and insurance in global capitalist dealings—the very engine itself. In terms of prompting the Great Recession, the apogee of such reliance on statistical engineering, technicist reduction, and fantasies of progress was seen in David Li's formulation of the Gaussian copula, which engendered the sorts of decisions via "algorithmic calculation" (Amoore, 2008, p. 116) that became culturally normative. The formula was as follows:

$$C_p(u,v) = \left(\phi_p(\phi^{-1}(u), \phi^{-1}(v)\right)$$

The problem was simple. Such calculations of risk, and securitizations of the same, ignored the black swan, most famously popularized by Taleb (2008): They assumed norms of activity and behavior that history clearly showed were unstable, not least in the tendency of capitalism to periodic crisis: "Black swans have now become the new orthodoxy" (Tett, 2011, p. 12). The black swan phenomenon can be illustrated vividly in the nature of risk-taking that prompted the current crisis. The subprime mortgage trigger in the United States involved a series of displacements of risk. First, individual contracts were made, often improbably optimistic in relation to their viability. Then the risk was insured and sold to others. Such risks were then bundled and sold again, with good credit ratings based on statistical probabilities of default from globally influential credit agencies such as Moody's and Standard & Poor's.[3]

The strategy was to make the loan, and then sell on the risk to someone else—"securitization" would "disperse risk" (Tett, 2009, pp. 56, 63). The investment bundles were CDOs,[4] wherein even the bundles themselves could be bundled together again to be sold as $CDOs^2$, and even $CDOs^3$. Finally, it was also possible to speculate in this market of sold-on risks through "synthetic" CDOs, whereby no actual CDOs were purchased and business relied on betting on future price movements of rebundled and by this time quite unassessable risks (Authers, 2010b; Chang, 2011). Indeed, these became an 'increasingly tall structure of financial assets teetering on the same foundation of real assets' (Chang, 2011, p. 239). They were all nevertheless assessed and assured by formulas derived from the Gaussian copula—"the combustion engine of the CDO world" (Tett, 2009, p. 121)—as low or no risk investments, and so long as the bubble persisted, everyone concerned made money. The resemblance to a pyramid scheme is remarkable. The apogee of such confidence in permanent economic boom, however, must be the U.K. chancellor's 2007 Mansion House speech, where the mantra of "no more boom or bust" had its climactic moment as "a new world order was created," "a new golden age for the City of London" (Brown, 2007, p. 1).

In the light of this formulaic madness, we therefore propose a new equation, an admitted spoof, for understanding this sort of process:

$$R = \frac{A}{V^n}$$

where $R$ = the real in a performative sense (see Baudrillard in Poster, 1988), as an effect rather than a truth of any kind; A = the actual event itself; $V$ the virtualization of the event through the sorts of proxy displacements we illustrated, and $n$ represents the number of these displacements. It's a postmodernist calculus, and things don't get much more paradoxical than that, but it makes more sense than the Gaussian copula applied to events in history. We confidently await our Nobel Prize in Economics. Nor is such a trade in virtual proxies by any means a thing of the past in terms of capitalist markets. Synthetic ETFs [Exchange Traded Funds] are somewhat similar to the CDOs that brought about the last collapse, and a concern for regulators (Moore, 2011). Note that such a formula is as easily applied to current knowledge economy worlds, beset by league tables, test outcomes, audit, and multiple proxies for educational actualities.

Thus far we have sought homologies between the parallel epistemologies of scientific socialisms and capitalisms. But they are also subject in China to a different kind of overlap, wherein the authoritarian, political, and military aspects of Chinese communism combine with revolutionary success in the global market. What greater "semantic collision" (Stronach 2010, p. 177) could we envisage than a *Capitalist Communism*? In an age now accepted as Uncertain and Unpredictable, we can only explore possible scenarios. Crisis is endemic; the emergency refuses to go away: "a situation in which precarity seems the norm below and Schmittian state of exception the norm above" (Foster, 2011, p. 117).

In relation to political as well as economic futures, as a *Financial Times* Leader (editorial) bemoaned: "Instability is the new certainty" (FT, 2011b). The old certainty is debunked from Right as well as Left as a mistaken "fundamentalism" (Norman, 2010, p. 101). We are (still) in a "crisis spiralling out of control," with sovereign default and potential euro collapse, and "from bad to worse for the UK economy" (Giles, 2011a, 2011b).

**Contention 6: That blame for such an economic collapse has been successfully deflected from its economic and capitalist origins to more palatable bogey-men in the public sector and the national memory.**

In 2007, the origins of the Great Recession were clear and unambiguous. First, there was large-scale and imprudent lending on the U.S. subprime mortgage market. The calculation of risk was no longer part of individual judgment (client/professional) but one of abstract statistical calculation, based on degrees of risk that could be bundled together and re-sold in such a way that no one individual quite knew what kind of risk had been bought or sold (Chang, 2011; Jones, 2009). Thus, decisions based on personal judgment and specific contexts were universalized via evidence-based procedures that had been normatively correlated in terms of their likely occurrence and outcomes. In this system, agents and principals had become strangers.

What went wrong? Lanchester (2010, pp. 73–74) offers a succinct account: "'The Credit Crunch was based on a climate (the post-Cold War victory party of free market capitalism), a problem (the subprime mortgages), a mistake (the mathematical models of risk), and a failure, of the regulators." He went on to argue that the "free market became a secular religion" (p. 201). It is equally possible to invert that term and argue that the problem was one of religious secularity. As Barber reported, the chairman of Goldman Sachs was clear about the warrant for their enterprise: "We are doing God's work" (Barber, 2009).

When the U.S. housing bubble burst, it became clear that major banks had invested rashly, and that their systems of risk assessment were inadequate and even inoperable. In the United Kingdom, Northern Rock and the Royal Bank of Scotland had, in effect, to be nationalized, since otherwise bankruptcy was inevitable. Worse, risk assessment agencies that variously accredited banks, bonds, and countries were wildly wrong. States had to intervene on an unprecedented scale to prevent or postpone the onset of another Great Depression. The events of 2007–2008 were no less calamitous than 1928–1929, and it is probably significant that the Great Depression also had its "green shoot" moments in its early phase. Nor does the Great Hypocrisy end there. States that bailed out banks now face banks apparently colluding to force them into default and bail-out.[5]

At first, the Conservative opposition in the United Kingdom was keen to acknowledge the scale of the disaster, but the electorate was reluctant in 2009–2010 to vote for an "age of austerity," and a 20-point Conservative lead began to shrink. The age of austerity temporarily disappeared, and the emphasis shifted to the New Labour government's "profligacy," according to the Conservative leader David Cameron, in relation to the country's finances. The public sector apparently was an unaffordable sybaritic paradise of "feather-bedded" pay and "gold-plated pensions" (Toynbee, 2010). A Conservative shadow minister cast an even wider net, blaming the baby-boomer generation for having sold out their children (Willetts, 2010). The baby boomers were suddenly the "baby busters." Thus was the relation of crisis to capitalism successfully inverted.

In 2007, it was universally acknowledged that the public sector had to bail out the private sector's self-engendered capitalist crisis. Proper market fundamentalists wished it hadn't, and that banks and building societies had been allowed to become bankrupt. That was "market discipline." But neoliberal governments had a sudden, if brief, Keynesian moment; they could not let that happen. By 2010, the banking crisis had more or less disappeared as a prime cause in the United Kingdom, along with much of the demand for greater finance-market regulation (Authers, 2010a; Gapper, 2010; Kleinman, 2011; White, 2010). As even the right-wing *Daily Mail* angrily noted, "bankers are running rings round politicians and regulators leading to a return to the grotesque bonus culture" (Brummer, 2010, para. 20).

Such criticism was resisted in 2011 by the sector calling for an end to "banker bashing" at Davos (Jenkins & Guerrera, 2011). As a result of such a public sector "binge," the new Coalition government decided that state spending would have to be pruned by some twenty to forty percent. It was the greatest debt cancellation in the history of global capitalism, because not only had the deficit been reversed, but also a series of "blame bubbles" shifted responsibility from capitalism to the state or rather the public sector and the citizen for causing the crisis in the first place. Note the relocated bubble in the following question: 'Was June's emergency budget the death knell for the public sector bubble?' (Shore, 2010). And then the bubble became a "public spending binge" that had to be ended (Hastings, 2011). As Polly Toynbee put it, the alchemy was impressive: "A crisis caused by an out-of-control finance sector is now blamed on rapacious teachers, midwives and road menders. This should be a prime case study for every student of political propaganda" (Toynbee, 2010).

Michael Moore called it "the robbery of the century" (in Žižek, 2009a, p. 12). To put it a little too simply, *we* bailed them out, but *they* demanded repayment.[6] Their greed was our fault and the price was an imposed virtuous austerity that excluded the guilty, who had to be "incentivized" to even remain in the United Kingdom and continue to be underregulated to remain competitive. Such a grand larceny involves a form of violence far in excess of any unrest as seen in current student occupations and demonstrations. Or indeed the August Riots in England in 2011.[7] It is "ethical violence" on a systemic scale (Butler, 2005, p. 5). The duplicity far exceeds that of 1928, when, as Galbraith noted: "Such was the fate of the bankers. For the next decade they were fair game for Congressional committees, courts, the press, and the comedians" (Galbraith, 1992, p. 136).

Attaching blame and avoiding responsibility is a dynamic process, however, and while important political purposes have been served in the last eighteen months by attempting to deflect anger from bankers and financial manipulators onto past governments and the public sector, the end of 2011 has seen the emergence of a new target in the form of the European Union. Here, what is presented are two very different objects of fear. The countries of the feckless and profligate south (Greece and Italy, for example) are presented as awful warnings of what might happen if countries do not cut back their deficits , while Germany re-emerges in its old guise, beloved of the Thatcher generation of the eighties who remain important on the Conservative backbenches, as the continental superpower eager to dominate Europe.

This twin evocation of "folk devils" (lazy Greeks, bossy Germans), which echo long-term atavistic stereotypes in the British vision of "abroad," also provides a new set of explanations for the fact that current economic prescriptions appear to be failing to generate growth. As David Blanchflower, a former member of the Bank of England Monetary Policy Committee points out, "It's always someone else's fault. No longer should we blame the weather or lots of bank holidays or the royal wedding but those pesky Europeans" (Blanchflower, 2011, para. 1). The uncertainties and hesitations of German policymakers in the face of demands that they authorize the printing of money by the European Central Bank to rescue the eurozone are the central focus of news reports. They arise, as Richard Evans points out, from the national memory of the 1920s inflation and the horrific political and social consequences that followed from the economic crash, yet they are presented as part of a model of German conspiracy to dominate their neighbors in a new "Fourth Reich," using fiscal constraints rather than panzer tanks as their first strike weapons (Evans, 2011).

**Contention 7: That the capitalist crisis, far from undermining its simulacrum, the knowledge economy, will intensify the drive toward making education serve capitalism**

This is counter-intuitive. But recall Festinger et al. (1964). In their study of a millenarian sect who confidently awaited the appointed date of the destruction of the world, disconfirmation merely strengthened their belief in the imminence of the event. Similarly, an intensified commitment to the knowledge economy and its (dys)functional relation to the needs of global capitalism and competition is perhaps the most likely outcome of the Great Recession, not least because such belief offers psychological comfort in times of great uncertainty.[8] Hysteria works so much better than history. And, as Mazower notes, it is based not on scientific capitalism so much as a "gospel of productivity," a "creed of growthmanship" (1999, p. 301). This may particularly be the case in countries where industrial capitalism has already given way to a financial capitalism that has proved both deceptive in its promises of growth and security, and footloose in terms of its allegiances.

Such a gospel drew both on a "modernization agenda" pursued by Blair and Clinton, which was united to a "Third Way" creed that asserted the superior wisdom of markets. The Department for Trade and Industry (DTI) in 1988 summed up the changes succinctly: "In the industrial policy making of the 1960s and 1970s to be modern meant to believe in planning. Now meeting the requirements of the knowledge driven economy means making markets work better" (DTI, 1998, p. 11, cited in Brown & Lauder, 2001, p. xx). The implicit theology of such belief is well expressed by Blair, when sound-biting his way toward a phrase stolen from Marx, and re-expressed in more Biblical terms: "We know what a 21st century nation needs. A knowledge-based economy. A strong civic society. A confident place in the world. Do that and a nation masters the future. Fail and it is the future's victim. ... People are born with talent and everywhere it is in chains. Talent is 21st century wealth" (Blair, 1999, para. 10).

Finally, we have seen how government policy directed inward toward the polity has been driven by statistical engineering of one kind or another—precise, measurable, targeted, and prefaced on the continuation of what came to be called the "great moderation" in the United States. Such a schema removed judgment, trust, and ideographic knowledge from decision-making. Expertise became increasingly located in the "symbolic services." As Reich (1992, p. 178) put it: "They simplify reality into abstract images that can be rearranged, juggled, experimented with, communicated to other specialists and then, eventually transformed back into reality." Or not, as it turned out in the 2008 meltdown.

Yet this was accompanied in foreign policy by a kind of arbitrariness that Agamben (2005) has called "exception," where rules of law/regulation/rights are permanently suspended—as in the case of Guantanamo—and where undeclared wars become more frequent.[9] It's as if over-predicting and over-controlling the local is to act as compensation for an increasingly uncertain and chaotic global world—a world gone *gloco*?

**Contention 8: That the current crises of both the economy and the role within it of knowledge insist on new analyses of possibility, which include the renaissance of forms of qualitative inquiry, from the anthropology and history of the global to the kinds of educational processes and outcomes that count for a post-global education**

If the 20th century has only now ended, *contra* Hobsbawm (1994), then we have some new thinking to do. Education cannot go on mimicking a failure-prone capitalism by way of whatever knowledge economy. Professionalism cannot be regulated and defined by its output contributions to that deeply mythicized game. Examples elsewhere warn against reconstructing the various phases of our education system into a "hierarchy of employability," an "unhealthy dynamic" that is especially well advanced in the U.K. higher education system (Chang, cited by Mroz, 2010). Note, however, the hypocrisy of *Times Higher Education,* which promotes its own global league tables for universities with messianic zeal. The commodification and audit regimes have shown their potential for sterility, contradiction, and regression to the measurable. Quality cannot be quantified without contradiction. We have tried and found wanting both scientific socialism and scientific capitalism. Current sloganeering about the "Big Society" will take us nowhere, and is little more than a way of not saying cuts.

So where can we look for radical solace? We have written elsewhere about the need for democratic schools and the paradox of a current educational system that is increasingly "Fordist" in its means and goals. Nor are its audit cultures a valid measure of educational quality. (Stronach, 2010). Here we want briefly to extend that argument, accepting that the depth of current capitalist crises may well be beyond acceptable remedy (Klein, 2007; Žižek, 2011). But what can an "anticapitalist" future look like? Žižek offers a very broad communist agenda: "The only sense in which we are communists is that we care for the commons. The commons of nature. The commons of what is privatized by intellectual property. The commons of biogenetics. For this and only this we should fight" (Žižek 2011, p. xx).

Žižek emphasizes that such a new communism would have to respond equally to environmental and technological crisis as well as the new forms of apartheid, new inequalities, and the privatization of different aspects of communal life. Such a society would need to move beyond property and markets in a new form of social existence. True, we have heard such things before and failed to bring them about. But if capitalism has finally engendered problems it cannot solve, this time we have no choice. There can be no Keynsian rescue.

Perhaps the most significant aspect of current protest is a new contrast between the "verticals" (of traditional Right or Left) with the "horizontals" (Graebner, 2002) of movements such as Occupy Wall Street and Occupy the City. Such horizontalism can perhaps be associated with Zapatistas or with Chavez, "more sympathetic with anarchistic principles of organization, non-hierarchical forms of direct democracy, and direct action" (Graebner, 2002, p. xx). At any rate, as the spirit of 9/11 gives way to the spirit of 1/99, there is good reason, as Žižek says, to begin at the beginning again.

It would be strange to end on an optimistic note with the assistance of Leonard Cohen. But recall that lyric: "First we take Manhattan, then we take Berlin!"

"It's a weird time. We've gone into a different world" (Warren Buffett, in Docherty, 2009, p. 684).

## Notes

1. We began with an in-house "Bring Back *Das Kapital* Punishment! Credit Crunch and the Fall of the Knowledge Economy" (Stronach & Clarke, 2009), developed the argument first doe *Research Intelligence* (Stronach, 2009) and then for *Forum* in 2010 (Stronach & Clarke, 2010). Thereafter, we were asked to do some more work for a book edited by Forbes and Watson (Stronach & Clarke, 2011b). Finally, a much-extended version was accepted by *Qualitative Inquiry* (Stronach & Clarke, 2011a). We had decided to tiptoe away from the topic until this edited chapter was requested. It contains much new material on the period following the "crunch," and we are pleased that our analysis thus far has turned out to be prescient. We're having a great Great Recession, thank you very much. On paper, at least.

2. There is, at the Operating Systems conference, the same dialectics between the external and the internal. An entrepreneur claims that running a business requires the same sorts of "tracking how business is going. So I started doing that with myself." Such monitoring returns to the material culture of capitalism by potentially generating a "huge market for consumer-focused health and wellness tools," not to mention a "personalized" health analysis, "disease management," and "personalized drug development."

3. These same agencies, and the same methodologies, failed to predict the credit crunch/Great Recession and are now used to assess the chances of sovereign default, and each government's credit rating in relation to bond issue. This may seem entirely foolish, but it must be remembered that predicting failure has elements of self-fulfilling prophecy that failing to predict failure lacks.

4. The financial instruments were variously named CDOs, CDSs, the former standing for collateralized debt obligation and the latter for credit default swap (Tett, 2009, p. 53). Astonishingly, they even involved loans to what were termed in the trade "ninjas" [no income no job]. George Soros called it "securitization mania" (2008, p. xviii).

5. An EU Commission is currently looking at sixteen global banks (including RBS, HSBC, and Barclays) to determine whether they "played a part in forcing Greece and Ireland to seek EU bail-out funds" (Goodley, 2011).

6. Harford is correct in noting the misuse of the notion of bail-out. It is possible for governments to make a profit from the bail-out, as was recently predicted since these are loans not grants (though current circumstances might confute that hope). Indeed, some have suggested that governments act as "vulture capitalists" in this respect. Harford concludes: Blame the banks, not the bail-out (Harford, 2011b).

7. Responses to the riots were predictable, dismissed as "pure criminality" by a "feral underclass" by government ministers. But the right-wing *Daily Telegraph* also blamed the "feral rich" of Chelsea for generating such extremes in society. Students of "states of exception" may also note that the punitive sentences for often trivial theft or damage broke all sentencing guidelines—"feral justice"?

8. Recent government statements on education, as reported especially in *Times Higher Education* (January–August 2010), indicate that this is likely. The Department for Business, Innovation, and Skills (DBIS) stressed the "continuing focus of the research councils in driving up the economic impact of the research base" (DBIS, 2009, p. 63), as part of that universal drive to deliver "the skills that globalization and a knowledge economy demand" (DBIS, 2009, p. 3). There is a demand for "industry-ready graduates" (Price, 2010), and U.K. universities rush toward employability divisions (e.g., Exeter University) and "world of work" remedies (e.g., Liverpool John Moores University).

9. Philip Alston, UN representative on extrajudicial executions, notes that an "ill-defined license to kill without accountability" marks the U.S. deployment of drone attacks in Pakistan in particular. Again, "exception" marks that political space (*Guardian*, 2011a). The assassination of Osama Bin Laden is yet another exceptional event, in Agamben's terms.

## References

Agamben, G. (2005). *State of exception* (K. Attell, Trans.). Chicago: Chicago University Press.

Althusser, L. (1971). *Lenin and philosophy and other essays* (B. Brewster, Trans.). London: NLB.

Amoore, L. & de Goede, M. (Eds). (2008). *Risk and the war on terror.* London: Routledge.

Arendt, H. (2006 [1963]). *On revolution.* London: Penguin.

Authers, J. (2010a). The Great Rescue regulation turns into Great Escape. *Financial Times*, July 17/18, p. 2.

Authers, J. (2010b). Why bets on synthetic CDOs must be banned. *Financial Times*, April 24/25, p. 4.

Authers, J. (2011). We need new models in an uncertain world (March 13, 2011). All *Financial Times*, p. 5.

Bachelard, G. (1994 [1958]). *The poetics of space* (M. Jolas, Trans.). Boston: Beacon Press.

Barber, L. (2009). The year in review. *Financial Times*, December 19/20, p. 1.

Blair, T. (1999). Keynote speech to Labour Party conference. *BBC*, September 28. http://news.bbc.co.uk/2/hi/uk_news/politics/460029.stm (accessed February 7, 2012).

Blanchflower, D. (2011). Something happened at the end of August to terrify policymakers. *New Statesman*, November 21. http://www.newstatesman.com/economy/2011/11/eurozone-bank-government (accessed February 7, 2012)

Brown, G. (2007). Speech by the Chancellor of the Exchequer, the Rt. Hon. Gordon Brown, Mansion House, London, June. http://www.hm-treasury.gov.uk/press_68_07.htm (accessed July 17, 2007).

Brown, P., & Lauder, H. (2001). *Capitalism and social progress: The future of society in a global economy.* Basingstoke, UK: Palgrave.

Brummer, A. (2010). Truth behind the Great Panic. *Daily Mail*, September 17. http://www.dailymail.co.uk/money/article-1313100/COMMENT-ALEX-BRUMMER-Truth-great-panic.html (accessed February 7, 2012).

Butler, J. (2005). *Giving an account of oneself.* New York: Fordham University Press.

Carrier, J. & Miller, D. (Eds.). (1998). *Virtualities. A new political economy.* Oxford: Berg.

Chang, H-J. (2011 [2010]). *23 things they don't tell you about capitalism.* London: Penguin 2011.

Dembosky, A. (2011). Invasion of the body hackers. *Financial Times* June 10. http://www.ft.com/intl/cms/s/2/3ccb11a0-923b-11e0-9e00-00144fe-ab49a.html (accessed February 6, 2012).

Department for Business, Innovation & Skills (DBIS). (2009). *Higher ambitions. The future of universities in a knowledge economy.* DBIS: London.

Docherty, T. (2009). *The snowball: Warren Buffett and the business of life.* London: Bloomsbury.

Evans, R. (2011). The shackles of the past. *New Statesman.* November 21. Kindle Edition.

Festinger, L., Rieken, H. & Schachter, S. (1964). *When prophecy fails. A social and psychological study of a group that predicted the destruction of the world.* New York: Harper.

*Financial Times* [FT]. (2011a). Democracy's slow cure for the Euro. Editorial, September 16. http://www.ft.com/intl/cms/s/0/2e4610f4-e069-11e0-ba12-00144feabdc0.html (accessed February 6, 2012).

*Financial Times* [FT]. (2011b). Instability is the new certainty. Editorial, February 12. www.ljmu.ac.uk/ecl/ecl_docs/unrulytimes-bera.doc *(accessed February 8, 2012).*

Foster, H. (2011). Towards a grammar of emergency. *New Left Review, 68,* March/April, http://www.newleftreview.org/?view=2888 (accessed February 7, 2012).

Galbraith, K. (1992 [1954]). *The Great Crash 1929.* London: Penguin.

Gapper, G. (2010). The world's banks take a holiday from regulation. *Financial Times,* July 31/August, 1, http://www.ft.com/intl/cms/s/0/5dee4f7a-9c1c-11df-a7a4-00144feab49a.html (accessed February 7, 2012).

Giles, C. (2011a). Global economy: Five warning signs to watch, *Financial Times,* September 24/25. http://www.ft.com/intl/cms/s/0/20df9584-e5c8-11e0-8e99-00144feabdc0.html (accessed February 7, 2012).

Giles, C. (2011b). The 14% question. *FT Investors Chronicle,* October 11. http://blogs.ft.com/money-supply/author/chrisgiles (accessed October 15, 2011).

Goodley, S. (2011). EU inquiry into claims of banks' collusion in credit derivatives market. *The Guardian* (London), April 29. http://www.guardian.co.uk/business/2011/apr/29/banking-credit-default-swaps-eu-investigation (accessed February 7, 2012).

Graebner, D. (2002). The new anarchists. *New Left Review, 13* (January–February), 61, 73.

Gramsci, A. (1971). *The prison notebooks*. New York: Columbia University Press

*Guardian.* (2011a). Drone attacks will escalate Libya war. April 23. http://www.guardian.co.uk/world/2011/apr/23/drone-attacks-escalate-libya-war (accessed February 7, 2012).

*Guardian.* (2011b). It's time we all paid off our debts. October 5, p. 2.

Harford, T. (2011a). Banks, bills, and bail-outs. *Financial Times*, June 10. http://www.ft.com/intl/cms/s/2/8f9f53e2-9172-11e0-b1ea-00144feab49a.html (accessed February 7, 2012).

Harford, T. (2011b). Mr. Prime Minister, we like our credit cards. *Financial Times*, October 8/9, http://timharford.com/2011/10/mr-prime-minister-we-like-our-credit-cards/ (accessed February 7, 2012).

Hargreaves, D. (1996). Teaching as a research-based profession. Annual lecture, Teacher Training Agency, London.

Hastings, M. (2011). Cameron's silent prayer for Clegg. *Financial Times*, January 7, http://www.ft.com/cms/s/0/a927bba4-1a9b-11e0-b100-00144feab49a.html (accessed February 7, 2012).

Hobsbawm, E. (1994). *The age of extremes. The short 20ᵗʰ century, 1914–91*. London: Michael Joseph.

Jenkins, P., & Guerrera, F. (2011). Stop attacking lenders and back growth. *Financial Times*, January 29/30, p. 6.

Jones, S. (2009). Of couples and copulas. *Financial Times*, April 25/26, p. 3.

Kapuscinski, R. (2007). *Imperium* (K. Glowczewska, Trans.). London: Granta.

Kettle, M. (2010). The credit agencies are leading an assault on all of us. *Guardian*, December 17. http://www.guardian.co.uk/commentisfree/2010/dec/16/credit-rating-agencies-downgrade-spain (accessed February 7, 2012).

Klein, N. (2007). *The shock doctrine: The rise of disaster capitalism*. Toronto: Knopf.

Kleinman, M. (2011). King's renewed banking flak points to testing times. *Financial Times*, March 12/13. http://www.ft.com/intl/cms/s/0/e0cdb7d6-4c0d-11e0-82df-00144feab49a.html (accessed February 6, 2012).

Lanchester, J. (2010). *Whoops! Why everyone owes everyone and no-one can pay*. London: Allan Lane.

Lanchester, J. (2011). The non-scenic route to the place we're going anyway. *London Review of Books*, September 8, p. 3.

Lather, P. (2009). Scientism and scientificity in the rage for accountability. In St. Clair, R. (Ed.), *Education science. Critical perspectives* (pp. 66–79). Rotterdam: Sense Publishers.

Mazower, M. (1999). *Dark continent. Europe's 20ᵗʰ century*. London: Penguin.

McCartney, M. (2009). Crossing the guideline. *Financial Times*, April 25/26. http://blogs.ft.com/mccartney/2009/04/25/crossing-the-guideline/ (accessed February 6, 2012).

Moore, E. (2011). Regulators fear risks for synthetics. *Financial Times*, October 15/16, p. 9.

Mroz, A. (2010). A tiger with a real sting in its tail. *Times Higher Education*, Leader, December 9. http://www.timeshighereducation.co.uk/story.asp?storycode=414536 (accessed February 8, 2012).

Mroz, A. (2011). Ape market or come together. *Times Higher Education*, Leader, April 21, p. 5.

Norman, J. (2010). *The big society. The anatomy of the new politics*. Buckingham: University of Buckingham Press.

*Observer*. (2011). Editorial. The coalition's strategy is courting disaster. June 5.

Poster, M. (Ed.). (1988). *Jean Baudrillard. Selected writings*. Cambridge: Polity Press.

Price, A. (2010). Becoming the entrepreneurial educator: Putting complexity into practice. Invited contribution to seminar on "Learning for Real World Complexity," Academic Enhancement Unit, Liverpool John Moores University, October 12.

Rancière, J. (2010). *Dissensus. On politics and aesthetics* (S. Corcoran, Ed. and Trans.). London: Continuum.

Reich, R. (1992). *The work of nations. Preparing ourselves for 21ˢᵗ century capitalism*. New York: Vintage.

Shore, G. (2010). If public begets private, small cap is a likely winner. *Financial Times*, July 3/4, http://www.ft.com/intl/cms/s/2/eeeccd04-85fa-11df-bc22-00144feabdc0.html (accessed February 6, 2012).

Soros, G. (2008). *The crash of 2008 and what it means: The new paradigm for financial markets*. New York: Public Affairs.

Strathern, M. (2000). The tyranny of transparency. *British Educational Research Journal*, 26, 3, 305–321.

Stronach, I. (1999). Shouting theatre in a crowded fire: "Educational effectiveness" as cultural performance. *Evaluation*, 5, 2, 173–193.

Stronach I. (2009). Appreciating failure, depreciating success: an antidote to the eulogies of departure. *Research Intelligence*, 14–16.

Stronach, I. (2010). *Globalizing education, educating the local. How method made us mad*. London: Routledge.

Stronach, I., & Clarke, J. (2009). Bring back *Das Kapital* punishment! Credit crunch and the fall of the "knowledge economy." *Innovations in Practice*, 2, 2, 16–20.

Stronach, I. & Clarke, J. (2010). Bring back *Das Kapital* punishment. The credit crunch and the fall of the knowledge economy. *Forum, 52*, 1, 119–123.

Stronach, I., & Clarke, J. (2011a). Eight contentions for an educational future: Timely rules for unruly times. *Qualitative Inquiry, 17*, 10, 986–996.

Stronach, I., & Clarke, J. (2011b). For whom the bell tolls: Education, care and professional practice in uncertain times. In J. Forbes & C. Watson (Eds.), *The transformation of children's services: Examining and debating the complexities of inter-professional working* (pp. 60–76). London: Routledge.

Swift, J. (2007). *Gulliver's travels, and, verses on "Gulliver's Travels" by Alexander Pope.* London: Vintage.

Taleb, N. (2008). *The Black Swan: The impact of the highly improbable.* London: Penguin.

Tett, G. (2009). *Fool's gold. How unrestrained greed corrupted a dream, shattered global markets and unleashed a catastrophe.* London: Little Brown.

Tett, G. (2011). Black swans, but no need to flap. *Financial Times*, March 26/27, p. 12.

*Times Higher Education* (THE). (2011). World University Rankings, 2011–12. Supplement, October 6.

Toynbee, P. (2010). Cameron and Clegg are like pre-modern leech doctors. *Guardian*, June 19, http://www.guardian.co.uk/commentisfree/2010/jun/18/cameron-clegg-leech-doctors (accessed February 6, 2012).

Trotsky, L. (1967 [1934]). *The history of the Russian Revolution.* Volume 3. London: Sphere.

Trotsky, L. (1971) [1907]. *1905.* Harmondsworth, UK: Penguin.

Uvalic-Trumbic, S. (2011). High scores in the wrong game. *Times Higher Education*, April 28, p. 17.

Webb, M. (2011). In spite of debt crises, Greece is in the core. *Financial Times*, December 4/5, p. 11.

White, M. (2010). Much talk about deficit, but no mention of debt. *Guardian*, August 12, p. 19.

Willetts, D. (2010). *The pinch: how the baby boomers took their children's futures—and how they can give it back.* London: Atlantic Books.

*WOW Star.* (2011). WOW careers review. Graduate Development Centre, Liverpool John Moores University.

Žižek, S. (2009). *First as tragedy, then as farce.* London: Verso.

Žižek, S. (2011). Speech at Occupy Wall Street/Liberty Plaza. (http://occupywallst.org/article/today-liberty-plaza-had-visit-slavoj-zizek (accessed October 21, 2011).

## Chapter 3

# "Answers," Assemblages, and Qualitative Research

Mirka Koro-Ljungberg and Tim Barko

*What is it that the man who says, "I want the truth" wants? He wants the truth only when it is constrained and forced. He wants it only under the rule of an encounter, in relation to such-and-such a sign. What he wants is to interpret, to decipher, to translate, to find the meaning of the sign*
—Deleuze (1972, p. 17)

*The truth is not revealed, it is betrayed; it is not communicated, it is interpreted; it is not willed, it is involuntary.*
—Deleuze (1972, p. 160)

"Corporative science" calls for truth and generalizable answers that are not to be interpreted, deciphered, or translated. Rather, the finality of these answers oftentimes implies epistemological control and a fetishization of systems of knowledge. This contemporary movement toward increased control of knowledge

*Qualitative Inquiry and the Politics of Advocacy,* edited by Norman K. Denzin and Michael D. Giardina, 79–100. © 2012 Left Coast Press, Inc. All rights reserved.

and research practice is troubling yet real. Various sociopolitical circumstances and grand-narratives enable and call for particular types of questions, thus enabling corporative science along with many scholars to effectively promote and seek for ultimate and reliable answers to these questions. We find these essentializing desires for answers and corresponding questions that are treated as verifiable truths exempt from critique problematic (see, e.g., Dynarski, 2008; Slavin, 2004). More specifically, we are concerned with social and political pressures to oversimplify and promote definite, simplified, and ultimate answers even when studying complex and multidimensional educational problems. These political pressure points steer researchers to focus on outcomes rather than paying more attention to the processes that generate particular types of answers.

Many scholars before us have raised concerns about simplicity, "easy think," "easy fix," and taken-for-granted answers to complex educational problems. For example, Schwandt (2008) referred to a quest for simplicity in educational researchers and problematized tendencies to engage in easy think that "flourishes in a climate of apathy, distrust, and cynicism" (p. 141). Dynarski (2008), in turn, emphasized educators' prioritization of answers arguing "educators perhaps are less interested in the routes taken to arrive at answers than in the answers themselves" (p. 29). When answers to research questions and complex educational problems are taken for granted and assumed to provide essential and evidence-based knowledge, answers are treated as an endpoint for research indicating a closure and the end of a text, interpretation, and dialogue (see Hostetler, 2005). This simplicity, a form of epistemological essentialism, can work against professionalism as a kind of trusteeship as Schwandt (2008) explained. Professionalism is replaced with "the notion of technical professionalism, with the professional reduced to a supplier of expert services" (Schwandt, 2008, p. 142).

Sometimes it is tempting to prefer easy think, to want the bottom line (the final product, the realization of the investment, the return of capital, removal of venture debt) over the possibility, potentiality, and futurity of what asking these questions and conducting research might bring. This return of capital and the realization of the investment can become problematic when research projects, inquiry, and interactions with participants might not have a clear endpoint or analytical ultimatum, as often experienced by many qualitative researchers. Scholars are not patient enough to tolerate "rifts between assemblages" or "elements that do not arrive on time," and it is difficult to "pass through fog, to cross voids, to have lead times and delays" (Deleuze & Guattari, 1987 [1980], p. 255).

Gordon (2007) argued that the quest for certainty in education reflects researchers, parents, teachers, administrators, and politicians' desires for psychological security and increased control. "This quest implies an unwillingness to live with the inherent complexities and risks of education" (p. 37). Similarly, Schwandt (2008) noted that the current trend to value optimal solutions "ignores all that we have learned about complexity, about bounded rationality, and about the virtues of seeking a satisfactory outcome versus a maximal one" (p. 143). According to Schwandt (2008), this trend is also disturbing because it reflects the lack of tolerance for ambiguity, it ignores variations, and it puts forward oversimplified view of the social order. Rilke (1993) challenged us to "live the question" rather than search for answers. He asks us to "try to love *the questions themselves* as if they were locked rooms or books written in a very foreign language" (p. 34). Furthermore, Rilke proposed that living the questions can possibly enable individuals to live their ways into the answers.

Many of us are trained to recognize an answer when we see it in the data or we are expected to conclude with an answer once we have completed the research and methodological processes. Less often, scholars are prompted to consider how they epistemologically and conceptually position the sign and concept of answer or how answers function in their research. Sometimes answers to research questions, especially those answers presented with authority and exclusion, are closing inquiries and terminating future processes of knowing. Deleuze (1972), influenced by Proust, said:

> We search for truth only when we are determined to do so in terms of a concrete situation, when we undergo a kind of violence which impels us to such a search. Who searches for truth? The jealous man, under the pressure of the beloved's lies. There

is always the violence of a sign which forces us into the search, which robs us of peace. The truth is not be found by affinity, or by good will, but is betrayed by involuntary signs. (pp. 15–16)

Additionally, some qualitative researchers are asked to generate and produce not only answers but also "calcifications that have come to be regarded not as answers at all but as truths exempt from critique" (O'Byrne, 2005, p. 393). Hostetler (2005) discussed the problems associated with desires for answers in the educational context and problematized the need to *"end* with the answers" (p. 21; emphasis added). This request to end with the answers can create spaces that avoid questions of ethics, communal responsibility, and contextual and situated decision making. By privileging answers over ongoing questioning and open-ended inquiry, researchers also tend to close dialogue between disciplines, literature, practitioners, and between researchers and diverse participant communities. Answers are considered to imply finality and an end to the inquiry and interpretation processes, which might remove the tension and movement that is oftentimes necessary for scientific encounters (see, e.g., Kuhn, 1977).

To promote this movement important for creativity and science, we now put forward dialogue and reflections on the correspondence between a question and answer or the relationship between inquiry and outcomes. We worry, like Bogue (2004), who said that in the world of recognition and representation learning is "simply the passage from non-knowledge to knowledge, a process with a definite beginning and ending, in which thought, like a dutiful pupil, responds to pre-formulated questions and eventually arrives at pre-existing answers" (p. 333). Furthermore, Bogue emphasized the role of paradox when thinking about novelty of answers by explaining that anything new does not confirm with expectations or does not represent orthodoxy. Instead, new seems paradoxical and nonsensical. Likewise, in this chapter it is our intention to present not an exact idea of what an answer could be only a representation of ideas how one can think about diverse ways answers are becoming, creating movement; moving to all directions at once (see also Deleuze & Guattari, 1987 [1980]). To support these intentions, we have also formatted our writing to illustrate how we make connections to existing texts and signs emphasizing multiple perspectives and lines of thought, hopefully without argumentative closure, rigidness of linear logic, and presence of textual stability.

## Assemblages

One can imagine answers as assemblages. Similar to Marcus and Saka (2006), we use the concept of assemblage to think with and to make connections to the texts we read. For us, assemblage represents a "structure-like surrogate" (Marcus & Saka, 2006, p. 101), an image of a jar, an opening among other things. In one context, we refer to a Wallace Steven poem as a point of departure. In later context, we will provide images of bottled water as an answer to a poor question and discuss the notions of the jar assemblage in the context of militarized finality and what responsibilities we might have for our culturally destructive tendencies. Furthermore, we see assemblage as an anti-structural concept that permits the researcher to speak of emergence, heterogeneity, the decentered, and the ephemeral in a nonetheless ordered social life.

Assemblage is opposed to modernist accounts of structured and ordered life or societal expectations related to grand narratives framing the appropriate uses of answers. An assemblage can be used as a catch-phrase or perhaps micro-"theory enabling a heterogeneous outlook within the "post-"understanding of ephemeral; that is, it allows for a discussion of the heterogeneous without loss of the modernist references, concepts, and presuppositions of structure and order. Assemblage can also reflect an image of structure. But assemblage is also a ruse: "Assemblage thus seems structural, an object with the materiality and stability of the classic metaphors of structure, but the intent in its aesthetic uses is precisely to undermine such ideas of structure" (Marcus & Saka, 2006, p. 102). It becomes, as Deleuze and Guattari suggest (1987 [1980]), a radical, deviant current in relation to the structural dependencies of modernist tradition.

One might argue that assemblage can be viewed as an excuse for textual messiness or irrational and disconnected flow of ideas. It is exactly this messiness and disconnection that put ideas, thoughts, and concepts in motion. Assemblage is the source of "emergent properties" of machinic processes and can be seen as a result of the intersection of two (or more) open systems. The assemblage is productive of difference (nonrepetition). It can be seen grounded and as a primary expression of qualitative differences. The notion of assemblage allows us to recapture (reterritorialize) the playful and profane notions difference and heterogeneity, in this case when thinking about answers in qualitative research. The modernist apparatus (rules of play) can be read also as the globalized apparatus, the desire to remove difference and add structure to thought. A globalized apparatus is designed to remove heterogeneity and facilitate an academic and economic process of McDonaldization, where the food for thought is ground up, bleached, sterilized, structuralized, and served under a singular, universally recognizable commodity label (the Golden Arches becomes a metaphor for all thought, cultural, social, spiritual, in general). Assemblage is opposed to globalization as imagined above.

Assemblage can also be seen as an evocation, a prayer almost, though not a prayer where we just mouth the words without meaning. Assemblage is not a dead metaphor, rather it evocates emergence of the heterogeneous within and from our data of inquiry; it attempts to remove the finality of the object of research, and in so doing, provides a basis for the imaginary shifting between open systems of thought without ultimately globalizing the substance of human experience.

## The Jar Assemblage: What Was the Question Again?

*"Anecdote of the Jar"*

*I placed a jar in Tennessee,*
*And round it was, upon a hill.*
*It made the slovenly wilderness*
*Surround that hill.*

*The wilderness rose up to it.*

Reading *Anecdote of the Jar* by Wallace Stevens (1923) reminded us of a whiskey jar, one of those old clay jars supposedly used by Tennessee wild men and mountain bootleggers and then by those more legitimate whiskey salesmen who wanted to put on airs of those rough-and-tumble days of mountaineer bootlegging. Even though Stevens's poem doesn't relate to whiskey or whiskey jars, it does relate to the cultural object of the jar and the jar assemblage, of which a whiskey jar represents one example. Jars have been used throughout human history to preserve cultural images (i.e., Greco-Roman urns, Egyptian canopic jars, Ming dynasty vases). In a sense, the jar as assemblage represents a practical answer to a universal question: How do I best transport difficult, hard-to-carry objects such as liquids and other malleable food ingredients, things that don't fit easily or neatly into a cart or don't lend themselves to being carried by hand or horse? Or one can consider Egyptian canopic jars used to preserve the organs and viscera for the recently departed's journey in the afterlife. Hence, we, as a species, have crafted jars or those other jar-like objects—for example, urn, vase, tankard, mug, cup, glass, and bottle, to name but a few—for a distinct purpose in response to distinct real-world problem. All these variations of a jar represent a distinctly utilitarian, hand-crafted or machine-created cultural assemblage of the jar and jar-like object, a solution to a universal problem: How do we best carry difficult substances?

Many cultures throughout time—there are always counterexamples—both prehistorical and historical, have seen fit to craft for themselves these jars for many different reasons, the most obvious of which is to help collect, carry, and hold difficult or easily lost things, to keep things hot, cold, or well preserved, but also, in later iterations, to act as adornments or decorations, obvious signifiers of status and social class. After all, why would Keats write an "Ode to a Grecian Urn" if not to celebrate on some level, the visual merits, and not the innate utility, of the jar assemblage as decorative and artistic signifier?

Because of the pervasiveness of the jar, we agree with Wallace Stevens, who, in his poem, expresses that jars, in themselves, represent a humanistic and holistic way of thinking and solving problems. Jars are crafted and created from the elements of the earth, made from baked clay, sand, and dirt. There are jars made from vegetative materials such as wood from trees and dried-out gourds. Recent archeologists have even discovered such macabre relics as human skull drinking cups, used by ancient ice-aged civilizations in the British Isles for consuming liquids (Bello et al., 2011). To Stevens, the jar represents our dominion over nature and our capacity to turn nature into something simply unnatural, something you would not find apart from human cultural influence. The jar becomes more than just a jar, it becomes a symbol for human culture and language, all those attributes that follow from the interwoven capacity to put language to use in order to fashion, craft, create, and use those creations to solve problems. Culture is seen by Wallace as being opposed to the natural condition. To create, and to use our creative capacity, we first exert control over the natural. In so doing, the jar, namely human culture, has taken dominion everywhere, to the point where, hiking through the mountains of Tennessee, it would be quite difficult to not stumble at some point or another on some discarded piece of our culture, often, some form of a jar: a bottle or beer can, haphazardly thrown out, just being there, in all its unnaturalness, a testament to our cultural ingenuity, our capacity to create, fashion and control "like nothing else in Tennessee."

## Speaking in Images, Again

For Deleuze, difference is a movement away from the same; it is no longer subordinated to the linear process of not-group to group. There is no end point, no destination, and no linearity. Difference becomes a process of creating the unique and the particular, the truly individual, an escape from sameness, stability and homogeneity. One can imagine answers as a processes becoming. Becoming is the creation of newness, it is opposed to sameness and repetition. Repetition is a form of difference, a form of movement away from the point of origination. Becoming as an intersection of the *molar*, the governing cultural apparatus, such as cheerleading in Jackson's (2010) example, containing overcoded and saturated ideas of femininity, service activity, seductive and coy routines, sexuality, and all that entails, with the *molecular*, the effect of breaking apart, fracturing, rupturing these overcoded and governing cultural distinctions into personal, creative, and individual processes. Becoming is how we withdraw from a majority and therefore also how we rise up from the minority. Becoming is a process of creating friction in the "molar machine."

Imagine answers as similar to the end of an essay or book, research or science. Feyerabend (1991) explained that "The end of an essay, or a book, though formulated as if it were an end, is therefore not really an end but a transition point which has received undue weight" (p. 163). In short, the notion of end, in science, is artificial, something researchers impose on the process when it could be argued that there is no barrier between the end and the experiment itself. According to Galison (1987), "there is no *strictly logical* termination point inherent in the experimental process," therefore any notion of ending is rendered problematic methodologically, just like our answers. In this sense, the goals of experimental discovery, if they exist, are a byproduct of multiple layers of interaction between measurement, theory, history, belief and the idiosyncrasies of the researchers (p. 3; emphasis in the original). It is not something that comes easy, the eureka moment of science is often an after-the-fact addition to simplify the narrative, to make it more heroic, giving the end and not the process itself Feyerabend's undue weight.

What else could philosophy teach us about different images of answers, practices of educational researchers, and their desires for ultimate or concluding answers? Nietzsche suggested that the search for truth and answers points to the limits of science, the irresolvable illusion that requires arts and other forms of knowing to survive. Nietzsche wrote in *The Birth of Tragedy* that, "Once truth has been seen, the consciousness of it prompts man to see only what is terrible or absurd in existence wherever he looks" (1999, p. 40). He continued: "Art alone can re-direct those repulsive thoughts about the terrible or absurd nature of existence into representations with which man can live; these representations are the *sublime*, whereby the terrible is tamed by artistic means, and the *comical*, whereby disgust at absurdity is discharged by artistic means" (p. 40; emphasis in the original).

Additionally, Nietzsche described how searching for truth is more meaningful than finding it. Nietzsche's suspicions of the possibility of truth problematized the good nature of science by casting doubt on science's intentions and presupposing the will-to-power as the ultimate core of human understanding. Tradition and the knowledge engendered from tradition become something to be mastered, controlled, or done away with completely. He also refers to "the imperturbable belief that thought, as it follows the thread of causality, reaches down into the deepest abysses of being, and that it is capable, not simply of understanding existence, but even *correcting* it" (1999, p. 73; emphasis in the original). This sublime metaphysical illusion and causality's capability of correcting existence ultimately will transform itself into art. Nietzsche was also worried about scientific illusion, science's hurry to its limits where optimism will come to an end. Then, scientist will see "how logic curls up around itself at these limits and finally bites its own tail, then a new form of knowledge breaks through, *tragic knowledge*, which, simply to be endured, needs art for protection and as medicine" (p. 75; emphasis in the original).

Whereas Nietzsche categorized knowledge through mastery, Gadamer rejected this suspicion and presupposes openness and trust as a condition for knowledge (see e.g., Gadamer, 1989 [1960]; Moran, 2001). In the context of hermeneutics, Gadamer proposed that texts (articulation of answers in the context of science and thought) represent different voices in larger historical dialogue. Individual thoughts are narrowly defined in the larger context of hermeneutics, as history, society, and the individual interact to reinterpret meaning and knowledge actively through the reading of a text. To Gadamer, texts were not created in order to record answers but to perpetuate dialogue and reinterpretation; individuals open themselves to the text. A text is not an *answer* but rather something that must be reinterpreted by each individual and reader. A text "explicitly and consciously bridges the temporal distance that separates the interpreter from the text" (Gadamer, 1989, p. 311). The text becomes a voice, a partner, in a growing historical dialogue as new meanings are created from old ideas. Hermeneutics becomes a generator of dialogue, opposing the finality of *answers* by presupposing movement of understanding from the whole of history to the part of the individual and back again to unity.

Derrida, in turn, wondered what "a well-put question" was. He argued that:

> The analysis that give rise to one another in this book do not answer this question, bringing to it neither an answer nor an answer. They work, rather, to transform and deplace its statement, and toward examining the presuppositions of the question, the institution of its protocol, the laws of its procedure, the headings of its alleged homogeneity, of its apparent unicity. (1982 [1972], p. xvi)

Additionally, Derrida further questioned the role of answer and question. He did not view answers as metaphysical objects rather he wondered about the benefits of using questions as one structural component of expected question/answer correspondence. For Derrida, even a question might be aside a point. "No answer, then. Perhaps, in the long run, not even a question. The copulative correspondence, the opposition question/answer is already lodged in a structure, enveloped in the hollow of an ear, which we will go into to take a look" (1982, pp. xvi–xvii).

Alternatively, one can imagine answers as invitations to conversation or as nutrients to dialogue. Deleuze (1990 [1969]) compared the notions of eating and speaking with defecating and thinking and he sought to relate the process of speaking and thinking with the ecological notions of nutrient cycle, with the byproducts of the process becoming nutrients for further growth (pp. 85, 193). The process of dialogue becomes a cycle of consumptions as words become *food for thought* and the nature of the nutrient cycle, as excremental object, becomes a form of decomposition, with the compost serving as renutrification for the rhizomes and other plant-like metaphors. Dialogue becomes ecological and process oriented; a multiplicity, not a finality (Deleuze & Guattari, 1987 [1980], pp. 8–10).

Answers could also be imagined as epistemological openings to the structures that shape and produce knowledge claims. Answers can be informative signifiers of language and social structures that shape the entire research process. In this case, instead of approaching answers as truths exempt from critique, answers might serve as basis for critique:

> So the sense in which truth is "relative," and not absolute, is just that because truths are representations of facts, and there can be no presentation of facts without language or something essentially similar; it follows that truths of any kind are subject to the conditions under which meaningful language is possible. (Baldwin, 2008, pp. 114–115)

From this perspective, answers become a transitional phase in the research process. In other words, answers are mere place holders, temporary signifiers whose ultimate goal is to draw our attention to the future work that yet needs be done: all the further questions, further discussions, and research that have yet to take place. Answers serve as transitions between our epistemological past, our present traditions of thought, and the futurity of the Derridian *to come* in science, philosophy, and society.

## The Water Bottle Question

We wonder what question bottled water was supposed to answer? For what reasons did someone decide to bottle, sell, and commodify something so readily available and practically free to the average consumer? While bottled water as an industry has been around for some time, companies like Perrier and Evian are over a century old. Evian, the first bottled water company, at least in the traditional sense of a company, began selling water in 1830 in earthenware jugs. Perrier as offered its spa-grade mineral water, distinct from the bland bottled waters consumed in the United States, since 1898. The water was bottled and sold at the Perrier spa in Vergèze, France, and moved outward to larger markets from France.

The cultural images of bottled water as a necessity are much more recent phenomena. According to Leonard (2010), the bottled water industry emerged as a byproduct of the soda industry of the late 1970s. As the soda industry's market projects began to plateau, they needed to find a new market niche to increase profit margins and water was chosen as the next big verdant market. So, initially bottle water industry had a question: How do we increase profits of a beverage industry? To answer this question, the industry had to find a new market and create a massive campaign to vilify tap water as dangerous, polluted, and just plain dirty (Gleick, 2010). Since the decision to commodify the water market in 1976, the average consumption for bottled water has: "doubled, doubled again, double again, and then doubled *again*" (Gleick, 2010, p. 24). As a result, consumers have begun to fear the commonly, freely available water of the tap and have consistently put their faith in the commodity of the bottle.

What question is bottled water an answer to? Is it a well-formed question? Is it the type of question that is beneficial for a society, a culture, or an individual? Does this question create positive effects on our daily lives? As stated earlier, the jar assemblage was initially an answer to the question: How do we transport difficult to carry substances, such as liquids, in such a way as to make them available when we need them. However, the jar assemblage is not the only answer to this question. Both modern and classical engineering have found and created mechanisms to bring liquids to us. Romans had aqueducts, now we have faucets and spigots, water fountains and household sinks. In short, using jars as a mechanism for liquid distribution is by no means the best of all possible solutions to the original question about how to transport difficult to contain and carry objects. That is not to say the jar assemblage is no longer needed or is no longer a valuable component to answering the question. After all, once we have the water in our houses or in a public space, we have to have an equitable delivery mechanism that allows us to move the water about from the source to wherever it is needed. Hence, jars are still viable in their role vis-à-vis distribution apparatuses.

In fact, the argument given by many for using bottled water is that it is more convenient, you don't have to be near a spigot or faucet or water fountain, you can carry it with you, as any good jar will allow. The question now becomes, why the specific use of a disposable plastic bottle as a delivery device for transporting and consuming water? Why not something more sustainable, reusable, and economical such as a canteen or cup? Bottled water, as instance of the jar assemblage when examined in this light, demonstrates a clear deficiency in what we mean by a well-formed question, of

Images taken by authors while walking through Florida's wilderness. Even in natural places, the jar becomes a jar-as-waste object.

course, unless we consider the bottled water as answer to the corporatist question: How do we diversify our product line and increase profits? After all, bottled water might not be any more convenient than most other mechanisms for obtaining and transporting water.

The bottled water as jar assemblage offers little in actual return when convenience is the primary consideration. In addition, the bottled water as jar represents a disposable commodity that often finds its way not into recycle bins, but rather out there "round upon the ground," as Stevens puts it, an unnatural object in a natural place. This returns us to the central nature of the jar assemblage: To make a jar, you must take available resources and fashion them into something distinctly usable to human culture. Bottled water industry uses obviously finite resources (e.g., natural oil) to create a commodity that, in itself, offers us little except a mechanism for increasing our dominion over the natural sphere in the form of mountains of discarded and used jars. The jar assemblage as cultural artifact has come to exert dominion, giving us nothing but a future of "slovenly wilderness" of discarded jars, a forest of commodified answers swelling the natural world, granting dominion of human culture over the natural domain: an answer to a question that in all reasonableness had already found a much more equitable solution.

### The Jar Goes to War: Assemblages and the "Finality" of Militarized Thought

The jar assemblage also has a more sordid and violent history. The Byzantine Empire made use of its "Greek fire" through a clay pot delivery mechanism. And, while the western Roman Empire was chipped away by invasions of the "barbarian" hordes, the eastern Empire was more than capable of defending its walls from encroachment through its use of weaponized jar-like delivery mechanisms. The jar, instead of providing a useful mechanism for delivering spoilable goods and liquids, became co-opted for purposes of war. Although the Byzantine Empire may not have been the first to make use of the jar assemblage for war it seems, for all practical purposes, the first distinctly martial use of a jar to deliver a dangerous chemical or explosive material in an act of aggression or defense against another human being.

With the Western discovery of gunpowder—which wasn't a discovery per se but an integration of eastern Chinese technology—the jar assemblage continued to progress in its potency as a mechanism for not just exerting humanity's dominion over nature but humanity's dominion over itself. The jar was used to extend the destructive and war-making capacity of those who were in possession of the appropriate technology. The jar assemblage became the repository of objects that served not just as utensils and decorations as discussed above but also those related genealogically to the clay pot Greek fire jars and even earlier projectile weapons: bombs, grenades, and bullets. As technology progressed, so did the destructive nature of the "war jars." Basic clay pots gave rise to more advanced explosive technologies, including the invention of dynamite and case-less ammunition. Greek fire gave way to the likes of the dreaded chemical weapons used in World War I and to its most obvious descendant, napalm, both used to horrific effects throughout the 20th century.

As technology has developed, so has our ability to find more devastating purposes for the jar assemblage. With World War II, both the axis and allied powers were busy in a race to develop perhaps the most horrific of all jars: the nuclear bomb. This has led us to ask what question the nuclear bomb was an answer to. Was it a question that had to inevitably end or lead to destruction? By the end of the war, when the bomb was officially developed, the Third Reich had fallen and the Japanese Empire was in a state of retreat, with its war-making ability reduced to a point where defeat was ensured. The question has been raised whether dropping two nuclear bombs was justified, considering how little offensive energy the Japanese Empire had left. An invasion of the Japanese islands by the Allies was imminent. According to historians, the Japanese military had planned for this contingency and had called it *Ketsugo* (Skates, 1994).

Regardless of the perceived or rhetorical estimates of American and Japanese lives that would have or could have been lost, it was deemed a more reasonable solution to use our newly created atomic arsenal, the fat man and little boy, on two Japanese cities and let the emperor know that it was not necessary to invade his country. The question still remains: Was the use of two nuclear bombs on actual humans a necessary and significant condition for the ending of hostilities between the Allies and the Japanese Empire? Was there a more reasonable solution? Would a demonstration on some uninhabited island have been better, and would the Japanese military decision makers realize the destructive capacity arrayed against them and surrender? Regardless of the possible answers to these questions, the atomic age had begun. The jar had played its part as a conveyor of difficult-to-control, difficult-to-hold, difficult-to-carry objects. What began as a clay pot designed to hold Greek fire had ended with a jar capable of producing destruction and deadly chemical reactions on massively large scales, jars-as-weapons-of-mass-destruction.

Industrialization led to militarization of the jar as weapons-grade assemblage in the 20th century. Top: U.S. soldiers put new gas masks to use. Middle: small crane swinging 400mm shell. Bottom: inside of ammunition car. (Photos used courtesy of the United States Army Heritage and Education Center. All photos are under the public domain, and may be used without permission.)

The jar has come a long way from a cultural object presenting our domination over the natural world and it has become much more than a means of protecting and conveying difficult to carry and control substances. It has transformed into a militarized cultural object capable of not just exerting domination over the natural world but possibly ending it as well. We wonder whether, in answering the most destructive questions posed by the precarious history of the 20th century, if the jar assemblage has been militarized to such an extent that, in the end, "Dante's Inferno will be made to look like a children's playground" as mused the poet Charles Bukowski in his apocalyptic eulogy *Dinosaria, we.* To what extent were culture, science, and the quest for a final solution to the war culpable for the militarization of the jar assemblage or any assemblage for that matter?

Rather than reading an apocalyptic finality into the invention of the atomic bomb, which seems to be the most obvious of readings, given the countless references to atomic finality throughout visual and literary media during the cold war, we want to present even the atomic bomb as not a finality, but a new beginning. This new beginning stimulates further questions, questions that perhaps require deeper and more prolonged thought. It raises new questions of implementation, questions of availability and control, questions of equitable distribution, of disarming, of retooling and of securing; questions about proper and fair use; questions about research programs, big science, little science, greener energy, and radioactive waste. Not an end but rather a continued process of new beginnings, new questions, and new ideas. Which leads to another question, always more questions: What responsibility do we have as researchers, educators, poets, and people for continuing progress not toward a final destruction but the realization of social justice?

## Ending or New Beginning?

Various grand narratives and training of educational researchers produce answers in research as an ultimate goal, objective and verifiable facts that end an inquiry. However, these perspectives can become problematic, especially when considering the persistent problems with improving practice, facilitating long-lasting changes in socially diverse communities, and promoting social justice in different educational contexts. In other words, answers are treated as arbitrary endpoints without further considerations of the impact of these pedagogical practices. We believe that during neoliberal and reductionist times and politics, it is important to consider how answers function in research and how scientific answers are shaped by larger sociopolitical discourses thus greatly influencing the work educational researchers do and will do in the future. Bogue (2004) proposed that "problems must be evaluated not according to their 'resolvability,' as often happens in philosophy [and in other disciplines], but according to their importance, their ability to generate new questions" (p. 334). Problems are not solved by resolutions and specific solutions but, according to Bogue, problems are "structured field of potential actualizations" (p. 335) and systems of differentially connected elements and points.

Deleuze (1972) suggested that orders of production and truth remain partitioned, fragmented, and "*without anything lacking*: eternally partial parts, open boxes and sealed vessels, swept on by time without forming a whole of presupposing one, without lacking anything in this quartering, and denouncing in advance every organic unity we might seek to introduce into it" (p. 143; emphasis in the original). We wonder what would happen if we imagine answers to our research questions and educational dilemmas as open boxes "without anything lacking" or as opportunities to reformulate old elements into new patterns (see Swearingen, 1990).

Hostetler (2005) connected answers to researchers' ethical responsibilities to work toward social good. Similarly, Schwandt (2008) called for:

> Citizens and professionals who are marked by their capacity to be inquisitive, systematic in their inquiry, judicious in their claims, truth seeking, analytical, intellectually humble, sympathetic to opposing points of view, self-critical, and open-minded—not simply open-minded in the sense of being tolerant to other points of view, but open-minded in the sense of recognizing the challenges to one's own way of seeing things that arise from others' ways of making distinctions of worth. (p. 149)

We would like to encourage qualitative researchers to think about answers to research questions as multiple images of beginnings, entry points, as an entrance to the ongoing dialogue; not an exit or the ending of research. Intertextuality, reflective readings, thinking with philosophers and theory, and focusing on images and different ways of knowing might help us avoid feeling trapped and controlled by fixed and essential questions. Thinking about answers as transitions, openings, jars, or other kinds of invitations and forms of dialogue does not diminish the value of research but it could avoid closure and finality that can possibly limit the impact and implications of educational research.

Applying Deleuze and Guattari's (1987 [1980]) idea of plane of immanence to our wonderings about answers, we also consider answers as "the infinity of the modifications that are part of one another on this unique plane of life" (p. 254). Thus, answers, for us, do not present organizations but compositions, movement, rest, speed, and slowness, borrowing from Deleuze and Guattari. Possibly it could be interesting, stimulating, and productively challenging to focus more on learning that could involve a reorientation of thought following its initial disorientation, to understand something new in its newness, and "as a structured field of potential metamorphic forces rather than a pre-formed body of knowledge to be mastered" (Bogue, 2004, p. 341) Or we could be guided by Proust's idea of possibilities of constrains and chance.

> In opposition to the philosophical idea of "method," Proust sets the double idea of "constraint" and of "chance." Truth depends on an encounter with something which forces us to think, to see the truth. The accident of encounters, the pressure of constraints are Proust's two fundamental themes. (Deleuze, 1972, p. 16)

Or maybe it would be best to focus on living the questions, as Rilke suggested. And while living the questions, staying confused and uncertain, we may be able to get to know ourselves better and make our lives and education more meaningful. Who knows?

## References

Baldwin, T. (2008). Presence, truth and authenticity. In S. Glendinning & R. Eaglestone (Eds.), *Derrida's legacies: Literature and philosophy* (pp. 107–117). London: Routledge.

Bello, S. M., Parfitt, S. A, & Stringer, C. B. (2011). Earliest directly-dated human skull-cups. *PLoS ONE* 6(2): e17026.

Bogue, R. (2004). Search, swim and see: Deleuze's apprenticeship in signs and pedagogy of images. *Educational Philosophy and Theory, 36*, 3, 327–342.

Deleuze, G. (1972). *Proust and signs.* New York: G. Braziller.

Deleuze, G. (1990 [1969]). *The logic of sense* (M. Lester, Trans). New York: Columbia University Press.

Deleuze, G. & Guattari, F. (1987 [1980]). *A thousand plateaus: Capitalism and schizophrenia* (B. Massumi, Trans.). Minneapolis: University of Minnesota Press.

Derrida, J. (1982 [1972]). *Margins of philosophy* (A. Bass, Trans.). Chicago: University of Chicago Press.

Dynarski, M. (2008). Comments on Slavin: Bringing answers to educators: guiding principles for research syntheses. *Educational Researcher, 37*, 1, 27–29.

Feyerabend, P. (1991). *Three dialogues on knowledge.* Oxford, UK: Basil Blackwell.

Gadamer, H-G. (1989 [1960]). *Truth and method* (J. Weinsheimer & D. Marshall, Trans.). New York: Continuum Publishing.

Galison, P. (1987). *How experiments end.* Chicago: University of Chicago Press.

Gleick, P. (2010). *Bottled and sold: The story behind our obsession with bottled water.* Washington, DC: Island Press.

Gordon, M. (2007). Living the questions: Rilke's challenge to our quest for certainty. *Educational Theory, 57*, 1, 37–52.

Hostetler, K. (2005). What is "good" education research? *Educational Researcher, 34*, 6, 16–21.

Jackson, A. Y. (2010). Deleuze and the girl. *International Journal of Qualitative Studies in Education, 23*, 5, 579–587.

Kuhn, T. (1977). The essential tension: Tradition and innovation in scientific research. In T. Kuhn (Ed.), *The essential tension: Selected studies in scientific tradition and change* (pp. 225–239). Chicago: University of Chicago Press.

Leonard, A. (2010). *The story of stuff: How our obsession with stuff is trashing the planet, our communities, and our health-and a vision for change.* New York: Free Press.

Marcus, G. & Saka, E. (2006). Assemblage. *Theory, Culture & Society, 23*, 2–3, 101–109.

Moran, D. (2001). *Introduction to phenomenology.* London: Routledge.

Nietzsche, F. (1999). The birth of tragedy. In R. Geuss & R. Speirs (Eds.), *The birth of tragedy and other writings* (pp. 3–116). Cambridge, UK: Cambridge University Press.

O'Byrne, A. (2005). Pedagogy without a project: Arendt and Derrida on teaching, responsibility and revolution. *Studies in Philosophy and Education, 24,* 5, 389–409.

Rilke, R. M. (1993). *Letters to a young poet.* New York: Norton.

Schwandt, T. A. (2008). Educating for intelligent belief in evaluation. *American Journal of Evaluation, 29,* 2, 139–150.

Skates, J. R. (1994). *The invasion of Japan: Alternative to the bomb.* Columbia: University of South Carolina Press.

Slavin, R. (2004). Education research can and must address "what works" questions. *Educational Researcher, 33,* 1, 27–28.

Stevens, W. (1923). The anecdote of the jar. *Harmonium.* New York: Knopf.

Swearingen, C. (1990). Dialogue and dialectic: The logic of conversation and the interpretation of logic. In T. Maranhao (Ed.), *The interpretation of dialogue* (pp. 47–71). Chicago: University of Chicago Press.

**Chapter 4**

# Turning the Next Wide 21st-Century Corner

## Holistic Restorative Justice as Science in Qualitative Inquiry

John H. Stanfield, II

Nearly forty years ago, as a young man, I embarked on the journey to become a sociologist as a graduate student at Northwestern University.[1] Howie Becker, the guru of qualitative sociological research in the department, and around much of the country, was on leave the fall quarter I entered. Nevertheless, each entering doctoral studies cohort had to take qualitative methods the first fall quarter. I recall vividly that John Kituse and a young colleague Marshall Shumway were Howie's replacements that quarter. I can still see the intimidating piles of studies recorded on the distributed departmental qualitative methods bibliography that students were expected to master by the time comps rolled around, if you were so blessed to get that far.

As I embarked on my qualitative research project, which was a participant observation study in a Hare Krishna temple conveniently located across the street from my apartment in Evanston, I became, as a novice researcher, sensitive to the many dos and don'ts of field research canons during our weekly debriefing seminars. One of the major concerns then and probably still today, was

*Qualitative Inquiry and the Politics of Advocacy,* edited by Norman K. Denzin and Michael D. Giardina, 101–120. © 2012 Left Coast Press, Inc. All rights reserved.

the danger of going native and protocol antibiotics to be administered if such a lapse in fieldwork dos and don'ts occurred. The going-native taboo became an unanticipated acute matter of deep concern to me. I recall now with great amusement, my great shock and confusion, when due to engaging too well in the practice of rapport, near the end of the fall quarter, the Hare Krishna temple leadership asked me to become their Northwestern University campus representative. This proposal inspired me so much that I made a mad dash to John Kituse, panic stricken, seeking advice about a concept we had not yet studied called "how to exit with grace from your field setting." An amused though wise John Kituse made the problem more complex by suggesting that perhaps I might want to stick around and make the setting my dissertation project, which I only faintly heard as I made my way out of the literal front temple door.

Although I had no desire to go native in the Hare Krishna temple, for years I never fully agreed with the conventional taboo in fieldwork protocol against going native in a particular field setting, especially when becoming one of the folks could be best for the researcher and the researched, not only in regard to engaging in some research design but good for all of us, becoming better and more humane people. Don't get me wrong, I continue to be a conventional social researcher in believing that it is important for the researcher to be an impartial observer, data collector, and data interpreter. In my opinion, that means being an insightful observing researcher who is fair minded, balanced, and ethical and knows all the appropriate validity and reliability logic of inquiry principles to assure adequate data collection and data interpretation. My definition of impartiality is in stark polar extreme to the 19th-century scientific notion of being objective—that is, being value free—which we now understand in the histories, sociologies, and politics of sciences to be of questionable merit and too often and usually inadvertently a self-serving myth for those with the power to determine what is and what is not valid and reliable knowledge and who has the right to define knowledge in the first place.

Except for reasons related to maintaining the dominance of elite institutions called the sciences premised on the priestly caste-like identity of the scientist, I continued to have a serious problem seeing and understanding why a researcher cannot have it both ways. Why can't a researcher be an impartial observer while becoming or being one of the folks being researched? Why can't researchers under certain conditions in which the researcher and the researched are safe and secure and benefit from authentic closeness as friends, as brothers and sisters, come together to not only do the science together but to work on becoming better human beings? In fact, why can't such efforts be viewed as science? Why can't I become close to the people who I encounter in my fieldwork settings who with genuine openness, open up their homes, religious and civic institutions, families, and, in many cases, their hearts to me? Yes, opening up to me, to me, that certified nosy-body called a sociologist or that teacher or that student or that professor, or that young or old man from over there, over there, from that strange forbidden place called the university.

Of course, when we get close to people who we have been trained to commodify as subjects and as informants or as participants, there is the danger, the high risk, of losing impartial perspective since one has become one of them, one of the folks. This has caused many a beginning researcher in the field to allow compassion to override impartiality and to never finish the study since to hand over the data in dissertation or book form would or could betray the folks. But, for those who learn how to balance impartiality with becoming one of the folks situationally or permanently, or is one of the folks just going back home and reporting on what is going on in the house, there is an even greater reward than being the proverbial distant researcher, caring and attentive perhaps with social justice values maybe but still going by the conventional rules of keeping your distance.

Again, under conditions of safety and mutual human betterment experiences, when we allow ourselves as researchers to become one of the folks, the more we do that, the more rich human experiences of those we are observing and living with will be revealed. The more we keep our selves distant in situations in which we should be willing to draw close to those we are examining, the less we will know about them, regardless of how good our statistical tables and thick descriptive narrative slices read in print. And consider how offensive it must be to those in the field setting to listen to my proclamations of caring for them when my actions prove otherwise. Not only my body language reveals how fearful we really are of them, but more importantly, since when I can and should, I choose not to spend the night in their homes, to eat their food, if they have any, and to be with them when their children are born and when their spouses die unless it is part of some darn study.

Perhaps for a distinct ethnic reason, I am uneasy about this Euro-centric researcher taboo of going native, which so falsely disconnects emotionality from professional practices, a delusionary separation of being human and feeling that runs and hides under the illusionary cover of objectivity ideology maintained through the rituals of arrogant distance between the researcher and the researched. Thus, in these still early years of the 21st century, I am delighted that we have finally begun to move slowly and somewhat surely toward a consensus in some circles of American social sciences with a humane bent that black researchers, like researchers from other ethnic backgrounds, do indeed have unique cultural values and identities and that our cultural values and identities, like researchers of other ethnic backgrounds, have a bearing on how we construct the epistemologies, theories, methods, and evaluations undergirding our research designs.

Thus, as a man with deep traditional black ethnic roots with an upwardly mobile working-class into upper middle-class status, I have become increasingly mindful that my uneasiness with the notion that I should not go native with the professional ideology that I cannot possibly become one of the kinfolks as I impartially study each one has much to do with my ethnic background that values closeness, and, more than that, family-like closeness or what the great African American ethnographer Hylan Lewis (1988) called friendliness in his 1955 seminal study *Blackways of Kent*.

Through the years—be it as an oral historian, ethnographer, or as a program evaluator or even as a minister in a church or a board member of a nonprofit organization in an inner-city community, as a brother man getting his hair cut in a hood barber shop—I have found that remaining as I am, as a black man, has enabled me to navigate well in any predominantly black setting and any other ethnic setting, for that matter. That is because my kinfolk elders taught me, well before I even knew a place called Northwestern, let alone university, as a first-generation college kid to always do my best to relate to people in genuine fashion, never be a phony, always remember where I came from, where I am at in the present, and where I want to go in the future. I learned such things from parents who taught me that I should always acknowledge people I knew and get to know those I did not know and never judge people from how they looked, dressed, or talked. I learned how to be just a good, friendly, welcoming person from that little church on the corner founded by Deacon John Stanfield, my paternal grandfather, chair of the deacon board of Mt. Calvary Baptist Church in Rome, New York, who, for thirty years, had older men and women in his congregation. Those older folks were like spare-wheel aunts and uncles for my sisters and me and the other young folks in the congregation, always teaching us by daily observed example to be authentically interested in people and be kind to them, no matter who they were.

This matter of why I do not hold the taboo of going native as a necessary universal in fieldwork protocol speaks of the long concern I have about the potential creative balance between researcher impartiality and going native. It registers as well my genuine desire as a human being to strive to become authentic more and more each day, including when I meet and engage with those who I am researching who are not my subjects but my folks, who embrace me as I embrace them. This on-going conversation in my head and with others over time gradually conditioned my subconscious and cognition to finally find a roosting place in the late 1980s and early 1990s in the midst of all the global excitement about the dramatic dismantling of white apartheid rule in South Africa and in its place, the emergence of black majority rule.

During the emergence of black majority rule days in South Africa, which began in 1994, I and others became fascinated by Anglican Bishop Desmond Tutu's Truth and Reconciliation Commission approach. President Nelson Mandela's administration endorsed this approach as a way to to work toward reconciliation in the aftermath of the state-sanctioned reign of terror instituted by the apartheid government (Tutu, 1999). What happened in South Africa brought to the global surface restorative justice as a highly visible worldwide movement with deep, hidden historical roots in numerous indigenous cultures around the world. It has become a well-known alternative public policy model largely rooted in comparative legal study debates and literature, discussing the best ways in these post–cold war times to transition states and rebuild societies devastated by exterminations of people sanctioned by states or/ and done through massive public atrocities. Restorative justice, in its numerous forms, calls for new alternative public policy experiments in places such as South Africa, the Balkan states, Rwanda, Southeast Asia, and Latin America. Restorative justice is proving to be a movement that is slowly changing how nations and people within them perceive each other and treat each other in areas related to human rights and human accountability.

For instance, even in recent months, the influence of restorative justice thinking and acting has dramatically impacted the democratization street movements in Middle Eastern countries significantly facilitated through Facebook and other social technologies. The Obama administration crafted a humanitarian rationale to develop an unprecedented collaborative military intervention in Libya, breaching longstanding UN covenants and traditions regarding the rights of nations not to have their internal affairs interfered with by outside states. This was the direct result of the failure of the U.S. government not to intervene in the 1994 Rwanda genocide in which Hutus killed nearly one million Tutsis and liberal-to-moderate Hutus. Susan Rice, President Obama's UN ambassador, was a first-hand witness in American and international foreign public policy circles as a lower-ranked State Department official in 1994 when the U.S. government and other Western powers refused to intervene in Rwanda in timely fashion. She decided then that if she ever had senior foreign policy decision-making power, she would do all she could to prevent such actions from recurring. This is why she recommended humanitarian intervention in Libya in the face of a head of state threatening to exterminate Libyan citizens en masse.

## Just What Is Restorative Justice Anyway?

As I say in my forthcoming book *Rethinking Race and Ethnicity in Research Methods* (Stanfield, 2011a), restorative justice is, in the face of an en-masse human extermination or other forms of dehumanization such as slavery, mass rape, or environmental disaster, the recovery of humanity through acknowledging and embracing the humanity of those one has been socialized to believe to not to be human, to be objects, to be furniture, to be chattel, to be lower animals, to be insects.

Usually, restorative justice is applied in piecemeal ways as state, community, or institutional actions such as confessions of wrong-doing, apologies, forgiveness, or reconciliation, which is why, as policies, such piecemeal efforts usually are not all that effective or miss the point of what it means to be restored as human beings. In the most ideal sense, what I call holistic, restorative justice is a process of authenticity and transparency to get to the bottom of the horrible en-masse episode or institutionalized system and to reestablish accountability human beings have to each other (Erikson, 1976; Gandhi, 1940; Greene, 1988; Helmick & Petersen, 2001; Higgins & Johnson, 1988; Johnstone & van Ness, 2011; King 1958; Lederach, 1998; Nouwen, 1992; Redekop, 2002; Stanfield, 1985, 2006a, 2006b, 2011a, 2011b; Tutu, 1999; Volf, 1996).

In the holistic sense of restorative justice, the horrible en-masse thing dehumanizes the entire society and communities and institutions within it. Perpetrator population members who are the direct dehumanizers—the ones who pull the trigger or swing the knife or who capture and sell the slaves—are not only the ones who do the horrible deeds. They are also victims in how damaging their actions are to their dysfunctional mental health and how their terrible treatment of other human beings cuts them and their descendants off from the rest of humanity. Perpetrators are victimized since their actions that dehumanize and kill others—physically or socially and emotionally without thought or care—dehumanizes the perpetrators as well. They can only do such hideous horrible things by victimizing themselves through schizoid moral character developments in which they treat their "own kind" more or less as human beings while disregarding the humanity of others. Perpetrators are dominant people who write and pass down official and unofficial histories and family and community traditions that are silent about what they did and why they did it. This produces a convenient amnesia commonly called massive ignorance or innocent naiveté among those of the perpetrator dominant population who were bystanders and descendants. Perpetrator population bystanders and descendants may not have been involved in the dehumanization directly and may not have been even born when it occurred. Nevertheless, they still benefit socially if not economically and politically due to their privileged population membership, so their hands are bloodied, too.

Victim populations are not only the targets of perpetrators. Victim population members can be perpetrators as well as collaborators of perpetrators or bystanders who think they will not become victims and do nothing to assist their own group or actual brothers and sisters. Being passive due to intergenerational fear of reprisal is not a form of collaboration necessarily, but it is a form of accommodation, which allows perpetrators to engage in their destructive reigns of terror. Like in any other sustaining state of social inequality, en-masse societal horror afflicted by one population unto another can occur not only through the dominance and the force of the powerful but also when the powerless allows such atrocities to happen to them via collaborative betrayal, indifference to the plight of their own people, or multigenerational passivity.

The restorative justice process involves bringing to the table, so to speak, an institution, a community, or an entire society, such as the South Africa Truth and Reconciliation Commission, perpetrators and victims to actively listen and see each other, probably for the first time. Perpetrators and victims at the table are required to communicate without cross-talking or cross-referencing. They must make eye-to-eye contact since dehumanization occurs and is maintained through talking to rather than talking with, through interrupting, and through being socialized not to look at the Other straight in the eyes. It is a process of becoming authentic, as perpetrators and victims tell their versions of the terrible thing that happened, which is called mutual remembering, then move into the phase of mutual admitting, that is confession. Perpetrators admit their deeds and victims admit what they could have done to prevent the deeds from occurring, then move on to the mutual apologizing phase, which is the Judeo-Christian word repentance, meaning acknowledging wrong and promising never to do it again. Perpetrators promise never to dehumanize again, and victims promise never to place themselves in position again to be dehumanized. Then comes the mutual understanding phase that is called forgiveness, which means that perpetrators and victims either decide to embrace and live totally together or to coexist—a growing area in the global restorative justice field metaphorically akin to the divorce and family literature, which tells us how parents who cannot and perhaps should not live together still cooperate for the sake of continuing to raise their kids. Perpetrators and victims in the same community with deep-seated dislikes realize that they must come together in the public sphere to collaborate on efforts to assure quality education for their children, decent health care for all, etc. Yet they cannot or should not live under the same roof though they are in the same community.

After forgiveness, there is reconciliation, meaning giving back deprived or stolen material or symbolic dignity or what is called reparations. Perpetrators not only give victims back their land, money, names, the bodies of loved ones or locations of mass graves and provide educational and health care resources, but victims provide perpetrators opportunities to learn how to be back in touch with their humanity emotionally and socially. In the case of Rwanda, for example, this entails that perpetrators live in restorative villages with survivors of victims and doing community service for their families and survivors doing the same for perpetrators.

While the previous steps and concepts of memory, confession, apology, forgiveness, reconciliation, and reparations have been developing significant literatures over the past twenty years, especially the last ten, the last step, coming out unified in restored lives sustained through new circles, networks, and environments is my own contribution to the field. As a sociologist, it makes no sense to me to go through a process of soul searching and life transformation such as this and continue to return back to one's old environments.

It is the basic reason why diversity and sensitivity programs and even college curricula do not work in many cases: Participants may become transformed in the classroom, but then go back to the same old prejudice-infested environments. How people over time, through their participation in the previous steps, come to develop and sustained opening intercultural living lives and environments, is an area of study worthy of future research.

Holistic restorative justice processing is far from easy. It is a painful, emotional, transparency-driving laborious process that can take months and years rather than minutes, days, and weeks before we can see any noticeable sustaining positive outcomes. It is also a lifelong experience for those involved; it never ends for those in the land of the living, and goes on for seemingly count-less future generations, since the memories of the dead, the loved ones of previous generations, are such integral parts of this rehu-manization process.

Unfortunately, as much as restorative justice has reached the level of national public policy setting to resolve horrible en-masse dehumanization incidents and well-institutionalized systems in numerous places around the world, this has yet to happen in the United States. At some local and state levels, we do observe some interesting efforts to employ restorative justice measures in crimi-nal justice areas such as victim rights, community courts, and, to a much lesser extent, programs that address perpetrator account-ability. Also, in piecemeal ways, we have seen occasional cases of universities, faith communities, and local and state governments apologizing for past wrongs such as their support of slavery or/and Jim Crow or the forced confinement of Japanese Americans during World War II. There are a few citizen movements such as Consent to Govern, which attempt to bring restorative justice measures to addressing the need to resolve drug problems in urban commu-nities through identifying managers of the highest levels of drug cartels in the United States to get them to confess and apologize in exchange for amnesty and providing reparations to communities. But there is no receptivity to employing restorative justice on the federal level, especially the described holistic approach.

Nevertheless, something very interesting has been going on in this country for a number of decades at the individual level. It reminds us that restorative justice is not just an alternative public policy possibility, but is also a way that some people, some communities, live out their lives in ways that actually involve the several steps of holistic restorative justice, call it normative holistic restorative justice–based mutual remembering, mutual confessing, mutual apologizing, mutual forgiveness, mutual reconciliation, and the sustained unity of all of us. Specifically, more than what the eye has been socialized to see in this society, in the area of racial justice, there has been an increasingly noticeable transformation process occurring that has a normative holistic restorative justice ring to it that is not being studied extensively. That is why, among other reasons, social scientists were caught so flat footed when then Senator Barack Obama seemingly came out of nowhere, made that rousing speech at the 2004 Democratic National Convention, and four years later landed in the White House as America's first African American president.

It is my firm belief, which is detailed in a book I am writing called the *Obama Phenomenon* (see also Stanfield 2008), that the reason why Barack Obama did so well as a campaigner, first against his Democratic Party rivals and then against his Republican Party rival, is that his civic unity message was very much a restorative justice message receptive to a citizenry on the ropes. It appealed especially to young people, disenfranchised urban and rural dwellers, a fractured declining middle class seriously distracted and disgruntled about economic woes, and American public's both young and old, cutting across all ancestries who understand how socially, emotionally, and economically we continue to be embedded in the atrocity of race.

## The Obama Phenomenon

The year 2008 was the first time in decades, and one of the few times in American history, that someone elected to the White House did so on a restorative justice campaign promise on societal healing. Others were Abraham Lincoln, Franklin D. Roosevelt, and John F. Kennedy, who President Obama used to be compared to, more in the past than now as his restorative justice-oriented charisma has dissipated. His civic unity message during his campaign days about coming together and working together across differences was especially thrilling to millions of disheartened Americans coming out from under eight depressive years of President Bush the second. Senator Obama's Philadelphia race speech, as the first restorative justice–oriented public speech on race by a front-running mainstream American candidate for the U.S. presidency, advocated acknowledging and working through the pains of racism as a national civic unity project.

For a number of complex reasons beyond the scope of this chapter, President Obama has disappointed his starry-eyed constituencies. President Obama is now perceived by many as being as a politician who has faltered badly as he moved from being a restorative justice campaigner with such brilliant public speaking skills to becoming a president with a reluctant if not timid leadership style about issues such as racial civil rights and other causes dear to the heart of those who assumed they were electing a change-oriented president (Stanfield, 1989). In too many cases, this view of Senator Obama was premised on widespread insidious racist presumptions that being black would make him a change agent since, stereotypically, "all black people, of course, are change oriented since we have, of course, experienced so much historical racism," without paying close attention to his previous political careers or even to the books and articles he wrote and published prior to his election.

Nevertheless, his rather sudden appearance and then extraordinary success on the American political scene symbolizes a number of chickens coming home to roost with regard to the historical construction and transformation of rural, urban, and suburban environments over the last ninety years. Since the end of World War I, and especially since the end of World War II, the Truman civil rights initiatives, the 1954 *Brown v. Board of Education*, and the 1955 Montgomery bus boycott years, the 1960s civil rights acts, the era of political assassinations, and the urban race riots have been increasingly played out on the expanding national television media, which meant that the American viewing public saw Jim Crow being ousted, exposed, and attacked in black and white or in living color.

Whether or not President Obama becomes a one-term president is certainly an interesting and important question for historians and political scientists to ponder. But to me, the more fascinating and crucial questions about what his emergence represents are sociological, anthropological, and Jungian psychological. The Obama Phenomenon, as I call this sociological and anthropological something, symbolizes a profound ontological trinity of societal transformation; that is, a cluster of symbolic historically embedded changes, technologically and globally derived present changes, and futuristic guideposts to changes that we are already in the midst of and those surely on the way that we know, may know, and do not know.

Historical and contemporary forms of racial prejudice, and its inequality and otherwise dehumanizing consequences, continue to exist as a grotesque multigenerational plague of human degradation for this society and for too many others with the same tragic plague. Racial prejudice continues to persist because for many, it is economically, politically, socially, and emotionally beneficial. As well, racial prejudice continues to persist since we refuse to be transparent about it in the public sphere. Instead, depending on the historical era, Americans have preferred to pretend that racial prejudice does not exist, or we water it down, or underestimate it with historical era specific trendy words such as such as melting pot, assimilation, integration, the declining significance of race, color blind society, and post-racial and post-civil rights society. This consequential continuation of racial prejudice and its persistent impacts on quality-of-life variables in American society certainly justifies why most American social scientists and foreign social researchers who specialize in American racial matters study racial prejudice and how it defines, structures, and transforms racialized inequalities.

But that said, there is a desperate need for a new kind of social research (Stanfield, 2011a). As social researchers committed to racial justice concerns, we need to turn the corner of our research focuses and look on the other side of the flipped coin. We must begin to more comprehensively examine how, what, and why since the ending of World War I, Americans have been on a remarkable societal natural experiment called desegregation. Desegregation is far from complete and certainly has had its negative impacts. Yet, we cannot and should not ignore its incredible positive impacts.

Desegregation and the changing demographics of immigration during the past forty or so years, first brought about through the liberalization of immigration policies in the 1960s, are not mostly stories of failure or negatively leaning mixed outcomes. Yes, the problems of racial exclusion and marginality are still with us, as are resistant pockets of white privilege. But even in the midst of these persistent problems of a society painfully transforming itself interculturally, there are also stories out there that document that Americans and non-Americans residing here have been experiencing far more transformation of values than what our outmoded survey questions and scales and fieldwork protocols tell us. These subtle, everyday interpersonal negotiations constitute normative restorative justice and are enhanced by a demographically integrating mass media and popular culture and globalization ranging from corporate outsourcing, social technology communities such as Facebook and Internet dating services to growing U.S. dependency on Chinese, East Indian, and other forms of global capital and technology. If I were a betting man, I would bet that if we were to study the lives of people daily going through normative restorative justice processes, that they are all going through the phases somewhere along their journey constituting the several steps of "holistic restorative justice processes" I outlined earlier. This probability is borne out when we dissect the biographies of, say, Americans, South Africans, and East Indians of various racial or caste backgrounds who became champions of racial or untouchable justice, or just ordinary everyday people who come to notice the materialization of the various holistic restorative justice phases in their life histories.

All of these complex holistic normative restorative justice processes are occurring in the along with dramatic changes in the cultural and ethnic demographics that have been accelerating in the United States since the 1970s; the traditional white-black color line has expanded into the complex mosaic of a rainbow in a salad-bowl society. Paradoxically, consequential critical sociological and cultural problems today in salad-bowl America result from the scarcity of effective mass-level "intercultural living" literacy infrastructures in public and private education, media, businesses, government agencies, faith communities, and nonprofit sectors. Effective intercultural living literacy, is, by the way, much more important than intercultural competence. This is because intercultural living literacy is premised on transforming the interior emotional life and cognitive perceptions and identities of people. Conventional intercultural competency, on the other hand, merely equips people with technical and professional interpersonal management skills without transforming them into authentically rehumanized human beings who reach out and embrace everyone especially those they were routinely taught to dehumanize, in this case racially.

Intercultural living literacy is a sorely needed on-going life transformation experience and critical-thinking skill in a society in which occupational place and institutional roles are becoming increasingly unpredictable in terms of demographic content, power, and authority. From the doctor's office, the courtroom, the classroom, the employment interview room, and even the White House Oval Office, who shows up to greet us, to tell us to sit down or to stand up, and to tell us if we are well or sick or will get the job or not or get hired or fired is becomingly increasingly uncertain, surprising, or both.

All these changes—the gradual or the rapid desegregation of living spaces, the heterogeneous immigrant population, the emergence of post–baby-boomer generations without the prejudices of their parents and grandparents, and others—is what made, I suspect, so many post–baby-boomer Whites and non-Whites receptive to then Senator Obama's restorative justice–oriented campaign rhetoric—and are now disappointed in his lack of follow-through on his civic unity campaign rhetoric.

## Coda

The national and global external environmental factors discussed above and others not discussed help explain the results of the 2008 election year and its restorative justice orientation. They also help explain the increasingly opening of a post-1980s American academy so long resistant to civil rights–oriented movements when it comes to transformative pedagogies, ethnic and cultural studies curriculum expansion, experiential education, globalization, and recruitment of black and other scholars of color in traditional departments rather than in ethnic studies units. As a post–cold war movement in higher education, not a few universities and their individual and institutional donors are becoming receptive to providing incentives to administrators, faculty, and students interested in transforming traditional 19th- and 20th-century definitions of sciences and about what sciences are supposed to do. This is especially seen in those academic sector movements that are collapsing the boundaries among the various sciences and between the sciences and theology and the other humanities, beginning to stress the moral, ethical, and historical dimensions of scientific inquiries, and searching for ways to tear down the ivy-covered walls of the academy too long separating us from outside worlds.

This growing academic receptivity to transformation, to the point of even redefining research, in this case, scientific research, has been coaxed not only by globalizations but also through government pressures over the past forty years. These pressures have encouraged if not required researchers to become much more sensitive about their ethical conduct in human subjects and animal research. There has also been growing pressure on private and public universities that apply for federal grants to be accountable to the public's growing cultural diversity and to demand that universities and colleges pay closer attention to people who look like them.

Corporate America, the sector that understands the value of cultural diversity the most, with its wealthy foundation subsector and high-status professional interest groups, has leaders who are applying increasing pressure on universities and colleges to do what is necessary to produce interculturally competent students, future managers, and workers. The expanding learning curve of the cultural diversity and inclusion needs of the salad-bowl society and of global survival is too steep for new employees to enter the workplace interculturally clueless and naive. For instance, I recall being a University of California-Davis professor and member of the Executive Committee of the UC system–wide Black Faculty and Staff Association in the mid-1990s when the UC Board of Regents passed its anti-affirmative action policies.

Soon thereafter, a delegation of managing partners of blue-chip law firms in California paid a visit to the UC president. They told the president they would not hire any UC law students until the regents' anti-affirmative action policies were rescinded; they needed culturally diverse and interculturally aware attorneys to join their firms and did not want attorneys educated in environments in which intercultureness was not valued, respected, and learned well.

This is why I believe strongly that the time is now for those of us involved in qualitative inquiry to seize the moment to engage in efforts to take some long steps beyond the postmodern pale of qualitative research. We need to identify and work with and within academic institutions and professional associations such as this one, The International Congress on Qualitative Inquiry, which are receptive to further transformation, which *get it* when it comes to understanding our need to change if we are going to remain or become relevant to outside world as well as on our own campuses. Within such institutions and associations, we need to begin to push the envelope of restorative justice about how we do our research and more than that, about how we define what research is, in this case, scientific research. It is a matter of realizing that there are occasions deserving of respect and embracing in which we all need to be transformed, we all need to get our humanity back, the researcher and the researched, not only as an arena of data collection and interpretation, not only in respecting the right of the researched to be heard, to be protected, and to participate in the research process.

Sometimes, there is the need for healing, especially intercultural healing and intracultural healing. There is a growing list of research settings and research questions for all involved, the researcher and the researched, to come together to remember together, to confess together, to apologize together, to forgive together, to reconcile together, and to live together, not over and beyond the needs of science but as a new expansive definition of what scientific inquiry is and is supposed to do in this day and age, in which norms of dominant paradigms of everything we do as academics are so dramatically being questioned, as all kinds of walls are tumbling down in academic circles such as between the humanities and social sciences; between theology and the social sciences; between national, international, and area studies; and between town and gown.

Thus, when it is feasible and safe for all to do so, why not make the walls come tumbling down between researcher and the researched? As we all search for and therefore shall find the humanity we have lost, therefore we shall recover when we all come together and break bread together, as researcher and the researched, as brothers and sisters, going and being native together for the good of all us.

The next wide turn in qualitative research is about turning to our humanity and that of those we research and walk out and live together in unity as we tackle quality-of-life problems that cannot be addressed through the mandates of 19th- and 20th-century research protocols requiring sciences—which fail to heal—and restore the researcher and the researched as a gesture of rehumanization of all of us.

## Note

1. This chapter was presented as the co-opening Keynote Address at the 7th International Congress of Qualitative Inquiry, University of Illinois, Champaign-Urbana, May 18, 2011.

## References

Erikson, K. T. (1976). *Everything in its path: Destruction of community in the Buffalo Creek flood.* New York: Simon & Schuster.

Gandhi, M. (1940). *An autobiography: The story of my experiments with truth.* Ahmedabad (India) and Boston: Navaiivan Publications and Beacon Press.

Greene, M. (1988). *The dialectic of freedom.* New York: Teachers College Press.

Helmick, R. & Petersen, R. (2001). *Forgiveness and reconciliation.* New York: Templeton Press.

Higgins, P. C. & Johnson, J. (1988). *Personal sociology.* New York: Praeger.

Johnstone, G. & van Ness, D. (2011). *Handbook of restorative justice*. New York: Willan.

King, M. L., Jr. (1958). *Stride toward freedom: The Montgomery story*. New York: Harper.

Lederach, P. (1998). *Building peace*. Washington, DC: United States Peace Institute Press.

Lewis, D. L. (2000). *W. E. B. Du Bois: The fight for equality and the American century, 1919–1963*. New York: Henry Holt.

Nouwen, H. J. M. (1992). *The return of the prodigal son: A meditation on fathers, brothers, and sons*. New York: Doubleday.

Redekop, V. (2002). *From violence to blessing*. Toronto: Novalis.

Stanfield, J. H., II (1985). *Philanthropy and Jim Crow in American social science*. Westport, CT: Greenwood Press.

Stanfield, J. H., II (2006a). Psychoanalytic ethnography and the transformation of racially wounded communities. *The International Journal of Qualitative Studies in Education, 40*, 387–399.

Stanfield, J. H., II (2006b). The restorative justice functions of qualitative research methods. *The International Journal of Qualitative Studies in Education, 19*, 723–727.

Stanfield, J. H., II. (2008). The reality of the impossible: Profound meanings of the Obama phenomenon in emerging America. Public lecture, London South Bank University, London, November 27.

Stanfield, J. H., II. (2009). The reluctant bystander: Why President Obama may be a one-term president. Public lecture, State University of Londrina (Paraná, Brazil), November 20.

Stanfield, J. H., II. (2011a). Holistic restorative justice methodology in intercultural openness studies. In J. H. Stanfield, III (Ed.), *Rethinking race and ethnicity in research methods* (pp. 27–42). Walnut Creek, CA: Left Coast Press, Inc.

Stanfield, J. H. II (2011b). Weberian ideal-type methodology in comparative historical research: Identifying and understanding African legacy societies. In J. H. Stanfield, II (Ed.), *Rethinking race and ethnicity in research methods* (pp. 293–312).Walnut Creek, CA: Left Coast Press, Inc.

Tutu, D. (1999). *No future without forgiveness*. New York: Doubleday.

Volf, M. (1996). *Exclusion and embrace: a theological exploration of identity, otherness, and reconciliation*. Nashville: Abingdon Press.

# Section II
# Method

## Chapter 5

# Mixing or Adding Methods?

## An Exploration and Critique

### Kathy Charmaz

My comments derive from three related areas of interest: grounded theory methods, qualitative inquiry, and reflections on a demonstration project, which later turned into a book, *Five Ways of Doing Qualitative Analysis: Phenomenological Psychology, Grounded Theory, Discourse Analysis, Narrative Research, and Intuitive Inquiry* (Charmaz, 2011a, 2011b), in which four psychologists and I analyzed the same qualitative data. As R. Burke Johnson, Marilyn W. McGowan, and Lisa A Turner (2010) propose, grounded theory fits mixed methods research particularly well. Constructivist grounded theory informs my exploration of mixed methods research below, but the voice of mixed methods practice will come from others in this volume.

In this chapter, I address three questions. (1) What are mixed methods? (2) Where do the discussions of mixed methods take us? (3) How do varied qualitative analytic approaches shape the research process and product? Throughout the chapter, I explore mixed methods assumptions and strategies and raise questions about them.

*Qualitative Inquiry and the Politics of Advocacy,* edited by Norman K. Denzin and Michael D. Giardina, 123–144. © 2012 Left Coast Press, Inc. All rights reserved.

## What Are Mixed Methods?

Perhaps the most immediate definition of mixed methods that comes to mind focuses on using both quantitative and qualitative methods in a particular study. Presumably the researcher aims to gain more knowledge about the research problem and to construct a more thorough analysis of it than would be possible by only using one method of data collection. Defining what mixed methods are and can be is crucial for developing research methods and methodologies. Leading spokespersons for mixed methods research (see, e.g., Cameron, 2009; Creswell, 2003; Morgan, 2003; Morse, 2011) view the turn to mixed methods as a paradigm shift of similar magnitude to the qualitative revolution that Denzin and Lincoln proclaimed in 1994. Even those who may view mixed methods research as less than a paradigm shift cannot ignore its increasing significance.

So how do we define mixed methods? How should we define them? Perhaps most researchers view mixed methods as projects that include both qualitative and quantitative components. Mixed methods proponents usually view their approach as combining qualitative and quantitative approaches including their respective perspectives, analyses, and forms of inference to gain breadth and depth of understanding and to corroborate the findings of the each method. The origins and objectives of mixed methods hearken back to Norman Denzin's (1970) original concerns with triangulation (Greene, 2006; Morse, 1991; Tashakkori & Teddlie, 2003). Mixed methods proponents have made a serious effort to take up the complexities that triangulation has occasioned. R. Burke Johnson, Anthony J. Onwuegbuzie and Lisa A. Turner (2007) conducted an exacting review of the definitions of mixed methods and concluded that mixed methods "combine elements of qualitative and quantitative research approaches ... for the broad purposes the breadth and depth of understanding and corroboration" (p. 123). Burke Johnson et al. contend that this combination of quantitative and qualitative approaches includes their accompanying perspectives, types of analyses, and forms of inference.

Burke Johnson et al.'s definition is sophisticated yet straightforward and useful, as it suggests directions for assessing mixed methods practice and products. Overall, however, definitions of mixed methods and what these definitions mean for inquiry are contested, multiple, and blurred. Does the definition include studies with distinctive quantitative and qualitative components that researchers treat as separate and often report in separate venues to different audiences? Should researchers define a multiple or sequential methodological approach as mixed methods research? Must a mixed method study require having both quantitative and qualitative components?

Most researchers define mixed methods research as including both qualitative and quantitative components. Do these components have an equal or complementary footing? To date, the logic and conduct of quantitative research have driven most mixed methods projects. Sharlene Hesse-Biber (2010c) contends that an orthodoxy favoring quantitative research has dominated mixed methods practice. Margarete Sandelowski, Corrine I. Voils, and George Knafl, (2009) go a step further and argue that quantitative data and analysis dominates mixed methods projects and, moreover, qualitative data become subject to "quantitizing"[1] through researchers transforming them into numbers. John Creswell and colleagues (2006; see also Creswell and Plano Clark, 2007), however, contend that qualitative methods extend mixed methods practice and may be given priority in mixed methods projects.

The quality of the qualitative component has been problematic. Janice M. Morse (2011) observes, "The majority of mixed methods designs are quantitatively driven, with small add-ons of a few interviews or focus groups as the qualitative supplemental component. I am constantly amazed at how sophisticated the quantitative components of these studies are, and how feeble the qualitative" (p. 1020).

Yet researchers have diverse reasons for adopting these tools, analyzing their findings, and deciding whether and to what extent to use each of the subsequent analyses. Researchers' reasons for adopting a quantitative-qualitative mixed methods design include: (1) constructing instruments; (2) corroborating findings; (3) reducing cultural and investigator biases; (4) improving clinical trials; (5) addressing research participants' experience;

(6) satisfying funding agencies; and (7) informing professional practice and/or public policy (Charmaz 2011c). The turn toward grounded theory studies in social justice inquiry may also spur development of quantitative-qualitative mixed methods, although as Christ (2009) observes, transformational research does not readily fit a quantitative framework.

Technical advancements may play a role in expanding qualitative components in quantitative-dominant mixed methods research designs. Morse (2011) writes that qualitative computer analysis programs seem to have made data management and analysis quicker, easier, and more reliable. Like me, she also questions whether speed comes at the cost of bringing critical and theoretical thinking to qualitative analysis. The characteristics of speed and ease, however, may make integrating qualitative research more appealing to quantitative researchers who wish to add a qualitative component to their projects. The next decade may bring technological advancements that can spawn new ways of doing mixed methods research. Nigel Fielding and César Cisneros-Puebla (2010) have already integrated CAQDAS and GIS methods in an innovative mixed methods approach.

The definition of mixed methods is expanding and simultaneously abandoning earlier taken-for-granted assumptions that mixed methods research required both quantitative and qualitative components. Numerous researchers now advocate methodological pluralism whether or not they invoke it. For increasingly more researchers (see, e.g., Hesse-Biber, 2010a, 2010b, 2010c; Morse, 2009; Morse & Niehaus, 2009; Nepal, 2010), mixed methods means using more than one method, whether or not these methods mix quantitative and qualitative research. In their book, *Mixed Method Design: Principles and Procedures*, Janice Morse and Linda Niehaus (2009) start from the assumption that mixed methods may consist of two or more qualitative methods.

Like Hesse-Biber (2010a, 2010b, 2010c), Morse and Niehaus (2009), and Creswell et al. (2006), I call for expanding conceptions of mixed methods to include different forms of qualitative research in the same project. Furthermore, I call for different forms of qualitative *analysis* as part of the mix—or use—of methods. In my view, whatever the mix or combination—be it qualitative with qualitative or quantitative with qualitative and all permutations within and among them—the criteria for effective mixed methods research rests on analytic coherence of the research product, integrated findings, and illumination of the research problem(s).

Do these criteria mean that researchers must be assured of effective mixed method outcomes before they start? No. They cannot. The inductive logic of most qualitative research precludes such assurances and serendipitous quantitative findings may supersede anticipated outcomes. A weak incorporation of one component in mixed method research, usually a qualitative method, does not necessarily mean that the other component fails to generate useful findings. What it may mean is the project does not represent best mixed methods practice.

Mixed methods may divide, collide, or cohere. Or a method may just be added but not mixed. Jennie Popay et al. (2003) conclude, as I do, that mixed or multiple methodologies can generate different and conflicting data. Popay et al. studied people's views of the causes of health inequalities and how their views varied in relation to their localities. These authors' abstract states the methodological significance of their findings.

> The findings, however, also illustrate how the ways in which questions about health and illness are asked shape people's responses. In the survey reported on here people had no problem offering explanations for health inequalities and, in response to a question asking specifically about area differences in health experience, people living in disadvantaged areas 'constructed' explanations which included, but went beyond, individualistic factors to encompass structural explanations that gave prominence to aspects of "place." In contrast, within the context of in-depth interviews, people living in disadvantaged areas were reluctant to accept the existence of health inequalities highlighting the moral dilemmas such questions pose for people living in poor material circumstances. While resisting the notion of health inequalities, however, in in-depth interviews the same people provided vivid accounts of the way in which inequalities in material circumstances have an adverse impact upon health. The paper highlights ways in which different methodologies provide different and not necessarily complementary

understandings of lay perspectives on the causes of inequalities in health. (p. 1)

Popay et al.'s statement serves as a reminder of Aaron Cicourel's (1964) insight: How researchers form their questions frames the answers they receive.

## Where Do the Discussions of Mixed Methods Take Us?

Much of the discourse about mixed methods starts from the *methods* rather than the research problem. Then methods become the focal point of attention with subsequent attention to research design. Yet methods are more or less useful tools to make the research problem visible and accessible. Research methods should flow from the research problem and the resulting questions it raises. We also need to think about the nature of the research problem. Despite moves to make qualitative research circumscribed and deductive (Burawoy, 1991, 2000; Lamont & White, 2009), the initial research problem may not be fixed and stable in qualitative research.

We grounded theorists aim to study what we define as significant in our data. The inductive logic of much qualitative research makes the initial research problem a starting point for inquiry rather than an end point of research design. Thus, the research problem(s) evolves. A grounded theorist refines the problem and may recast it as the study proceeds. Thus, grounded theorists will adopt emergent methods to fit the developing research problem.

The turn to mixed methods fosters looking at traditional methods of data collection and analysis anew. Which data we collect, how we collect them, and what kind of analytic approach we take to them all come into purview. Earlier mixed methods discussions that treated qualitative research as a single entity (i.e., interviews) have given way to more nuanced considerations. Which data collection methods will prove to be complementary and advance the researcher's goals depends on the research problem and what happens in the field.

One of the ironies in qualitative research today is that researchers often only use one source of data collection such as interviews, focus groups, or Internet postings. Yet the tradition of Chicago School field research has long encouraged gathering data that sheds light on the research problem. Thus, Chicago School qualitative researchers have long used multiple sources of data. I doubt that many of them would view themselves as mixed methods researchers because they typically do not cross the quantitative-qualitative divide that until recently has characterized mixed methods research. In his new study, Jason Eastman's (2011) approach exemplifies Chicago School methods. Eastman used multiple forms of data to study the hegemonic masculinity of southern rock musicians, their worlds, and their music. Eastman writes:

> I complemented a qualitative ethnographic content analysis of Southern rock lyrics and websites with more traditional ethnographic methods, including musician interviews and participant observation of their concerts (Altheide 1987). Once I identified a band as part of the underground Southern rock scene, I downloaded their websites and MySpace pages biweekly while collecting their recorded music for a lyrical content analysis. Thus far I have analyzed 52 websites and 1,063 songs. I focused on strategic and intentional representations of rebel manhood in songs, from the stage and on websites to capture how musicians construct an ideal Southern identity in the abstract—or as unrestrained by the limits of everyday life.

> …. In the contemporary Southern rock underground, musicians not only express "Southernness" but fans assume their transient lifestyles enable musicians to embody rebel manhood in ways few others can. Furthermore, musicians' central place in the scene commissions them as the public role models of Southern, masculine rebelliousness, and musicians undertake identity work efforts to publically reflect this ideal. However, by also interviewing musicians in addition to examining their artistic expression, I was able to explore the backstage ways they construct idealized rebel masculinity along with how they navigate the rebel identity in their personal lives.

> I conducted thirty-nine formal interviews and five follow-up interviews with informants I first spoke with in the early stages of the project. These follow-up sessions along with adjustments

made to the topic list throughout the study enabled me to theoretically sample conceptual issues that arose. When conducting
interviews with rebels who are antagonistic toward educated men,
I tried to cede power to informants and make them feel in control of our discussions (Hoffman 2007; Schwalbe & Wolkomir
2001). For instance, instead of strictly administering questions in
a predetermined order, I let informants guide the subject matter
and simply checked off topics as they arose in conversation or I
gently steered the subject of discussion. (pp. 5–6)

The theoretical level and analytic density of Eastman's report
reflects the thoroughness of his data collection. His combined
modes of analysis, analytic induction, and grounded theory
fostered developing an incisive analysis and demonstrating the
strength of its empirical foundation.

Discussions of mixed methods can disrupt common assumptions about a hierarchy of methods in qualitative research. Like
the assumption that random clinical trials represent the gold standard in evidence-based health research, ethnography has been
taken as the gold standard in qualitative research. But what is ethnography? It does not consist of a single data collection method.
Without even taking up all the knotty problems of standpoints,
allegiances, and representation of participants, what stands as
ethnography raises questions.

In my view, ethnography is an approach to a community, setting, group, issue, or category of people in which the researcher
has a sustained involvement in the studied world. Ethnography
means more than an observer who visits, may engage in limited
participation, but does not become a part of this world. Certainly
ethnographers observe and record their field notes. They may also
conduct informal and/or formal interviews, video-tape conversations, analyze documents, and use surveys. And they may not
know all the methods they may need to use when planning their
research. Long before the days of Institutional Review Board
legitimation, I concluded an ethnographic study with distribution
of a carefully designed survey that focused what I had learned in
the six months during which I lived in the setting. My decision to
gather survey data arose during the research process rather than
before it. Now qualitative researchers need to leave openings in

their proposals that allow flexibility for such strategies as adding methods or returning to earlier settings and participants.

An emergent logic can mean adding or abandoning a method during the research process. Despite stinging critiques of interviews as an inferior method compared to ethnography (Atkinson & Silverman, 1997; Barbour, 1998; Becker and Geer, 1957; Silverman, 2007), interviews may allow access to data that remain unavailable to ethnographers. Lee F. Monaghan's (2002) depiction of his study, "Vocabularies of Motive for Illicit Steroid Use among Bodybuilders," provides a telling example. Monaghan engaged in lengthy ethnographic research and viewed himself as accepted in the bodybuilding culture. Yet he could not obtain the data he sought about steroid use precisely because he fit into the scene. In his formal role as an interviewer, he could ask questions that his ethnographic participation had precluded. Monaghan conducted sixty-one in-depth interviews and described his methods as follows:

> This paper draws primarily upon transcribed data generated while interviewing male (steroid-using) bodybuilders. There are three main reasons for this. First, as elaborated below, bodybuilding is male dominated and steroid use was particularly common within this group. Second, I was unable systematically to obtain naturalistic observations of bodybuilders giving steroid accounts to non-participants. Identity switching and secrecy seemed to be the most common strategies employed by steroid-using contacts when interacting with inquisitive non-participants. Third, there were distinct ethnomethodological reasons for me obtaining drug accounts in interview situations. Interviewing was an important strategy for asking potentially awkward questions in a cultural environment where steroid use is simply taken-for-granted (cf. Scott & Lyman, 1968, 46–47). The usefulness of this strategy was underscored given the disadvantages associated with my otherwise valuable field role or, to be more specific, the image which most respondents had of me. (pp. 696–697)

A major goal of mixed methods research is to demonstrate integration of the methods and to create a finished product that shows the whole is greater than would have been gained by only using separate methods (Barbour, 1999; Bryman, 2007). In their spirited response to critics of their study of teaching reading in elementary classrooms, Robert G. Croninger and Linda Valli (2009) spell out what they tried to do and found using mixed methods research. Although their critics may disagree with their approach and conclusions, they captured the spirit animating mixed methods research goals.

> We used interview data, field notes, local artifacts, and classroom observations to demonstrate the corrosive power of high-stakes testing, especially in schools that lack a strong tradition of collaboration, a clear sense of professional community, and leadership supportive of teachers and students. These data—taken from both the quantitative and qualitative streams of our study— painted a picture of school life that was increasingly test driven and decreasingly focused on more engaging forms of instruction in reading and mathematics, especially as the school calendar moved toward the time for the state assessments. (p. 544)

A thorough description of methodological decisions and approaches in mixed methods practice provides readers with crucial information to understand and assess the rationale for a study and its methods and findings. Linda I. Reutter and her colleagues (2006) engaged in a mixed methods project that focused on the stigma of poverty and examined research participants' views of why poverty occurred. The study participants lived in both high and low income localities. Reutter et al. write:

> The 110-item survey instrument was constructed by the investigators specifically for this project, using relevant subscales from validated measures as well as items developed by the research team on the basis of the findings of Phase I [individual interviews with low-income and higher-income people and group interviews with low-income people]. Information was obtained on various aspects of exclusion/inclusion and isolation/belonging, including perceptions about the causes of poverty. (pp. 5–6)

The authors describe their quantitative procedures in detail and later state, "This paper focuses on results of Phase II, with Phase I data included to provide elaboration and interpretation of the quantitative findings, as appropriate" (p. 6). In this case, the qualitative component contributed both to forming survey questions for the quantitative study and to explaining and elaborating the interview participants' structural attributions for poverty. The findings from this mixed method approach complement each other. In a later paper from the same study, Reutter et al. (2009) report their qualitative findings. Here, they offer much greater detail about the qualitative design and their individual and group interview participants than in the 2006 article. Their statement, however, about their use of a mixed method approach does not inform the reader of their methodological rationale. In a single sentence, Reutter et al. state, "We employed mixed methods in the study, incorporating a qualitative descriptive approach (Sandelowski, 2000) using individual and group interviews (Phase I) and a representative survey of neighborhood residents conducted by telephone (Phase II)" (Reutter et al., 2009, p. 299). Scrutiny of the methods discussions in both articles, however, does afford the reader a strong grasp of how Reutter and her colleagues designed and conducted their study.

Taken together, the work of Reutter and her various coauthors (2006, 2009) reveal both potentials and problems in presenting and assessing mixed methods research. As I have noted, reporting the components of mixed methods research separately is common. As a consequence, how, when and what extent the other project components figure in the research likely remains opaque.[2]

Assessment of mixed qualitative methods raises other complexities. Morse (2011; Morse & Niehaus, 2009) advocates having one method serve as a core component and another method as a supplementary component. This approach works well when considering certain types of data collection. For example, the main method of gathering data for my studies of chronic illness (see, e.g., Charmaz, 1991) consisted of intensive interviews of people who had intrusive chronic illnesses. As a supplement, I analyzed published personal accounts by people who had such conditions. Morse (2009) correctly points out that one researcher may call a study mixed methods research whereas another researcher would not. My definition of ethnography is a perfect case in point. I do not see ethnography as a single method, while other researchers, who might well invoke the same data-collecting methods that I would, do.

When we consider analytic approaches, the questions and quandaries increase. Barbour (1998) was among the first to recognize that not all qualitative methods are compatible. Inherent incompatibilities may not be discernible until the analysis phase of inquiry. Until recently, researchers in some disciplines and professions, such as nursing, aimed for methodological purity and bemoaned what they construed as straying from an accepted standard. Other disciplines and professions treated methods as more fluid, flexible, and mutable. The same method may differ considerably when adopted by representatives of different disciplines who hold different theoretical perspectives. Psychoanalytic theory and feminist perspectives inform Ruthellen Josselson's (2011) narrative analysis. Catherine Riessman's (2008) rendering of narrative analysis invokes feminist and sociological perspectives and thus would generate different findings and conclusions. Similarly, constructivist grounded theory treats action and meaning in different ways than objectivist grounded theory. What constructivist grounded theorists take as data, the stance we take toward collecting them, our data collection practices, and our engagement with data all differ from researchers who subscribe to objectivist grounded theory.

Subsequently, what stands as grounded theory reflects how researchers define, use, and represent the method. Although I view grounded theory as an umbrella covering several different approaches, other grounded theorists do not. Grounded theory is particularly contested because numerous researchers have claimed that they conducted a grounded theory study when they used inductive qualitative research. Some researchers have claimed grounded theory to legitimize their studies, but many who have claimed the method do not understand it.[3] Relatively few researchers take grounded theory to its logical extension of theory construction. Instead, they engage in some sort of coding and memo writing that may be more or less consistent with one of the three major variants of grounded theory.

Grounded theory poses interesting problems for mixed methods research, precisely because grounded theory is contested from both within and without. That makes it difficult to establish the kind of guidelines for mixed qualitative methods research that

Morse (2009) advocates. My view ultimately rests on the answer to this pragmatic question: Does the analysis work? Steve Robertson (2006) analyzed relationships between men's understandings of what they needed to do to preserve their health and their constructions of masculinity. His mixed methods approach consisted of complementary qualitative analytic strategies. He first conducted a thematic analysis of their views of health and subsequently engaged in abductive analysis that interrogated the tensions between control to realize a "healthy lifestyle" and release from such control to achieve a "healthy balance" and thus permit pleasurable and risky behaviors. A thematic analysis is a typical qualitative approach. Abduction entails considering all possible theoretical explanations of an intriguing finding and lies at the core of grounded theory. Robertson describes developing a model that:

> Signifies a relationship between the "don't care/should care" dichotomy and narratives of "control" and "release" and how they are mobilized in regard to the construction of hegemonic masculinity. Just as masculinities are not static but rather represent configurations of gender practice that men move within and between, so the four health discourses that form the axes in the model are mobilized in different ways at different times in order to achieve (or reject) hegemonic ideals. (p. 185)

Robertson's substantive contribution fosters taking a nuanced view of men and risking behavior. He states:

> This model allows a challenge to assumptions and stereotypes that simplistically construct men as innate risk-takers (see also Lyons & Willott, 1999) and opens up a conceptual space for considering how, when, where and why men take responsibility for their health and well-being. (p.186)

## How Do Varied Qualitative Analytic Approaches Shape the Research Process and Product?

This question brings me to a brief discussion of the implications of the multiple method demonstration project in which I participated, *Five Ways of Doing Qualitative Analysis: Phenomenological*

*Psychology, Grounded Theory, Discourse Analysis, Narrative Research, and Intuitive Inquiry* (Charmaz, 2011a, 2011b). The book focuses on five qualitative researchers analyzing the same data. We studied the personal narrative and subsequent interview of a young woman we called "Teresa" who had life-threatening anaplastic cancer of the thyroid at age nineteen. I argue in the book that standpoints and starting points matter among qualitative researchers. We compared our completed analyses with each of the four other researchers, later Teresa (Emmalinda McSpadden) responded to each of our five analyses.

Through the comparative process, methodological assumptions and analytic styles became visible. My position resonates with Norman Denzin's (2008) contention that interpretation is inherently political. I argue that *our* purposes, as well as those of our research participants, shape what we do (Charmaz, 2011b, pp. 291–292). This point affects which questions we ask, the kind of data we collect, our modes of analysis, and what we take as evidence. Our purposes reflect professional biographies, personal experience, and political proclivities in addition to specific methodological preferences and skills.

My sociological background entered my views when I read each coauthor's chapter. I viewed our diverse analyses of the same data as echoing rhythms of collective life from our respective past experiences in graduate school and subsequent involvement in scholarship and research. Each one of us brought a worldview to our analysis that arose from these experiences and assumed both taken-for-granted and explicit theoretical allegiances.

Sociologists have long distinguished between research that takes an insider view, as contrasted with most research that begins and ends from outside the studied experience. I had come to view insider-outsider conceptions as quaint notions that barely tapped the complexity of researchers' positions. But our varied analyses testified to the significance of whether and to what extent a researcher begins from inside or outside of the experience. Our analyses also revealed that what we would define as inside or outside differed.

At the time we finalized our chapters, Fred Wertz was the only one of us who knew Teresa. I began from the standpoint of the rather typical insider qualitative approach of studying the texts with empathetic understanding. This understanding means trying to understand the logic of the person's experience from his or her point of view. It attributes a certain rationality to this experience and assumes the researcher's openness to it. In contrast, Fred Wertz and Rosemarie Anderson suggest a more intensive involvement with the research participant when they talk of doing research with love. Rosemarie begins her analysis with the following statement:

> The impulse to conduct an intuitive inquiry begins like a spark in the dark of winter because this impulse to explore a topic claims the researcher's imagination, often in an unconscious and uncanny way. She cannot stop thinking about the topic. Almost everything seems to remind her of the topic in some way. A yearning begins to understand the topic fully. This yearning to understand is Eros, love in pure form, because the intuitive inquirer wants to know her beloved topic fully. The researcher examines the fine points of a research account in a manner akin to a lover exploring a beloved's hand. Details matter. Secrets matter. The ordinary is extraordinary. The particular is favored. Everything related to the topic has meaning and significance, drawing her closer to understanding. She yearns to know more. Named or unnamed, conscious or unconscious, an intuitive inquiry has begun. (pp. 243–244)

Rosemarie writes here of love of the topic and her yearning to learn more. Yet you can sense Fred and Rosemarie's respective connections with Teresa beyond those portrayed in ordinary research reports. Their willingness to claim and express their feelings reminded me of the tacit limits of a sociologist's insider perspective. Ruthellen Josselson's narrative inquiry bridges insider and outsider strategies because she is simultaneously empathetic and professionally clinical. Linda McMullen did not aim to analyze either Teresa's experience or her story. Rather she looked for discursive patterns and focused on demonstrating one discursive pattern in the data, which she titled, "Enhancing Oneself, Diminishing Others." Linda started analysis from outside Teresa's experience and remained there. She aimed to show how her interpretations of were grounded in the texts. Linda described her work as removed from the individual but as accounting for how this discursive pattern is located in historical, social, and cultural conditions. Fred, Ruthellen, and Rosemarie all made interpretations of Teresa's psychological structure and brought in unconscious processes. As a grounded theorist, albeit an interpretive one, my analysis stuck more closely to the texts.

Linda's discursive analysis was the most sociological among my four colleagues in psychology. She emphasized action, performance, and language, all major interests of symbolic interactionists. However, when I compared my analysis with each researcher's, the differences with Linda's were the most striking. In my view, taking an insider view accounts for this difference.

In her reflection on the project, Linda raises an important but subtle point about methods. The approach a researcher assumed and used during data collection may pose sharp contrasts with the analytic methods he or she employs. Linda noted that ethical questions arise when interviews are conducted with empathy and aimed toward understanding but then these interviews are analyzed that does not aim for an analysis of experience. Linda was thinking of her situation as a discourse analyst who analyzed materials collected in a very different context. But the issue she raises crystallizes knotty ethical problems with ethnography and with some types of social justice research and qualitative interviewing.

This issue speaks to reporting qualitative research as well. Even if we aim for an analysis of experience how we portray that experience can foster diminishing the participants and thus contribute to distancing ourselves from them. Our language counts. This issue underscores my point that researchers need to ask whether, how, to what extent, and with which conceivable implications are the data gathering, analysis, and reporting congruent—and recognize when such congruence is not possible.

## Conclusion

The issues that arose in our demonstration project have strong similarities to the kinds of issues that may arise in mixed methods research practice. Researchers who take an insider's perspective have different starting points, hold different assumptions, and likely move in different directions. Similarly, ethical questions and dilemmas may arise that reflect the component methods of a mixed method project as well as from the disparities between them.

## Acknowledgments

This chapter builds on my comments about mixed methods in "Grounded Theory Methods in Social Justice Research," which appeared in Norman K. Denzin and Yvonna S. Lincoln (eds.), *The Handbook of Qualitative Research* (4ᵗʰ ed.) and a presentation in the plenary session: "Postmodernism, Triangulation, and Mixed Methods Research," at the International Congress of Qualitative Inquiry. Urbana, Illinois, May 20, 2011. Thanks are due to Michael Giardina, Sharlene Hesse-Biber, and Norman K. Denzin for encouraging me to participate and to finish this chapter.

## Notes

1. These authors affirm that "qualitizing" quantitative data also occurs.
2. Editors of substantive journals may also enforce limited discussions of methods. These discussions more likely include strategies for data collection rather than data analysis.
3. The claims and counterclaims do, of course, extend to those of us who are spokespersons of the method and have appeared in Internet discussions as well as in published works. Various proponents draw different lines as to what makes a piece of research a genuine grounded theory study.

## References

Altheide, D. L.( 1987). Reflections: Ethnographic content analysis. *Qualitative Sociology, 10*, 65–77.

Atkinson, P. & Silverman, D. (1997). Kunderas immortality: The interview society and the invention of the self. *Qualitative Inquiry, 3*, 3, 304–325.

Barbour, R. S. (1998). Mixing qualitative methods: Quality assurance or qualitative quagmire? *Qualitative Health Research, 8*, 3, 352–361.

Barbour, R. S. (1999). The case for combining qualitative and quantitative approaches in health services research. *Journal of Health Services Research and Policy, 4*, 1, 39–43.

Becker, H. S. & Geer, B. (1957). Participant observation and interviewing: A comparison. *Human Organization, 16*, 28–34.

Bryman, A. (2007). Barriers to integrating quantitative and qualitative research. *Journal of Mixed Methods Research, 1*, 1, 8–22.

Burawoy, M. (1991). The extended case method. In M. Burawoy, A. Burton, A. A. Ferguson, K. Fox, J. Gamson, N. Gartrell, L. Hurst, C. Kurzman, L. Salzinger, J. Schiffman, & S. Ui (Eds.), *Ethnography unbound: Power and resistance in the modern metropolis* (pp. 271–290). Berkeley: University of California Press.

Burawoy, M. (2000). Grounding globalization. In M. Burawoy, J. A. Blum, S. George, G. Sheba, Z. Gille, T. Gowan, L. Haney, M. Klawiter, S. A. Lopez, S. O' Riain, & M. Thayer (Eds.), *Global ethnography: Forces, connections, and imaginations in a postmodern world* (pp. 337–373). Berkeley: University of California Press.

Burke Johnson, R. McGowan, M. W., & Turner, L. A. (2010). Grounded theory in practice: Is it inherently a mixed method? *Research in the Schools, 17*, 2, 17.

Burke Johnson, R. Onwuegbuzie, A. J., & Turner, L. A. (2007). Toward a definition of mixed methods research. *Journal of Mixed Methods Research, 1*, 112 –133.

Cameron, R. (2009). Mixed methods research in the business world. *5th International Mixed Methods Conference & Workshops, 2009*. Harrogate, UK, July 9.

Charmaz, K. (1991). *Good days, bad days: The self in chronic illness and time*. New Brunswick, NJ: Rutgers University Press.

Charmaz, K. (2011a). Constructivist grounded theory analysis of losing and regaining a valued self. In F. J. Wertz, K. Charmaz, L. J. McMullen, R. Josselson, R. Anderson, & E. McSpadden (Eds.), *Five ways of doing qualitative analysis: Phenomenological psychology, grounded theory, discourse analysis, narrative research, and intuitive inquiry* (pp. 165–204). New York: Guilford.

Charmaz, K. (2011b). The lens of constructivist grounded theory analysis of losing and regaining a valued self. In F. J. Wertz, K. Charmaz, L. J. McMullen, R. Josselson, R. Anderson, & E. McSpadden (Eds.), *Five ways of doing qualitative analysis: Phenomenological psychology, grounded theory, discourse analysis, narrative research, and intuitive inquiry* (pp. 291–304). New York: Guilford.

Charmaz, K. (2011c). Grounded theory methods in social justice research. In N. K. Denzin & Y. S. Lincoln (Eds.), *Handbook of qualitative research*, 4th ed. (pp. 359–380). Thousand Oaks, CA: Sage.

Christ, T. W. (2009). Designing, teaching, and evaluating two complementary mixed methods research courses. *Journal of Mixed Methods Research, 3*, 4, 292–325.

Cicourel, A. V. (1964). *Method and measurement in sociology.* New York: Free Press.

Creswell, J. W. (2003). *Research design: Qualitative, quantitative, and mixed methods design* (2nd Ed.). Thousand Oaks, CA: Sage.

Creswell, J. W. & Plano Clark, V. L. (2007). *Designing and conducting mixed methods research.* Thousand Oaks, CA: Sage.

Creswell, J. W., Shope, R., Plano Clark, V. L., & Green, D. O. (2006). How interpretive qualitative research extends mixed methods research. *Research in the Schools, 13*, 1, 1–11.

Croninger, R. G. & Valli, L. (2009). Mixing it up about methods. *Educational Researcher, 38*, 7, 541–545.

Denzin, N. K. (1970). *The research act in sociology: A theoretical introduction to sociological methods.* London: Butterworths.

Denzin, N. K. (2008). *Searching for Yellowstone: Race, gender, family, and memory in the postmodern West.* Walnut Creek, CA: Left Coast Press, Inc.

Eastman, J. T. (2011). The hegemonic masculinity of the southern rock music revival. *Journal of Contemporary Ethnography, 28*, 10, 1–31.

Fielding, N. & Cisneros-Puebla, C. (2010). CAQDAS-GIS convergence: Toward a new integrated mixed method research practice. *Journal of Mixed Methods Research, 3*, 4, 349–370.

Greene, J. C. (2006). Toward a methodology of mixed methods social inquiry. *Research in the Schools, 13*, 1, 94–99.

Hesse-Biber, S. (2010a). Emerging methodologies and methods practices in the field of mixed methods research. *Qualitative Inquiry, 16*, 6, 415–428.

Hesse-Biber, S. (2010b). *Mixed methods research: Merging theory with practice.* New York: Guilford.

Hesse-Biber, S. (2010c). Qualitative approaches to mixed methods research. *Qualitative Inquiry, 16*, 6, 455–468.

Hoffman, E. A. (2007). Open-ended interviews: Power, and emotional labor. *Journal of Contemporary Ethnography, 36*, 318–346.

Josselsson, R. (2011). Narrative research: Constructing, deconstructing, and reconstructing story. In F. J. Wertz, K. Charmaz, L. M. McMullen, R. Josselson, R. Anderson, & E. McSpadden (Eds.), *Five ways of doing qualitative analysis: Phenomenological psychology, grounded theory, discourse analysis, narrative research, and intuitive inquiry* (pp. 224–242). New York: The Guilford Press.

Lamont, M. & White, P. (2009). Workshop on interdisciplinary standards for systematic qualitative research. Washington, DC: National Science Foundation.

Lyons, A. C. & Willott, S. (1999). From suet pudding to superhero: Representations of men's health for women. *Health, 3*, 283–02.

Monaghan, L. F. (2002). Vocabularies of motive for illicit steroid use among bodybuilders. *Social Science & Medicine, 55*, 3, 695–708.

Morgan, D. L. (2003). Paradigms lost and pragmatism regained: Methodological implications of combining qualitative and quantitative methods. *Journal of Mixed Methods Research, 1*, 1, 48–76.

Morse, J. M. (1991). Approaches to qualitative-quantitative methodological triangulation. *Nursing Research, 40*, 120–123.

Morse, J. M. (2009). Mixing qualitative methods. *Qualitative Health Research, 19*, 11, 1523–1524.

Morse, J. M. (2011). Molding qualitative health research. *Qualitative Health Research, 21*, 8, 1019–1021.

Morse, J. M. & Niehaus, L. (2009). *Mixed method design: Principles and procedures.* Walnut Creek, CA: Left Coast Press, Inc.

Nepal, V. P. (2010). On mixing qualitative methods. *Qualitative Health Research, 20*, 2, 281.

Popay, J., Bennett, S., Thomas, C., Williams, G., Gatrell, A., & Bostock, L. (2003). Beyond "beer, fags, egg and chips"? Exploring lay understandings of social inequalities in health. *Sociology of Health & Illness, 25*, 1, 1–23.

Reutter, L. I., Veenstra, G., Stewart, M. J., Raphael, D., Love, R., Makwarimba, E., & McMurray, S. (2006). Public attributions of poverty in Canada. *Canadian Review of Sociology and Anthropology, 43*, 1, 1–22.

Reutter, L. I., Stewart, M. J., Veenstra, G., Love, R., Raphael, D., & Makwarimba, E. (2009). Who do you think we are, anyway?: Perceptions of and responses to poverty stigma. *Qualitative Health Research, 19*, 3, 297–311.

Riessman, C. K.. (2008). *Narrative methods for the human science.* Thousand Oaks, CA: Sage.

Robertson, S. (2006). "Not living life in too much of an excess": Lay men understanding health and well-being. *Health, 10*, 2, 175–189.

Sandelowski, M. (2000). Whatever happened to qualitative description? *Research in Nursing and Health, 23*, 3, 334–340.

Sandelowski, M., Voils, C. I., & Knafl, G. (2009). On quantitizing. *Journal of Mixed Methods Research, 3*, 208–222.

Schwalbe, M. S., & Wolkomir, M. (2001). Interviewing men. In J. Gubrium & J. Holstein (Eds.), *Handbook of interview research: Context and method* (pp. 203–19). Thousand Oaks, CA: Sage.

Scott, M. B., & Lyman, S. (1968). Accounts. *American Sociological Review, 22*, 6, 664–670.

Silverman, D. (2007). *A very short, fairly interesting and reasonably cheap book about qualitative research.* London: Sage.

Tashakkori, A. & Teddlie, C. (2003). The past and future of mixed methods research: From data triangulation to mixed model designs. In A. Tashakkori & C. Teddlie (Eds.), *Handbook of mixed methods in social & behavioral research* (pp. 671–701). Thousand Oaks, CA: Sage.

Chapter 6

# Pulling Together

## Postmodernism and Multiple Method Research

Nigel G. Fielding

In this chapter, I argue that there is common ground between the contemporary practice of mixed methods research and the theoretical position of postmodernism. I position the argument in the context of the evolution of the objectives of mixed methods research from naive triangulation for convergent validation to that of combining methods for greater analytical depth, and in the context of the parallel development of an empirically oriented postmodernism that acknowledges community standards of truth even as it problematizes the notion of truth.

There has always been a tension in mixed methods between the flexibility required to provide openings for integrating multiple methods, and laying down systematic procedures to achieve such an integration with rigor. The canonical modernist statement of triangulation was Campbell and Fiske's (1959) "multi-trait, multi-method matrix," whose approach was preoccupied with taming rather than analytically exploiting the tendency of methods in combination to produce incommensurate, puzzling, or contradictory findings. To equally overdraw the case, whereas postmodernism

*Qualitative Inquiry and the Politics of Advocacy,* edited by Norman K. Denzin and Michael D. Giardina, 145–162. © 2012 Left Coast Press, Inc. All rights reserved.

has often been received as a nihilism that implies that, in the absence of agreed epistemological standards, anything goes, it can alternatively be read as setting such stringent standards for demonstrable, agreed knowledge that "nothing goes," where nothing means "conventional methodology." The point is that at an epistemological level, both positions make play with nuanced conceptions of flexibility and rigor.

The relationship of mixed methods and moderate postmodernism suggests that it is possible to have rigor without rigidity. The two positions come together in their common emphasis on the value of documenting and embracing multiple perspectives. Incorporating postmodernist positions in mixed method research can help mixed method researchers engage with the complexity of social phenomena, and the engagement of postmodernists with mixed methods can extend postmodernism's empirical reach by providing it with methodological resources that are sensitive to the limitations of mono-methods and whose analytical affordances have been tested through their combined application to social phenomena.

What Rosenau (1992) calls "affirmative postmodernism" has deep doubts about the established methodological assumptions underpinning conventional social research, especially social research done in the quantitative tradition, but does not regard these doubts as insuperable. Indeed, in fields like the sociology of technology and the sociology of everyday life, postmodernist work on substantive topics builds on mainstream work (Wakeford, 2004). Empirical postmodernism is particularly associated with methods like deconstructionism. Postmodernism's analytic organized around a de-centered subject informs a methodological posture of valuing multiple perspectives that quite readily connects with a central premise of mixed methods.

An abiding criticism of the classic convergent validation approach to mixed methods emerges from the observation that different methods make different ontological and epistemological assumptions. The classic approach gave us an analogy based on the land-surveying term "triangulation" as a marker of its conviction that mixing methods was an effective means of convergent validation. Convergent validation is centrally concerned with whether findings from different methods agree, in the same way that a land surveyor precisely assigns a point to a map on the basis of fixing a view of it with measurements from several viewing positions. By analogy, if findings from different methods agree, the researcher may assume that the findings are more likely to be valid, since different methods display different kinds of error, and thus, if the same finding emerges from more than one method, it is more likely to be correct (Webb et al., 1966, p. 3). If the methods being combined had the same biases, combining them would just multiply error.

However, sociology concerns itself with phenomena and conceptual relationships that are not analogous to simply locating where one is on a map. The main criticism of the classic approach is that triangulation cannot provide a validation strategy where different epistemological assumptions inform the different methods being combined (Blaikie, 1991). A characteristic that functions as a threat to validity in the epistemology associated with a given method may reflect an assumption that contradicts the epistemology of another method. Similarly, something that is undermining in one method may be an irrelevance or even an analytical resource in another method. As we will see, short of unconvincing appeals to methodological pragmatism, mixed methods researchers lack a compelling rebuttal of the epistemological critique, and this has led to a move away from the original convergent validation rationale and, with it, a retreat from the notion of triangulation to the more flexible formulation of mixed methods.

There are also empirical criticisms of convergent validation. These relate to the phenomenon of "bogus triangulation." In Ronald Burt's (2005) "echo hypothesis," similar opinions expressed by different sources are often not independent validation but rather individuals echoing one opinion, such as that of a high-status person, and therefore highly redundant. Related psychological research on false rumors suggests that denying them only reinforces and further disseminates the rumor (Rucker & Dubois, 2009). With each repetition, skepticism diminishes. Such research suggests that convergence between accounts should not automatically be taken as validation but as something to be further investigated. As a source of skepticism, postmodernism can be a resource for mixed methods in developing a more discriminating approach to findings that emerge from a mix of methods.

For critics, including postmodernists, the contemporary practice of mixed methods can be read as attempting to play down the differences in epistemological assumptions that configure the paradigm wars dividing quantitative and qualitative research. That kind of naive pragmatism is in tension with a take on mixed methods, which seeks a more self-aware and considered analytic integration of results from different methods. This is well put by Cronin et al. (2008), who treat such integration as "a process which *creates*, and analytically exploits, a particular relationship between different sets of data" (p. 583; emphasis added). The vital word in the quoted statement is "creates." By writing creates instead of discovers or demonstrates, Cronin et al. keep convergence on hold and highlight the analyst's role in mediating the relationship between different data sets.

The empirical and epistemological critiques of the original doctrine of convergent validation have cleared ground for a new understanding of the rationale and value of mixing methods. Rather than seeing the practice of mixing methods as a means to secure valid findings, many now acknowledge the force of the critiques and argue instead that the benefit of combining different methodologies and interpretive approaches is that it can extend the scope and depth of analytical understanding (Denzin & Lincoln, 1994; Fielding & Fielding, 1986; Fielding & Schreier, 2001). This "analytic density" rationale is skeptical that mixing methods will provide more reliable and valid findings but instead sees the virtue of mixing as being its provision of a wider and deeper picture from all angles (Shih, 1998, p. 633). This represents the current theoretical turn in mixed methods, which belatedly acknowledges that every mixed methods research strategy bears an implicit theory of meaning. It calls for a recognition that theory animates any analysis (Kelle, 2001)—including the theory that it is possible to produce atheoretical research findings—and seeks to draw out the implicit theories of meaning embedded in mixed methods work so that they may be used as an analytic resource.

So where does postmodernism stand in relation to such perspectives? Postmodernism is undoubtedly a contested school of thought with several branches. While severe postmodernists hold as a central tenet the death of the subject (as in the subject/object distinction), Rosenau's (1992, pp. 15–16) "affirmative postmodernists" believe it is not necessary to eliminate the concept of a subject to maintain a posture that is cautious about generalization and a unified frame of reference.

Similarly, McRobbie locates postmodernism's anti-foundationalism in "being attentive to the assumptions which shape social theory, the criteria which it uses, [...] to boundary-marking, and to what exactly is being excluded from or included in the fields of knowledge" (1994, p. 5). Along with postmodernism's interest in difference and its vision of "a fragmented and diverse social reality" (Turner, 2004, p. ii), these parts of the postmodern canon readily connect with mixed methods. Laclau's (1991) "radical incommensurability" of social divisions like age, sex, nation, ethnicity and class, feeds postmodernism's insistence on the elusiveness of a unitary vision. This insistence can be analytically fruitful. Spivak (1988) offers the example of analyses of the situation of black women, for whom the women's movement—a product of modernity—does not speak. The postmodernist criticizes the idea of a single womanhood, insisting that analysis must accommodate the view of those who dispute the terms in which they are represented.

While they repudiate the grand sweep of generalized theory, and its suppression of inconvenient contradictions and details that threaten the reductionist mono-causal vision, the affirmative postmodernist's focus on everyday life is "empiricist in character [and] emphasises concrete reality" (Rosenau, 1992, p. 16). The roots of this approach go far back and connect with some surprisingly mainstream approaches to epistemology. Where decentering the subject is construed as perspectival relativism, postmodernism is indeed on common ground with established perspectives in qualitative methodology—preferring a reflexive to a positivist epistemology, being dubious about claims to objectivity, and valuing difference over similarity.

As previously noted, the affirmative postmodernists hold a constructivist theory of reality. The methodological implication is that postmodernism is interested in complex, dynamic categories.

It seeks an analysis that reflects the way that differently located social actors apply distinctive perspectives on the same social phenomenon, an interest that connects with versions of mixed methods that regard different methods as capturing prismatic refractions of social phenomena (so that no single perspective can provide a full picture, nor can any method or combination of methods give *direct* access to the phenomenon). Thus, moderate approaches engage with different subjectivities, pointing out, for example, that black women do not read patriarchy as do white women, and that young women do not read the feminism/feminity dualism as do women who experienced the adversities of the early women's movement.

Moreover, the belief in "intertextuality"—the connection of everything with everything—that problematizes causal explanation for postmodernists can plausibly be read as an insistence that causal explanation is complex. Postmodernists assert the difficulty in establishing the temporal (chronological) priority that is a precondition of causal explanation in a social world where everything is related to everything else in an absolutely interactive way (Tyler, 1986). Such concerns were registered by social theorists prior to the emergence of postmodernism. Engagement with the temporal complexity of the causes of social phenomena and their instantiation in the interaction of structure and action has long been the business of systems theory (Buckley, 1967) and is at the heart of Archer's (1982) concept of "morphogenesis," the principal (and empirically more tractable) alternative rendering of instantiation to Giddens's notion of "structuration" (Fielding 1988).

Affirmative postmodernists acknowledge both obdurate social realities and "specific, local, personal and community forms of truth" (Kvale, 1995, p. 21). Arguing that social realities cannot be directly represented does not mean different empirical analyses cannot be evaluated, as postmodernists readily do when critiquing positivist empirical research. Postmodernist concerns here are consistent with those raised from the earliest days in qualitative methodology, covering such matters as the relationship of research to its social and political context (Bogardus, 1924; Ervin-Tripp, 1967; Rice, 1929); the location of research in its own micro-history and its temporal anchor in the development of the phenomenon at the time of the research intervention (Riesman & Benney, 1955; Wax & Shapiro, 1956; Whyte, 1953); and the multidimensional and sometimes ambiguous character of social reality (Becker, 1956; Dean & Whyte, 1958; Lazarsfeld 1944). The old dates on these references suggest how long these concerns have troubled and intrigued qualitative sociology. They considerably precede the emergence of a recognizable postmodernism.

Skepticism about epistemological assumptions underlying standard research methods such as interviewing is not the monopoly of postmodernists. It features prominently in the work of Burawoy (2000) and is a current issue in the wider field of methodology, as evidenced by Gobo (2011). From a postmodern perspective, McRobbie (1994) charges that sociology treats interview data "as transparently meaningful and as evidence in themselves, rather than as complex social constructs which are the products of pre-given discourses" (p. 180). However, this neglects Lyman and Scott's (1970) critical view of interview data as "accounts," Cicourel's (1982) treatment of the interview as a ritual interaction, and Holstein and Gubrium's reflexive conception of the relationship between validation and pre-theoretical orientations to empirical reality (Brekhus et al., 2005; Gubrium & Holstein, 1997; Holstein & Gubrium, 1995), all being non-postmodernist moves to treat interview data as topic rather than resource. For these authors, the fact that fieldwork is not a conduit tapping directly into empirical reality, and that it carries implicit theories, does not mean that the ontological status of field data affords researchers no analytic purchase at all.

Attempts to negotiate a middle way between naive objectivism and crude relativism began with foundational sociologists such as Max Weber, endure as features of the mediated approach to social reality based on community standards of validity found in contemporary hermeneutics (Bernstein 1983), and are found in applications of Peircian abductive logic (Shank, 2001) and of pragmatic philosophy to sociological conceptualization, for example, Malcolm Williams's (2000) work on "moderatum generalisation." These positions acknowledge that values and interests may lie behind consensus within a research community but do so without abandoning a concern with reliability and validity—a position seen in Denzin and Lincoln's (1994) criteria of "credibility, transferability, dependability and confirmability" (p. 14) and Tashakkori & Teddlie's (2003) notion of "inference quality," which combines internal validity with community standards of trustworthiness and credibility but downplays external validity/transferability (Bryman, 2006).

The connection between postmodernism's emphasis on the need to reflect different constructions of social reality and the contemporary practice of mixed methods is that incorporating multiple perspectives helps us look at the research issue from all angles. By revealing related but distinct dimensions of the phenomenon, mixed methods can act as a corrective to analytic tunnel vision. In philosophy, the classic account is Lesniewski's (1992) demonstration that multiple conceptual schemes can be used to describe the same reality. The value of mixing methods is not that it enables researchers to demonstrate that their findings mutually reinforce each other—the convergent validation idea—but that it "give(s) different viewpoints the chance to arise, and postpone(s) the immediate rejection of information or hypotheses that seem out of joint with the majority viewpoint" (Trend, 1978, p. 353).

Indeed, multiple method inquiry may challenge the researcher's assumptions in ways that are consonant with postmodernism but that arise empirically rather than by theoretical fiat. A researcher who engages with accountants' job satisfaction may begin by assuming that the phenomenon of job satisfaction is a tangible object of study, but become less certain as her or his awareness grows of competing conceptualizations. She or he may find that the cultural significance imputed to the phenomenon does not register with research participants, or that the indicators taken as signs of the phenomenon are so extensively mediated that "sign" cannot be distinguished from "noise." Self-reflexive engagement with multiple methods can lead researchers to open up what was first taken as a tangible and discrete research problem to reformulation in a similar way to postmodernism's heuristic. It may require the researcher to consider whether the research problem is actually a normatively based construction behind which sits a more profound social phenomenon, as in Grey's (1994) postmodernist analysis of accountants' careers. Thus, the researcher who engages with accountants' careers may be led to reject both member-validated accounts of the pleasures of calculation and the idea of "career" as a form of "*déformation professionelle*," but come to see the concept of career as a story that professionals tell themselves to counter the sense of contingency arising from the evidence daily before them of the risks posed by market economies.

Whether engendered as a starting assumption, as in postmodernism, or provoked by confrontation with empirical data, as in mixed method research, the impetus toward analytic density is a productive skepticism. It is skeptical in its alertness to the weaknesses in given methods, sampling strategies, and analytical approaches, but it is productive in making assumptions explicit and in making analyses that explicitly negotiate the basis for, and limits of, any generalization. These virtues are not unique to multiple method research but mixing methods does provide opportunities and make demands that encourage researchers to pursue such qualities. Multiple methods require a relativist element, so the mixed methods research design can sincerely engage with difference. Mixing methods puts findings from different methods into dialogue.

To illustrate this, we might take the case of a highly developed field of study, such as the effects of social disadvantage on educational achievement, which has been one of the most enduring concerns of sociology in its engagement with the concerns of social policy. Such highly developed fields of research as educational disadvantage are recognized as mature. When we describe a research field as mature, we mean that a substantive problem has been addressed by a variety of methods and theoretical orientations, with attention to its historical, structural, and cultural dimensions. This approach also connects with the affinities of affirmative postmodernism. McRobbie (1994, p. 39) commends analytical work that is "structural, historical and ethnographic" and calls for an "integrative" and "connective" mode of analysis. For McRobbie (p. 26), this will shift fields like the study of mass media from textual analysis of the underlying narratives borne by advertising and other cultural products toward a more holistic frame that includes the ownership and control of communications media.

As an instance of the interplay between methods, data, and theory in interpreting findings from mixed method research, we might consider Erzberger's (2000) account of the workings of the job placement scheme that was designed to facilitate the labor market entry of university graduates into employment in the once socialist East Germany. The system was generally seen as successful on the basis of quantitative analyses of official labor market statistics. However, qualitative research suggested that what was really happening was that the job placement system was being manipulated by job-seekers. They were actually finding their own work using informal channels, but then colluded with their would-be employers to report a "vacancy" to the job placement bureau. This was then immediately taken up by the supposed job-seeker in a process that, from the outside, seemed to show another success for the job placement system.

In such an example, the standard mixed methods case would be that, without the quantitative data providing one version of social reality, we would not know how to treat the finding from the qualitative study about job-seekers manipulating the system. To see the importance of the finding from the qualitative study, researchers had to have the quantitative data suggesting the official system was working. But the standard mixed methods approach would still leave doubts. For instance, it could be that the characteristically small sample of qualitative fieldwork had simply uncovered a few renegades who distorted the system that most graduates sincerely adhered to. To handle this doubt, the conventional mixed methods approach might involve a further quantitative enquiry that, rather than use the official data, mounted an independent survey that asked respondents precisely how they had learned of the job vacancy they took up. So the standard mixed methods approach would use initial quantitative data to understand the official version of the job system, explore the system with qualitative fieldwork, and then seek to resolve the conflicting versions of how the system was operating by testing whether the informal process found by the qualitative fieldwork was applicable more generally.

However, what a postmodern perspective might interject into such an approach relates to Kelle's insistence that theory must drive mixed methods enquiries. Such a theory might work from the fact that at the time of German reunification, one case after another emerged of the manipulation of official data by the former German Democratic Republic. This raised skepticism about any alleged successes of the GDR. It was this skepticism that drove researchers to use qualitative fieldwork to look behind the official statistics. The mixing of methods came about because of theory—driven by the wider political picture and the general suspicion of GDR information. That skepticism led researchers to see the interview data as a challenge to official employment statistics. From this perspective, the actual benefit of mixing methods is not that they enhance the likelihood that conclusions are valid and reliable but that they delay the hasty drawing of conclusions when evidence is thin, equivocal, or contradictory.

Like postmodernism, mixing methods encourages researchers to take a more critical stance. In particular, it encourages mixed methods researchers to recognize the naivety in imagining that any research inquiry can begin without positioning itself. Decisions about positioning are implicit in every preliminary preparation for doing research as much as they are present in collecting and interpreting the data. The practices of research design, instrument design, and sampling all necessitate that researchers look ahead to what the findings might be and make a research design employing methods that have the best chance of capturing what they anticipate will be the nature of the phenomenon. Celebrating multiple perspectives, experiences, and dimensions in the way that is characteristic of postmodernism facilitates this thinking ahead. It means that research design is not the arid application of a set of conventions and standard procedures but a creative, imaginative act. One of the great virtues of the mixed methods literature is that it has opened up the research design step of a research inquiry to that kind of attention. This approach promotes more complex research designs that help researchers be clearer about what their findings demonstrate and produce analysis that engages with qualifiers and constraints on the relationships it reveals.

An interesting (and appealing) view is that mixed methods "provides a rationale for hypotheses/theories/guiding assumptions to compete and provide alternatives" (Niaz, 2008, p. 287). This is a perspective that stands in tension with the more formulaic textbook renderings of mixed methods. Declining emphasis on creativity, inventiveness, and risk-taking is often a mark of methodological innovations when they move to the mainstream. Ivankova and Kawamura (2010, pp. 587–578) cite a stream of "how to" literature that profiles and exemplifies the application of mixed methods research designs in disciplines and subdisciplines, and meta-reviews assessing the purposes of, and trends in, such research. Interestingly, the actual analytic integration of quantitative and qualitative results is generally neglected in this literature. Since the presumable point of mixing methods is to explore the analytic implications of linking data derived from different methods rather than have different methods "talk past each other," the neglect of data integration is a troubling matter.

Ivankova and Kawamura (2010) seem to want to treat creativity and flexibility in mixed methods research design as a defect. They suggest that "interdisciplinary fields that seek understanding of more complex research problems calling for a pragmatic approach to research are more open to variability in the methods and the use of integrated designs" (p. 604). Since every social researcher of whatever discipline is highly likely to regard their discipline as addressing complex problems, that assessment boils down to two of the words in the quoted extract: interdisciplinary and pragmatic. From this chapter's perspective, a tendency to adopt mixed methods as a response to circumstances where research requires a pragmatic, interdisciplinary effort is problematical. Integrating different kinds of data derived from applying different methods is a particularly large challenge where researchers also have to negotiate unfamiliarity with where their different disciplines are coming from. Further, taking pragmatism as an overriding value is likely to work against efforts to integrate data in a well-considered analysis that knows when to synthesize some findings (because they are equivalent and commensurate) and when to respect and investigate contradictory findings (because the contradiction reflects epistemologically based differences that cannot be resolved empirically, only conceptually). No doubt there is excellent pragmatic, interdisciplinary mixed methods research out there, but it is not hard to imagine mixed methods projects where interdisciplinary teams working pragmatically produce findings and analyses that satisfy no one.

An older system of thought offers a more compelling approach than simple pragmatism and has affinities with this chapter's approach to mixed methods and postmodernism. As the branch of reasoning concerned with interpretation and meaning, *hermeneutics* is premised on the idea that we cannot directly apprehend the original against which a given reproduction must be compared. However, hermeneutics does not take this posture because it is founded on the impossibility of truth or the equivalence of all accounts of empirical phenomena. There being no prospect of a single account offering the transcendent universal truth, hermeneutics addresses each account for the particular elements of the phenomenon it may distinctively reveal. No single account may offer the whole truth, but each single account may contribute additively to a progressively richer understanding (Tate, 1998).

In hermeneutics, the interpretive process involves a circular movement between one's own and others' perspectives (Bentz & Shapiro, 1998). Both are regarded as partial, incomplete representations but their distinctiveness also enables different facets of the phenomenon to be glimpsed. The account built up through the dialogical circle of reasoning is an iterative understanding proceeding from the tradition of previous interpretations. For Gadamer, the essential thing is calibrating Heidegger's (1962) "foreconceptions" (derived from existing interpretations), with the phenomenon being interpreted is for analysts to be aware of their own biases, "so that the text can present itself in all its otherness and thus assert its own truth against one's own fore-meanings" (Gadamer, 1975, p. 259). No object of interpretation is uncolored by the previous interpretations that have been applied to it. To speak in terms of bias and tradition is not to suggest an opinionated approach but one mindful that all interpretation contains sediments of the particular analytic inheritance of the interpreter. "Hermeneutics aims at being open to understanding the other person. ... (T)he researcher aims to ... hear some things that might be inconsistent with the researcher's pre-existing theory" (Ezzy, 2001, p. 37).

The colorations comprising this tradition are exposed by debate in an intellectual community.

> What is essential ... is a dialogue in which there is a search for common ground and an attempt to work back from this to resolve disagreements, plus a willingness to revise views about previously accepted assumptions. ... What research offers from this perspective is not knowledge that can be taken to be valid because it is based on a certain foundation, but rather knowledge that can reasonably be assumed to be ... less likely to be invalid than information from other sources. This is because ... dialogue ... functions to expose and eliminate errors. (Hammersley, 1992, p. 200)

It is through dialogue with others in an intellectual community that understandings are refined (Gadamer, 1975, p. 209). This is, then, analogous to the local, community versions of truth to which moderate postmodernism subscribes.

This position particularly suits that form of sociological research that seeks application, for example, in policy evaluation, while being alert to the contextual and dynamic factors that undermine simplistic control design methodologies (Pawson & Tilley 1997; Tilley, 2000). Tilley (2000, p. 110) describes a process of "realistic evaluation" that negotiates "that aspect of postmodernism which casts doubt on the possibility of objective knowledge and ... that aspect of modernism that promises universal unconditional truths." Pawson and Tilley's (1997) "realistic evaluation" includes several techniques to attune the research intervention to contextual factors affecting program implementation, including a "teacher-learner function" between researcher and program participants by means of which the emergent theory of program functioning is explained to participants and adjusted in light of their response, a move that also enables participants to adjust program delivery in light of the theory. Such procedures aim for "something like objective understanding of contingent regularities and changes in regularities in behavior" (Tilley, 2000, p. 110). The desirability of a middle ground between what Tilley called the

Scylla of relativism and the Charybdis of absolutism is recognized by postmodernists, too, as in McRobbie's (1994) call for "a research mode which prioritizes multiple levels of experience, including the ongoing relations which connect everyday life with cultural forms. This would be a way of breaking down the division which has emerged between the study of cultural texts and the study of social behaviour and experience" (pp. 184–185).

In this discussion, I have argued that, since mixing methods has moved away from convergent validation toward the pursuit of analytic richness, and encourages us to recognize multiple perspectives, there is a connection with postmodernism's interest in multiple subjectivities. Taking a reflexive approach, engaging with the enigmatic, and being alert to facets of the phenomenon that can only be pursued with methods not already used is important common ground between postmodernists and practitisoners of mixed methods research. Neither postmodernism nor mixed methods are as inflexible as their critics claim. Both contain an impetus for making connections and a potential to deliver rigor without rigidity.

## References

Archer, M. (1982). Morphogenesis versus structuration: On combining structure and action. *British Journal of Sociology, 33,* 4, 455–483.

Becker, H. (1956). Interviewing medical students. *American Journal of Sociology, 62,* 199–201.

Bentz, V. & Shapiro, J. (1998). *Mindful inquiry in social research.* London: Sage.

Bernstein, R. (1983). *Beyond objectivism and relativism,* Philadelphia: University of Pennsylvania Press.

Blaikie, N. (1991). A critique of the use of triangulation in social research. *Quality and Quantity, 25,* 115–136.

Bogardus, E. (1924). Methods of interviewing. *Journal of Applied Sociology, 9,* 456–467.

Brekhus, W., Galliher, J., & Gubrium, J. (2005). The need for thin description. *Qualitative Inquiry, 11,* 6, 861–879.

Bryman, A. (2006). Paradigm peace and the implications for quality. *International Journal of Social Research Methodology, 9,* 2, 111–126.

Buckley, W. (1967). *Sociology and modern systems theory*. Englewood Cliffs, NJ: Prentice Hall.

Burawoy, M. (2000). Introduction: reaching for the global. In M. Burawoy (Ed.), *Global ethnography* (pp. 1–18). Berkeley: University of California Press.

Burt, R. S. (2005). *Brokerage and closure: An introduction to social capital*. New York: Oxford University Press.

Campbell, D. & Fiske, D. (1959). Convergent and discriminant validity by the multi-trait, multi-method matrix. *Psychological Bulletin, 56*, 81–105.

Cicourel, A. (1982). Interviews, surveys and the problem of ecological validity. *The American Sociologist, 17*, 1, 11–20.

Cronin, A., Alexander, V., Fielding, J., Moran-Ellis, J., & Thomas, H. (2008). The analytic integration of qualitative data sources. In P. Alasuutari, L. Bickman, & J. Brannen (Eds.), *The Sage handbook of social research methods* (pp. 572–584). London: Sage.

Dean, J. & Whyte, W. F. (1958). How do you know if the informant is telling the truth? *Human Organization, 17*, 34–38.

Denzin, N. K. & Lincoln, Y. S. (1994). Introduction: Entering the field of qualitative research. In N. K. Denzin & Y. S. Lincoln (Eds.), *Handbook of qualitative research* (pp. 1–18). London: Sage.

Ervin-Tripp, S. (1967). An Issei learns English. *Journal of Social Issues, 23*, 2, 78–90.

Erzberger, C. (2000). "What can we learn from Potemkin?": Quantitative results as optical illusions. *Social science methodology in the new millennium: Proceedings of the Fifth International Conference on Logic and Methodology* [CD-ROM]. Cologne, Germany: Zentralarchiv fur Empirische Sozialforschung.

Ezzy, D. (2001). *Qualitative analysis: Thinking, doing, writing*. Crows Nest, New South Wales, Australia: Allen & Unwin.

Fielding, N. G. (1988). Between micro and macro. In N. G. Fielding (Ed.), *Actions and structure* (pp. 1–19). London: Sage.

Fielding, N. G. & Fielding, J. (1986). *Linking data*. Beverley Hills CA: Sage.

Fielding, N. G. & Schreier, M. (2001). On the compatability between qualitative and quantitative research methods. *Forum Qualitative Sozialforschung, 2*, 1. http://qualitative-research.net/fqs/fqs-eng.htm (accessed December 7, 2011).

Gadamer, H. (1975). *Truth and method*. London: Sheed and Ward.

Gobo, G. (2011). Glocalizing methodology? The encounter between local methodologies. *International Journal of Social Research Methodology, 14*, 6, 417–437.

Grey, C. (1994). Career as a project of the self and labor process discipline. *Sociology, 28*, 2, 479–497.

Gubrium, J. & Holstein, J. (1997). *The new language of qualitative method.* Oxford, UK: Oxford University Press.

Hammersley, M. (1992). Some reflections on ethnography and validity. *International Journal of Qualitative Studies in Education, 5*, 3, 195–203.

Heidegger, M. (1962). *Being and time.* Oxford: Blackwell.

Holstein, J. & Gubrium, J. (1995). *The active interview.* London: Sage.

Ivankova, N. & Kawamura, Y. (2010). Emerging trends in the utilization of integration designs in the social, behavioural and health sciences. In A. Tashakkori & C. Teddlie (Eds.), *Sage handbook of mixed methods in social and behavioural research*, 2nd ed. (pp. 581–611). London: Sage.

Kelle, U. (2001). Sociological explanations between micro and macro and the integration of qualitative and quantitative methods. *Forum: Qualitative Social Research, 2*, 1. http://qualitative-research.net/fqs/fqs-eng.htm (accessed October 31, 2011).

Kvale, S. (1995). The social construction of validity. *Qualitative Inquiry, 1*, 1, 19–40.

Laclau, E. (1991). *Reflections on the new revolutions of our times.* London: Verso.

Lazarsfeld, P. (1944). The controversy over detailed interviews. *Public Opinion Quarterly, 8*, 38–60.

Lesniewski, S. (1992). *Collected works.* Dordrecht, The Netherlands: Kluwer.

Lyman, S. & Scott, M. (1970). *A sociology of the absurd.* New York: Goodyear.

McRobbie, A. (1994). *Post modernism and popular culture.* London: Routledge.

Niaz, M. (2008). A rationale for mixed methods (integrative) research programmes in education. *Journal of Philosophy of Education, 42*, 2, 61–68.

Pawson, R. & Tilley, N. (1997). *Realistic evaluation.* London: Sage.

Rice, S. (1929). Contagious bias in the interview. *American Journal of Sociology, 35*, 420–423.

Riesman, D. & Benney, M. (1955). The sociology of the interview. *Midwest Sociology, 18*, 1, 3–15.

Rosenau, P. (1992). *Postmodernism and the social sciences.* Princeton, NJ: Princeton University Press.

Rucker, D. D. & Dubois, D. (2009). The failure to transmit certainty: Causes, consequences, and remedies. *Advances in Consumer Research, 36*, 131–134.

Shank, G. (2001). It's logic in practice, My Dear Watson: An imaginary memoir from beyond the grave. *Forum: Qualitative Social Research, 2*, 1. www.qualitative-research.net (accessed November 14, 2011).

Shih, F-J. (1998). Triangulation in nursing research. *Journal of Advanced Nursing, 28*, 3, 631–641.

Spivak, G. C. (1988). French feminism in an international frame. In, G. C. Spivak (Ed.), *In other worlds: Essays in cultural politics* (pp. 134–154). London: Routledge.

Tashakkori, A. & Teddlie, C. (2003). The past and future of mixed methods research. In A. Taskakkori & C. Teddlie (Eds.), *Handbook of mixed methods* (pp. 671–701). Thousand Oaks, CA: Sage.

Tate, J. W. (1998). The ermeneutic circle versus the Enlightenment. *Telos 110*, 9–38.

Tilley, N. (2000). Doing realistic evaluation of criminal justice. In V. Jupp, P. Davies, & P. Francis (Eds.), *Doing criminological research* (pp. 97–113). London: Sage.

Trend, M. G. (1978). On the reconciliation of qualitative and quantitative analyses. *Human Organization. 37*, 345–354.

Turner, B. (2004). Foreword. In R. Boudon (Ed.), *The poverty of relativism* (pp. i–ix). Oxford: Bardwell.

Tyler, S. (1986). Postmodern ethnography. In J. Clifford & G. Marcus (Eds.), *Writing culture*, (pp. 122–140). Berkeley: University of California Press.

Wakeford, N. (2004). Developing methodological frameworks for studying the World Wide Web. In D. Gauntlett & R. Horsley (Eds.), *Web studies* (pp. 210–235). London: Arnold.

Wax, M. & Shapiro, L. (1956). Repeated interviewing. *American Journal of Sociology, 62*, 215–217.

Webb, E. J., Campbell, D. T., Schwartz, R. D., & Sechrest, L. (1966). *Unobtrusive measures: Nonreactive research in the social sciences.* Chicago: Rand McNally.

Whyte, W. F. (1953). Interviewing for organisational research. *Human Organization, 12*, 2, 15–22.

Williams, M. (2000). *Science and social science: An introduction.* London: Routledge.

Chapter 7

# Vulnerability and the Politics of Advocacy

## Challenges for Qualitative Inquiry Using Multiple Methods

Uwe Flick

## Introduction

Social vulnerability is an increasing phenomenon in Europe (see Ranci, 2010). Vulnerable populations (e.g., those facing unemployment, institutionalized people in nursing homes, or homeless adolescents) live in situations of reduced autonomy. Such discrimination can be a double challenge: to do qualitative inquiry exploring this situation and to contribute with research to improving the participants' living situations. Such a claim for advocacy leads to specific dilemmas. (1) We need to identify impacts of certain problems (e.g., lack of sleep in residents in nursing homes). (2) With advocacy in mind, we should identify and respect the needs and wishes of the members of such a population. (3) We should determine professionals' specific understandings of advocacy, which may differ from those of the vulnerable people.

If we want use our research to help improve residents' living conditions, we need multiple methods—one for identifying the impact of the problem (lack of activity and sleep problems

*Qualitative Inquiry and the Politics of Advocacy,* edited by Norman K. Denzin and Michael D. Giardina, 163–182. © 2012 Left Coast Press, Inc. All rights reserved.

in assessments, for example) and one identifying the problem awareness (of the professionals, for example, in interviews). With a mixed methods approach, we might produce data that show differences between practice and knowledge. However, if we really want to understand the multiple realities involved in such an issue, we need a triangulation of research perspectives that allows integrating theoretical perspectives of several methodological approaches and their findings. This specific potential of triangulation in the context of vulnerability and advocacy will be discussed in this chapter on a methodological level for multiple methods approaches and for examples of research.

## Background and Example 1: Unemployment as a Collective Experience

The idea of using multiple methods in the study of vulnerable populations has been pursued in social research since its early days. It goes back much further than the periods in which these concepts were formulated or became prominent in the research. While the discussion about triangulation has been going on since the late 1960s—in particular since Denzin's publications (e.g., 1989 [1970])—and the discussion on mixed methods has developed since the 1980s (e.g., Greene et al., 1989), the idea of using multiple approaches in a study can be traced back at least to research like *Marienthal: The Sociology of an Unemployed Community*. This study was run by Marie Jahoda, Paul Lazarsfeld, and Hans Zeisel (1971 [1933]) in the late 1920s and is one of the classic studies in social research (see also Fleck, 2004).

After the main employer of the inhabitants of an Austrian village went bankrupt, the authors studied psychological coping with unemployment in a broad and comprehensive sense. One major result is the elaboration of the leitmotif of a "tired society" as a condensed characterization of the attitude toward life and the day-to-day practices in the village. Various types of practices in reaction to unemployment (e.g., the "unbroken," the "resigned," the "desperate," and the "apathetic") were identified. Much later, Jahoda (1995, p. 121) summarized the methodological approach leading to these insights in the following rules:

1. for catching social reality, qualitative and quantitative methods are indicated;
2. objective facts and subjective attitudes should be collected;
3. observations at present should be complemented by historical material; and
4. inconspicuous observation of spontaneous life and direct planned interviews should be applied.

Applying these rules included linking multiple methodological approaches (qualitative, quantitative, interviews, and observation). Several methodological perspectives (objective facts, subjective attitudes, current, and historical issues) were pursued. Jahoda et al. (1971 [1933]) list the following types of data in their study: Cadastre sheets of about 500 families; life histories; sheets for documenting the use of time, protocols, school essays; various statistics; and historical information about the village and its institutions. Lazarsfeld (1960, p. 14) has made the link of qualitative and quantitative data and strategies a principle at least for this study. Lazarsfeld (1960, p. 15) mentions "three pairs of data": "natural sources" (statistics of library use) and data that were collected for research purposes (sheets of time use); "objective indicators" (e.g., health statistics) and subjective statements (interviews); and "statistics and empathic descriptions of single cases."

Why is this study instructive for the discussion about advocacy for vulnerable people based on research? The starting point for this study was the shock of a relatively new phenomenon (unemployment as a mass phenomenon after the first wave of industrialization). The scientific intent was to explore this phenomenon and how people individually and as a community (a village) deal with it. Maybe an even stronger force for commissioning this project was the wish to contribute to finding solutions for the problem and its victims. Jahoda (1995; see also Fleck, 2004, p. 59) describes how the impulse for the study came from the Austro-Marxist theoretician Otto Bauer, leader of the social democrat party in Austria. From this general impulse, Jahoda, Lazarsfeld, and Zeisel wanted to learn what the attitude of the population toward unemployment and what the social consequences of unemployment were like. However, the research did not provide immediate solutions or improvements for the participants.

Why is this study instructive for current discussions about triangulation and/or mixed methods? It is an example of how multiple methods contributed to providing a multifaceted understanding of a complex social problem and of the experiences of those who were exposed to it. The need for multiple methods resulted from the complexity of the phenomenon and from the fact that all people in the community were affected by it. Finally, the effects of the problem had to be analyzed on different levels. Here we find a research group facing a new problem with little earlier research or methods to apply for analyzing it. To understand the problem more comprehensively and from several angles, various approaches were used and methods were developed and related to each other. A variety of different forms of data was produced. Here it was not a principle—like triangulation or mixed methods—that was the starting point. Nor was it the intention to combine methods—or different types of methods, like in mixed methods research. Nevertheless, we find many characteristics of a good example of triangulation here.

## Current Concepts of Using Multiple Methods: Triangulation or Mixed Methods?

Despite the long tradition of using triangulation in social research, much recent attention has been focused on a specific form of combination. In the last twenty years, the combination of qualitative and quantitative methods using the keyword mixed methods (e.g., Tashakkori & Teddlie, 2010 [2003]) has attracted most of the attention. The concept of mixed methods has been developed distinct from approaches like triangulation and defines a rather limited space for the latter. Bryman (1992, pp. 59–61) identifies eleven ways of combining quantitative and qualitative research. Among these, the logic of triangulation (1) means for him to check for example qualitative against quantitative results. Qualitative research can support quantitative research (2), and vice versa (3), both are combined in or to provide a more general picture of the issue under study (4), etc. In a similar way, we find five justifications of such combinations in Greene et al. (1989). *Triangulation* is limited to looking for convergence of results. *Complementarity* refers to elaborating and enhancing results. *Development* intends to use results from one method to inform the other method (e.g., develop a survey after doing an interview study). *Initiation* focuses on the discovery of paradox and contradictions in the results coming from using two methods. *Expansion* extends the breadth and range of enquiry.

In such programmatic outlines of the field, triangulation is given a rather limited relevance. However, the discussion has developed a specific direction: We do not so much find issues of research or specific forms of data, which orient the general stream of discussion. Instead, methods have come to the foreground of the whole discourse about mixed approaches in research. This strong orientation on methods is also apparent in the basic structure of Tashakkori and Teddlie's handbook (2010). Here the central part (Part Two) is about methods issues—like design, control, analysis, and display—which is framed by two other parts. The first one is about background theories and history of mixed methods research, and the third one gives a survey of fields of application of mixed methods.

Not mentioned as a prominent issue for the discussion are specific issues of research that call for using mixed methods. This would help researchers decide when and why to use mixed methods approaches for their own issues of study—and when it would be better to refrain from this strategy. Also not mentioned are what *kinds* of data or combinations of data to use in mixed methods research. What does it mean for research to have specific diversity in different forms or sets of data? What are the implications of different forms of data for analyzing them? All this is more and more subordinated to the claim of a general strategy of mixed methods research, which is ready to replace other forms of research. This has also to do with the claim that mixed methods research is a third movement of research ready to replace earlier movements (quantitative being the first, and qualitative as the second; see Tashakkori & Teddlie, 2003). This is embedded in the far-reaching claims made for combinations of qualitative and quantitative research in general, which could raise the expectation that the strongly differentiated range of methods in both areas should be used and combined in mixed methods research.

## More than Just Methods: A Strong Program of Triangulation

If we want to address issues of advocacy and vulnerability, we need more than just a combination of several methods. We should start from a "strong program of triangulation" (Flick, 2011a) of research perspectives. This program seeks enhancing knowledge by using a number of research perspectives instead of looking for corresponding results coming from the second approach confirming those of the first one (as Bryman [1992] holds for triangulation). This strong program will also include the theoretical and methodological perspectives linked to various methods in the triangulation. Most important is that triangulation always has been more than just a combination of methods.

Denzin (1970) suggested several levels of triangulation. Besides methodological triangulation, which is differentiated in "within-method" (e.g., the use of different sub-scales within a questionnaire) and "between-method" triangulation, which will allow the triangulation of data, he suggested triangulation of several investigators and of various theories. Triangulation of various methods can be applied by combining qualitative methods—like interviews and participant observation—quantitative methods—like questionnaires and tests—or qualitative and quantitative methods. Within-methods triangulation can be realized in approaches like the episodic interview (see Flick, 2008), which combines question-and-answer parts with invitations to recount relevant situations. The forms of triangulation Denzin suggested can be integrated in a comprehensive way of doing triangulation: Investigators with differing backgrounds will bring various theoretical perspectives in the study, leading to using several methods that produce a variety of data (investigator triangulation→theoretical triangulation→methodological triangulation→data triangulation). This comprehensive triangulation will allow grasping the differences in the perspectives of vulnerable people and those who provide services for them or could do so. This will enable researchers to understand the complexity of research oriented on advocacy issues of vulnerable people.

## Triangulation in the Framework of Integrated Social Research

In what follows, the combination of qualitative and quantitative approaches will be in focus in the context of a concept of *integrated social research* (see Flick, 2011b, Chap. 10). This means that we first should ask: How developed is the knowledge about the issue of the study? Which empirical approaches make sense, are necessary, and should be combined for studying it? For planning such a study, the designs suggested by Miles and Huberman (1994, p. 41) give an orientation: Qualitative and quantitative methods can either be linked in parallel or one after the other in various sequences—depending on the research question and the point of departure. Data collection and analysis are based on methodological and data triangulation. This approach of using triangulation in the context of integrated research will be spelled out in a second example.

## Example 2: Sleeping Problems in Nursing Homes

This research[1] focuses on sleeping problems in nursing homes for the elderly and ways of dealing with this often underestimated problem. The main questions pursued here are: How relevant is the problem in an institutional setting? How aware of this problem are professionals working there? For answering them, we triangulated qualitative and quantitative approaches: In interviews with physicians ($n=20$) and nurses ($n=32$), we analyzed their awareness of the problem and how each group deals with it. The interviews focused on knowledge, understanding, and problem awareness of the interviewees concerning the sleeping problems of nursing home residents. To analyze the relevance of the problem, we took a second approach and reanalyzed assessment data of 10 percent of the nursing home residents in Berlin ($N=2,577$). These assessments included several variables about sleep, its quality and disturbances (non-restful sleep, insomnia, duration of sleep), and treatment variables (medication, physiotherapy, etc.).

These data revealed that almost two-thirds of the residents had sleep disorders (see also Flick, 2011a). More than 33 percent suffered from severe problems like insomnia (around 5 percent, some every night). Another 33 percent suffered from non-restful sleep, which means they are tired in the morning after a night of non-restful sleep. These data also show that around 5 percent of the residents were awake less than 33 percent of the day, so they spent more than 66 percent of the day dozing, sleeping, taking a nap, etc. Almost 20 percent of the residents were awake less than 66 percent of the day. These data show the relevance of the problem, often neglected in research and nursing practices (see Flick 2011a). They also show the impact of sleep problems on multi-morbidity (see Garms-Homolovà et al., 2010) and specific diseases. And they demonstrate that residents with sleeping problems participated in social activities much less than those without problems.

The physicians we interviewed either worked as employees in the nursing homes or came from their private facilities to treat the residents on a contract basis. Among other issues, we asked them about their practice of treating sleep problems with medications based on the fact that the causes of insomnia need to be clarified before medical treatment is prescribed. For the elderly, sleeping problems are often an epiphenomenon of a psychiatric or internist basic disease. If the cause is dementia, depression, or physical disease, that should be treated before undertaking therapy with sleeping pills. For symptomatic treatment of sleep disorders, hypnotics are available; these often have considerable side effects and danger of abuse and addiction (particularly in the case of benzodiazepines). Treatments of sleep disorders with hypnotics (like benzodiazepines) therefore should be limited to three to four weeks (DGSM, 2009) or given in intervals of two or three nights per week. Hypnotics also include the newly developed benzodiazepine-like Z-drugs with less severe side effects.

To understand how physicians regard this kind of therapy for sleep disorders of the elderly, we asked them questions like: "Which role do medications play for reducing residents' sleeping problems according to your experience?" "Could you please tell me a situation, how it happens that you prescribe a sleeping medication?" "Which advantages and disadvantages do sleeping pills have for your target group according to your experience?"

The interviews were analyzed by constructing comparative dimensions like the doctors' attitudes toward treating sleeping problems with drugs; relevance of hypnotics in the treatment routines; risk awareness, especially concerning medication addiction; and dealing with the risk of medication addiction. We found three patterns of interpretation and practices in the doctors' attitudes.

### Interpretive Patterns: Doctors' Attitudes toward Medical Treatment of Sleep Problems

The first pattern was called "by request." The characteristic for this attitude is that the residents' expectations are decisive for the doctor's decision to prescribe a sleep medication. The consumption of hypnotics is a tried and tested form of coping with sleeping problems. Residents are perceived to claim a right to receive sleeping pills as they have been prescribed over longer periods. To prescribe hypnotics helps maintain the self-perception of being a good doctor who helps the residents. The risk of a medication addiction in old age is not an issue or is accepted with resignation. Finally, medicine deprivation should not be expected by old people.

The second pattern ("ambivalence") is characterized by rejecting a permanent prescription of sleep medications for normative reasons. The relevance of hypnotics in the routine of caring is denied. While nonmedical interventions are often seen as ineffective, hypnotics are employed as a sheet anchor. The residents are finally responsible for abuse of and addictions to sleeping pills. These doctors' statements reveal rather indifferent ideas about the addiction potentials of sleep medications.

The third pattern ("reflected prescription") is characterized by differentiated ideas about the risks of addiction. Sleeping pills are only prescribed according to strict indications, not by residents' request. It seems possible to deprive residents of medications. The doctors see the need to fill a subjective emptiness experienced after medicine deprivation with appropriate nursing interventions. The integration of nurses, relatives, and residents in planning the treatments of sleeping problems is seen as improving the residents' compliance.

Table 1 summarizes the patterns in both groups of physicians. In this overview, we find a not very restrictive attitude toward prescribing hypnotics for treating sleep disorders: Almost half of our interviewees say they are ready to do so by request of their patients, and three-fourths of them tend to do so on request or if other interventions are not effective.

| Pattern | Professional group | | |
| --- | --- | --- | --- |
| | Employed physicians | Physicians in private practice | Total |
| | $N = 11$ | $N = 9$ | $N = 20$ |
| By request | 5 | 4 | 9 |
| Ambivalence | 4 | 2 | 6 |
| Reflected prescription | 2 | 3 | 5 |

Table 1: Patterns of Attitudes toward Medical Treatment of Sleeping Problems

## Representations Compared to Prescription Practice

That image of an ambivalent form of advocacy—doctors giving residents the pills they ask for despite side effects and risks of addiction—results if we see pattern one and two together. But does this reflect the actual practice? We did a secondary analysis of prescription data coming from a health insurance. These data directly refer to a part of the residents covered in the assessment data for a period of three years (2006–2008) and the nursing homes the interviewed doctors work for. For 2008, we found for example that less than 8 percent of the residents received hypnotics. We can assume that only 2 percent of the residents experience long-term consumption of benzodiazepines with a higher risk of addiction. A high consumption of more than 180 standardized daily doses of a Z-substance can be identified for 1 percent of the residents. This prescription prevalence contradicts the rather uncritical attitudes we found in interviews with the physicians about medical treatment of sleep disorders using medications with addictive potential.

In this example, quantitative approaches were integrated to complement the qualitative approach analyzing the professional practices of physicians in two ways: Analyzing the assessment data helped document the relevance of the problem in focus (how many residents have sleep problems, which health problems do they correspond to, what other features are linked to them?). Interviews permitted an analysis of professional practices as reflected by the participants. The final quantitative approach revealed discrepancies between the documented prescription practices and the perception of the interviewees.

The study revealed different ways of treating sleep disorders and how they were negotiated in concrete situations. With the focus of the politics of advocacy, we see a lack of knowledge and readiness to pursue treatments other than medication in cases where this would be possible, thus saving residents from risks of addiction and side effects of sleeping pills. To improve this situation, a follow-up study to the one presented here will try to determine effects of interventions for improving the sleep situation. For example, training the nursing staff will enable participants to activate residents during the day to give them the chance of sleeping better at night. The application of such activation by physiotherapists and occupational therapists will be studied to show the effects of this intervention on the sleep and health patterns of the residents. Thus, the results of the first study are a starting point for changing the routines in the nursing homes in favor of the participants.

## Triangulation in the Framework of Qualitative Research

Multiple qualitative methods have been shown to be useful over the years. However, this strategy is in danger of being pushed aside in the mixed methods rhetoric of overcoming qualitative and quantitative research discourse. In the context of vulnerability and advocacy, we should again sound out what triangulation means from a qualitative background. For example, we can focus on the professional side of dealing with the claims and needs of people in such situations.

## Example 3: Being Chronically Ill and Living on the Street

The third example addresses the life and treatment situation of homeless adolescent living on the street with a chronic disease.[2] Three methodological approaches were taken:

1. a longer period of participant observation focused on health-related actions and interactions among the adolescents;

2. episodic interviews (see Flick, 2008), with the adolescents focused on their health concepts and treatment experiences; and

3. expert interviews focused on social workers and physicians' perceptions of the adolescents and their estimations of the adolescents' treatment.

The interviews with the adolescents covered areas like their entrance into street life (how did that happen?), their health concepts and life situation, and factors such as housing, money, and eating. We also addressed how interviewees deal with health risks (like drugs, alcohol, sex) and problems. The male and female participants suffered from one or more chronic diseases like allergies, asthma, hepatitis C or obesity and were between fourteen and twenty-five years old.

### Patterns of Adolescents Coping with Their Diseases

In their interviews, adolescents mentioned various ways of coping with their diseases. These can be summarized in three patterns:

1. *Ignorance*. In this pattern, adolescents typically deny the severity of their diseases and potential consequences. They try to live as if nothing had happened and see their diseases as something to get used to. Negative consequences might

only happen in the distant future. Physicians are distrusted, as they lack insight in the adolescents' situation of living and do not take the adolescents seriously.

2. *Embittered.* The adolescents see serious consequences of their disease for their current everyday lives and further development. They feel marginalized by other members of the homeless peer group and fear being abused by the others because of their physical weakness resulting from their diseases. People perceived as friends deny support. Street life demands looking for shelters and money rather than taking care of their health and seeing a doctor. They only seek for medical help when the disease has become so dramatic it is unbearable.

3. *Facing the disease.* The adolescents seek information about their disease from friends and if possible in TV and the Internet. This makes the disease look less threatening and perhaps treatable. They try to talk to peers with the same disease about how to deal with it. Alcohol is not necessary for coping with the disease.

In our observations, we found another pattern that we labeled (4) *Fatalism.* This is marked by a lack of expectations concerning treatments and the further development of one's own life and the disease.

If we take a comparative perspective on the adolescents' patterns of coping with their diseases, we find a continuum of how adolescents believe they can actively steer their (coping) behavior and thus influence the development of their illness. At one end, we find those adolescents who ignore their disease and see themselves as victims of the street, with no other option than to endure their diseases. At the opposite end, we find adolescents who face their disease and show a high degree of self-responsibility for its development. Self-responsibility would also mean that it is the interviewees' "own fault" for developing the disease and they have "failed" to deal with it.

## Experts' Patterns of Representing the Adolescents and how They Manage their Diseases

To understand the relation of vulnerability and advocacy from a perspective of "social problems work" (see Flick, 2011a), we should complement the perspective of the adolescents with that of service providers they could or do address about health and social problems. In the interviews with the experts, we found three patterns of how they represent the adolescents and how the adolescents deal with their diseases:

1. *Ignorance.* The adolescents seem not to take their diseases seriously because of their lack of knowledge and wrong perceptions. The adolescents cannot allocate symptoms to diseases and avoid contact with medical experts as their own ignorance serves for a subjective relief.

2. *Disease as turning point.* Two social workers mention that for some adolescents the disease is a turning point to critically reflect their current way of living. In particular, hospital stays can increase the sensibility for health issues and lead to avoiding certain risks (like alcohol and drugs). Changing the way they live then leads to a partial withdrawal of adolescent from street life.

3. *Utilization.* Some physicians and social workers mention how adolescents seek help for their diseases. First they contact their peers who send them to the doctor or they give advice and practical help (e.g., putting on a bandage). This peer support is regarded with ambivalence by the experts, because the adolescent peers, who are acting as medical laypersons, are not skilled at exercising these (self-) treatments and might actually increase their peers' health problems.

The experts' interpretations are similar to the adolescents' views: According to the experts' experiences, the adolescents' behavior can be located along a range between "their own fault" to "victim of the street." The latter means that the adolescents have limited options as to appropriate illness behavior in their current situations. They rely on their social environment for help in case of disease-related stresses and strains. The experts mention a number of obstacles that prevent the adolescents from utilizing professional medical or social support. These obstacles result partly from administrative problems and partly from the service providers' attitudes toward the adolescents or from the adolescents' personal attitudes.

Beyond these similarities, we find differences between the professionals' and clients' perspectives. The professionals assume that the adolescents ignore their diseases. They see the adolescents' playing down of their illness as explicitly dysfunctional since it does not help with their illness problems in the short run. Rather, problems are aggravated in the long run and a further chronification of the disease has to be expected. In the light of such consequences, the experts see it as the adolescents' own fault when they deny their disease. However, such denial is often a short-term solution. In their current situation, the adolescents see no chance of mitigating or preventing certain symptoms. They resign and accept their "fate" and seem to be "victims of the street."

To experts, the adolescents' peer network is not helpful for their illness behavior. The network may bridge short-term gaps by providing a provisory shelter, where an adolescent may withdraw in case of acute symptoms. Peers may also provide provisional care for wounds. However, according to the physicians, the peers lack necessary knowledge. At the same time, such support often produces new dependencies. The individual will get thanks from their ill friend, and that increases loyalty to the peer network and its risky norms.

The adolescents are seen as refraining from consulting doctors because they are busy just surviving. This struggle can be so demanding that no resources remain for taking care of health issues. One's own chronic illness seems normal because of its persistence. This normality, then, means that there is no longer a need for action.

Different from the adolescents, most experts see the adolescents as being under a lot of pressure due to their life on the street and their chronic disease and in an urgent need of help. Like the adolescents, the experts see basic social coverage as a precondition for any readiness to become proactive for one's own health. In some cases, the intent to first secure the adolescents' survival and the basis for an autonomous way of living prevent social workers in our sample from feeling responsible for the adolescents' health problems. They see physicians as responsible for such problems or assume that the adolescents' social stabilization will automatically lead to their health improvement.

## Comparing Both Perspectives

The adolescents' and the experts' ideas of how to deal with chronic illness on the street differ slightly in some ways and differ completely in others. Major differences exist between seeing alcohol and drugs as problem solvers (as the adolescents do) and as problem intensifiers (as the experts do). Another difference refers to the need for help in relation to health. The adolescents see a rather limited need, whereas the professionals see very strong needs.

The three qualitative methods—episodic interview, participant observation, and expert interview—reveal three different perspectives about "living on the street with chronic illness" (see Flick & Röhnsch [2008] for details). The triangulation went beyond just combining multiple methods. The first approach focused on a more biographically oriented subjective perspective regarding the current situation and what has led to it. The second approach took an interactionist perspective for analyzing practices and discourses referring to the same issue. The third approach switched to an outside perspective and focused on expert estimations of the needs and problems of a hard to reach clientele. All three perspectives addressed different aspects of the field and issue and produced different sorts of data, which illuminated both from several angles.

Coming back to the politics of advocacy, this study intended to contribute to improving the situation of the participants by developing a number of suggestions for shaping the services of institutions and their collaboration (see Flick & Röhnsch, 2008). It was also the starting point for contributing to the report "Cooperation and Responsibility. Prerequisites for Target-Oriented Health Care" by the Advisory Council on the Assessment of Developments in the Health Care System (SVR, 2007) concerning primary prevention for vulnerable groups in particular homeless people.

## Methods, Issues, Data, or Knowledge Interests as Starting Points

Similar to the study of Jahoda et al. (1971 [1933]), the starting point of using multiple methods in our examples was a field and its complexity (specific forms of vulnerability: homelessness in adolescence or sleep disorders in institutionalized living). For studying this complexity, a number of qualitative or quantitative methods were selected. The decision to combine methods was driven by the aim of including subjective experiences of a specific group (adolescents with chronic diseases on the street) for understanding practices and interactions in their lives.

For the first perspective, interviewing the adolescents was necessary; for the second approach, an ethnographic/observing approach was used. A specific issue was in the focus—chronic illness—that leads to needed but sometimes postponed or rejected contact with the professional health system. Thus, it became necessary to study what happens at the interface of the life world and the professional system. This has led to taking expert interviews into account. In the second example, we combined quantitative analyses of the treatment practices (assessments and prescription) and compared them with the interviews of practitioners (e.g., physicians). In both cases, the tensional fields of vulnerability and advocacy required including more than one perspective in the research.

The examples may illustrate how particular methods were selected for the specific project—a question Greene (2008) has mentioned as open for mixed methods research. The linking of the methods happened around specific issues: What are representations of the other side in the potential or failing interaction between client/homeless adolescent and expert/health system in studying of utilization behavior and barriers? This may answer the second question Greene has raised for "around what the mixing in mixed methods happens." A methodology (that she misses for mixed methods research) of triangulation should be worked out around the point that data should be produced on different levels. In our example of studying adolescent homelessness, we realized this by integrating several perspectives on the issue—professional and clients' views—and data on several levels—representations and practices. This methodology should also include planning for the research and any combination of approaches that goes beyond combining methods per se and refers linking different theoretical perspectives and perhaps researchers with different backgrounds.

## Triangulation: Toward a More Systematic Use of Multiple Methods in the Context of Studying Vulnerability and Advocacy

This chapter referred to three settings of vulnerability:

1. A collective experience, which could not be influenced by the community confronted with it. Advocacy meant first understanding the complexity of the phenomenon in order to develop interventions for improving the situation.

2. An institution in which vulnerability (of residents in need of professional nursing) was about to be increased or reduced by the way the staff treated a specific problem (sleep disorders).

3. An individual situation and an open setting (homelessness) in which access to and response by professional service providers may contribute to increasing or reducing the vulnerability of adolescents.

Advocacy in the second setting refers to adapting routines to the needs of a target group without increasing their vulnerability (e.g., by producing addictions to sleeping pills). In the third setting, advocacy means contributing to establishing and improving structures of easily accessible services in an open field. Advocacy with qualitative inquiry can mean seeking to change a situation through research, making suggestions for changing routines, or making suggestions for changing structures of service provision, both based on the insights coming from the research.

Rather than seeking confirmation of findings, we should take approaches in our research on vulnerability that allow setting up mosaics of research issues. All this can be relevant for testing the limits of research methods and crossing their boundaries within qualitative research (as in the third example), but it can also be necessary and relevant for going beyond that area and for advancing to a more comprehensive approach of integrated research (as in the second example). Here, theoretical perspectives of vulnerability and marginalization can be addressed—as in both examples. We then can disentangle the various perspectives involved in the politics of advocacy when it comes to questions of how to improve the situation of vulnerable people.

## Notes

1. Funded by the German Ministry of Research—01ET0707. The research was done with V. Garms-Homolovà, G. Röhnsch, and J. Kuck (see also Flick et al., 2010, and Garms-Homolovà et al., 2010).

2. Funded by the German Research Council (DFG)-FL245/10-1-2. The research was done with G. Röhnsch (see also Flick & Röhnsch, 2007).

## References

Bryman, A. (1992). Quantitative and qualitative research: Further reflections on their integration. In J. Brannen (Ed.), *Mixing methods: Quantitative and qualitative research* (pp. 57–80). Aldershot, UK: Avebury.

Denzin, N. K. (1989 [1970]). *The research act* (3rd ed.). Englewood Cliffs, NJ: Prentice Hall.

DGSM (Deutsche Gesellschaft für Schlafforschung und Schlafmedizin) (Ed.). (2009). S3-Leitlinie—Nicht erholsamer Schlaf/Schlafstörungen. *Somnologie, 13*, (Supplement 1).

Fleck, C. (2004). Marie Jahoda. In U. Flick, E. v. Kardorff, & I. Steinke (Eds.), *A companion to qualitative research* (pp. 58–62). London: Sage.

Flick, U. (2008). *Managing quality in qualitative research*. London: Sage.

Flick, U. (2011a). Mixing methods, triangulation and integrated research— Challenges for qualitative research in a world of crisis. In N. K. Denzin & M. D. Giardina (Eds.), *Qualitative inquiry and global crisis* (pp. 132–152). Walnut Creek, CA: Left Coast Press, Inc.

Flick, U. (2011b). *Introducing research methodology—A beginners' guide to doing a research project*. London: Sage.

Flick, U., Garms-Homolová, V., & Röhnsch, G. (2010). "When they sleep, they sleep"—Daytime activities and sleep disorders in nursing homes. *Journal of Health Psychology, 15*, 755–764.

Flick, U. & Röhnsch, G. (2007). Idealization and neglect—Health concepts of homeless adolescents. *Journal of Health Psychology, 12*, 737–750.

Flick, U. & Röhnsch, G. (2008). *Gesundheit und Krankheit auf der Straße— Vorstellungen und Erfahrungsweisen obdachloser Jugendlicher.* Weinheim, Germany: Juventa.

Garms-Homolová, V. Flick, U,. & Röhnsch, G. (2010). Sleep disorders and activities in long term care facilities—A vicious cycle? *Journal of Health Psychology, 15,* 744–754.

Greene, J. C. (2008). Is mixed methods social inquiry a distinctive methodology? *Journal of Mixed Methods Research, 2,* 7–22.

Greene, J. C., Caracelli, V. J., & Graham, W. F. (1989). Toward a conceptual framework for mixed-method evaluation design. *Educational Evaluation and Policy Analysis, 11,* 3, 255–274.

Jahoda, M. (1995). Jahoda, M., Lazarsfeld, P. & Zeisel, H.: Die Arbeitslosen von Marienthal. In U. Flick, E. v. Kardorff, H. Keupp, L. v. Rosenstiel, & S. Wolff (Eds.), *Handbuch Qualitative Sozialforschung* (2nd ed.). (pp. 119–122). Munich: Psychologie Verlags Union.

Jahoda, M., Lazarsfeld, P. F., & Zeisel, H. (1971 [1933]). *Marienthal: The sociology of an unemployed community.* Chicago: Aldine-Atherton.

Lazarsfeld, P. F. (1960). Vorspruch zur deutschen Ausgabe. In M. Jahoda, P. F. Lazarsfeld, & Zeisel, H. (1971 [1933], Eds.), *Die Arbeitslosen von Marienthal* (pp. 11–23). Frankfurt: Suhrkamp.

Miles, M. B. & Huberman, A. M. (1994). *Qualitative data analysis: A sourcebook of new methods* (2nd ed.). Newbury Park, CA: Sage.

Morse, J. & Niehaus, L. (2009). *Mixed method design: Principles and procedures.* Walnut Creek, CA: Left Coast Press, Inc.

Ranci, C. (Ed.) (2010). *Social vulnerability in Europe: The new configuration of social risks.* Basingstoke, UK: Palgrave.

SVR. (2007). Advisory Council on the Assessment of Developments in the Health Care System. Cooperation and Responsibility. Prerequisites for Target-Oriented Health Care (http://www.svr-gesundheit.de/Gutachten/ Gutacht09/KF%20engl%20final.pdf9 (accessed November 8, 2011).

Tashakkori, A. & Teddlie, C. (Eds.). (2010 [2003]). *Handbook of mixed methods in social & behavioral research* (2nd ed.). Thousand Oaks, CA: Sage.

# Section III
# Politics

## Chapter 8

# Researching against Othering[1]

### Michal Krumer-Nevo

As both a social work practitioner and an academic, I find research that is motivated by the energy of social activism and the effort to change the world most appealing. Research with a social change agenda can take various forms, the most popular arguably being the documentation of the suffering and the resistance of marginalized groups. However, in this chapter I would like to invite you to think about the possibilities that qualitative inquiry opens for research with a social change agenda, by means of writing against Othering. In employing the phrase "writing against Othering," I follow Michelle Fine (1994), who used it as a subtitle for her article "Working the Hyphens," which has become a cornerstone of qualitative inquiry. Indeed, I am proud to follow her and to be influenced by her work. Fine (1994) claims that "Self and Other are knottily entangled. This relationship, as lived between researchers and informants, is typically obscured in social science texts, protecting privilege, securing distance, and laminating the contradictions" (p. 72). During the last three decades, the crisis of representation has engendered a massive corpus of writings by

*Qualitative Inquiry and the Politics of Advocacy,* edited by Norman K. Denzin and Michael D. Giardina, 185–264. © 2012 Left Coast Press, Inc. All rights reserved.

anthropologists, feminists, post-structuralists, and other qualitative researchers dealing with the relationships between researchers and informants (Clifford & Marcus, 1986; Denzin & Lincoln, 2008; Lather, 2007; Marcus & Fischer, 1999; Pillow, 2003; St. Pierre & Pillow, 2000).

In this chapter, I will examine closely some of the crossroads researchers face during various phases of the research process. The different paths actually taken at these junctions can mean the difference between battling Othering and enhancing it. I point to these decisional crossroads as political and to research in general as a political activity, which plays a role in the crowded market of representations.

## Othering

In psychoanalytic theory, the category of the *Other* is as primordial as consciousness itself. The self needs an Other to know its boundaries and to define itself. In this sense, the quintessential characteristic of the Other is its difference from the self and the very fact that the Other is distinct from or outside of the self. Anthropologists have used the concept of the Other in a similar manner.

However, "Othering," as I use the term here, is the result of a social process of differentiation and demarcation between social groups (not merely between individuals), groups that are subjected to differing standards and moral codes (Lister, 2004; Pickering, 2001; Schwalbe et al., 2000). This entails not only differentiating between me and other people who belong to the same social group, but the harsh and harmful distinction between the "We," who are perceived as subjects, who have emotions, rationality, capabilities, experiences, knowledge, and will, and the Others, who are perceived as objects lacking in complexity, motivation, rationality, and capabilities and who serve as the carriers of what is undesirable in ourselves or repressed and buried in our unconscious (Kristeva, 1991; Pickering, 2001). Through Othering, the Other is deprived of visibility, uniqueness, subjectivity, voice, and knowledge (Lister, 2004; Riggins, 1997). The quintessential characteristic of the Other is not merely its difference from the self but the assumed inferiority of the difference (Jensen, 2011). Othering thus is the translation of difference to inferiority (Pickering, 2001).

The oppressive power of Othering derives from the social distancing it creates and the impassable barrier it raises between us and them (Hall, 1997; Lister, 2004; Pickering, 2001; Schwalbe at al., 2000). No one volunteers to become an object. People are positioned and fixed as Others through power structures that enable certain rules of behavior, discourse, and performance to become signifiers of the "right," hegemonic self. Divergence from these rules is conceptualized as deficit or inferiority. Othering thus becomes a rationale and a justification for inequality. Schwalbe and his colleagues (2000) explain that identity rules that define the adaptive or dissident behavior of subordinates as signs of inferiority can become a powerful means of turning acts of resistance into evidence that the subordination is deserved and the inequality legitimate.

Qualitative research is deeply involved with the concept of the Other (Fine, 1994). The desire to know the Other, which lies at the heart of the desire to do research, carries in it a potential for both emancipation and oppression. In the case of emancipation, the encounter with the Other has the potential for empowerment, for experiences of trust, support, and understanding. The feminist interview, for example, was regarded through the 1980s as a version of research interview that resists the exploitation of the interviewee by the interviewer through utilizing attitudes of empathy, sensitivity, and respect (Oakley, 1981). On the other hand, the potential for oppression can realize itself when the desire to know becomes the desire to vanquish the informant, to make him or her the essential alien Other (Levinas, 1969).

The understanding that the representation of the Other is always the beginning of a process of reduction, since there is no representation that can fully catch the complexity of the other person, has aroused the awareness that the danger of Othering is an enduring aspect of research. Very often, Othering is the result of misunderstanding or paternalism on the part of the researcher. However, researchers can also enhance Othering while aiming to be objective, to describe truly the essence of the Other, or to write for Others (Fine, 1994). Recently I was asked by policy makers to describe the DNA of an ethnic group. This use of DNA as a metaphor to describe a whole social group is absurd and, in fact, a very good example of Othering. Any answer I would give claiming to provide the true or essential characteristics of the culture or behavior of the group would be falling into this trap.

My proposal to construe research as a potential weapon against Othering is based on two convictions: First, that researchers play a role in the textual constitution of vulnerable persons as Others (Smith, 1987, 2005), and, second, that qualitative inquiry may make a specific contribution to the advocacy of social change through its power to challenge social constructions and representations (Denzin & Lincoln, 2008). Researchers, I suggest, can and should make a conscious effort to combat Othering.

The dangers of Othering lie in the facts that its mechanisms are often hidden, embedded as it were in seemingly neutral or even positive discourse. The very difficulty of discerning its more subtle (but not less pernicious) performances makes the analysis of Othering essential to any critical assessment of social and cultural power mechanisms and dynamics (O'Barr, 1994).

Othering is often manifested in academic research and writing through four features: (1) *Objectification* of the research participants by the reduction and subjugation of their common humanity and their individual complexity and by ignoring their personal perspectives. This turns them into stereotypes composed of inferior, mostly negative features. (2) *De-contextualization*—a focus on behavior abstracted from the context in which this behavior was developed and continues to exist. De-contextualization can take various forms: detachment from a general context of policy and social economic structures (such as policies regarding health, housing, education, and the job market); detachment from a general context of symbolic structures, such as racism; or detachment from the immediate context of place and time in which the behavior occurs. De-contextualization contributes to the portrayal of certain behaviors as having no reason or rationality. Behaviors and occurrences become generalized features of the group rather than specific characteristics or specific responses to particular circumstances. (3) *De-historization*—the focus on the present, which is based on detachment from the personal individual history of the research participants. This distorts the researcher's understanding of the present situation. (4) *De-authorization*—the creation of text that is supposedly autonomous, objective, and authorless. Representation without an author means the use of an omniscient narrator and a perspective external to the subjects of study. This presents the subjects as given objects, not as products of an author's selective interpretation.

## Two Critical Moments

I have lately experienced the danger of Othering in a study I am carrying out on and with a community of immigrants who came to Israel from the Caucasus. The community originates in the Caucasus, a region in the southern former Soviet Union that embraces a diversity of ethnic groups and nations. The immigrants are termed in Hebrew "Kavkazi"—from the Hebrew word for Caucasus. While retaining their Jewish religious beliefs and Zionist aspirations, the Kavkazi Jews were also influenced by the region's dominant Muslim culture, traditions, and way of life (Altshuler, 1990; Yosephov, 1991, p. 169). The community's integration into Israeli society has been hampered by the fact that stereotypes, such as "primitive" and "violent" that were ascribed to Muslim culture in the Caucasus, were ascribed to these immigrants in Israel (Bram, 1999; Cohen & Magor, 1982). The roots of this perception lie in the Orientalist discourse adopted in the Soviet Union that distinguished between Ashkenazi Jews (originating in the European republics of the Soviet Union) and Mizrachi Jews who lived in the Asian republics, among them the Kavkazi (Bram, 2005; Shumsky, 2004). This distinction, along with the discrimination that accompanied it, was imported to Israel and dovetailed into the local social dichotomies that increased the stigmatization of the community (Bram, 2000; Shumsky, 2004).

The members of the Kavkazi community are unique in their keen awareness of the dangers of Othering. Though they do not use the word Othering, they openly talk about their stigmatization and object to it. When I first came to the community center looking for allies for my research, I met Hanoch, one of the community's leaders, who echoed the response of the colonized, indigenous people, described by Linda Tuhiwai Smith (1999), saying that he does not want any research carried out and doesn't see any good coming out of it. For him, research was a tool of cultural colonialism, and he refused to let me in. If you're interested in the Kavkazi community, you can come to the Kavkazi dance class, he said. I came and stayed for a year, once a week.

The class turned out to be very loaded with respect to Othering; I will focus on two "critical moments," as I term them. These are moments when the researcher must struggle to find a way of avoiding Othering—moments of struggle to find an interpretation that is rich, esthetic, and serving a social change agenda without violating or being disrespectful toward the people involved.

One critical moment involved the youths' attitudes to the dance class. These boys and girls, aged five to eighteen, who attended the class, emphasized and defended their ethnic identity and saw in the dance class a powerful celebration of pride in their heritage and community. Ofir (eighteen years old) said:

> Always when I saw Kavkazi people dancing, I wanted to dance like them, 'cause it's beautiful, 'cause it's fast, 'cause it's interesting. So I always looked for it, till a friend told me about the dance class. I thought to myself, I'll dance with them, it's a matter of your pride, when you know the dance of your [ethnic] group, and I started to dance in the class.

This attitude was interpreted by some teachers and social workers as a dangerous demonstration of ethnocentrism reflecting an unwillingness, or even resistance, to integrate into Israeli society. It was rather easy for me to see that this interpretation was based on and enhancing Othering, since through my talking and listening to the young people, I could provide an alternative interpretation. According to my interpretation, the dance class was a means of resisting the stigmatization to which the community was subjected in Israel, and their emphasis on their ethnicity was a way of treating their "identity wounds"—protecting their self-respect in a society that devalues it—and a way of gaining cultural recognition in Israel (Krumer-Nevo & Malka, 2012). This latter interpretation works against Othering because it breaks the Gordian knot between difference and inferiority.

A caution is in order here, though. Taking the side of vulnerable groups is easier when you focus on the pain and scars caused by injustice, inequality, and stigma and on the struggle of the people against their circumstances. However, this may mask other aspects of reality that are harder for the researcher to explain, to justify, or to identify with. This is what happened to me at the second critical moment, which was more difficult.

Part of the boys' struggle to augment their self-respect and the respect of their community via the dance involves the superior status that the dance gives them in comparison to the girls. The boys explain to me that the dance describes their ethnic group. It's the way you dance it. The girls are gentle so they dance gently, and the boys dance with power, vigorously. The dance shows beautifully the difference in our ethnic group, that the woman is inferior to the man. He gets more respect, and the woman less.

> In performances, when I come to the stage, I say to myself, thank God I'm not a Russian, or any other ethnic group, and I don't have to dance their dances. Because other dances are gentle, while the Kavkazi dance shows one's masculinity, you can see that we dance it with a hot blood.

The dance is an embodiment of the gender hierarchy. In my field notes I wrote:

> Only recently I realized that the girls and boys use the same movements in their dance, but they hold their bodies so differently that it took me a while to see it. The boys' back is straight, almost stiff, the movements of their hands are angular, fingers tensed, their eyes look directly ahead or follow the girls' movements. The girls lower their glance and never meet the boys' eyes, their hands movements are gentle, soft, and flowing. The boys stamp on the floor, the girls trip lightly on it.

When I read this and similar passages in my notes, I see the eyes of Hanoch, the community's chair, warning me not to join in stigmatizing the community. But can I look at patriarchy and not accuse the community of being patriarchal? How can I talk about the community's patriarchy and still avoid Othering?

Other researchers struggle with similar issues. In a talk she gave, Michelle Fine (2006) told how when writing her study of women prisoners at a maximum security prison in New York, she had difficulty "remembering" and taking into account the horrible crimes the women had committed. She was discussing the simi-larities between them and herself as women who are victims of all sorts of violence, when they insisted, "Yes, but there are also some differences between us, since some of us killed people." Michelle Fine read this as the women's insistence against avoid-ing Othering through romanticization or through "forgetting" or ignoring the difficult aspects of their reality and behavior.

## Resisting Othering by Partnership

Partnership with the people studied is no doubt the most pow-erful and systematic vehicle for struggling against Othering. A paradigmatic example of this approach is Participatory Action Research, PAR, in which persons with the relevant personal experience participate in choosing the research questions and research tools and in interpreting and presenting the findings (Chataway, 2001; Fine, 2007; Lykes & Coquillon, 2007; Reason & Bradbury, 2001). PAR is a research approach that acknowl-edges the knowledge, point of view, meanings, and theories that the people studied hold. The outside researcher joins the inside researchers in defining and determining the research goals, ques-tions, and procedures. Chatawy (2001) claims that more than anything, PAR is an attitude of commitment to a way of being with people, of responsiveness to their needs and concerns, and to the acceptance of one's own vulnerability that comes with full participation in multiple layers of social complexity. But how does this partnership works against Othering?

I will expand on this point by sharing with you a phone con-versation I had with a BSW (Bachelor of Social Work) student at the Hebrew University of Jerusalem by the name of Shai. He called me after reading a paper I had published describing a PAR with people in poverty. He found this approach very attractive and said he might want to go on and study it. Before committing himself, he wanted to know whether the research made any real change and, if so, what?

Before recounting the conversation, I will briefly summa-rize what the article was about (Krumer-Nevo & Barak, 2007). The article describes a PAR in which Adi Barak and I conducted discussion groups with people living in poverty all over Israel. We conducted thirteen groups with a total of seventy-eight participants. The focus of the groups was on the participants' experiences of, attitudes toward, and recommendations regarding the country's welfare, housing, and education systems. Although the groups enabled the participants to sound their voices, our emphasis was on their *knowledge*. As I use the terms here, "voice" refers to the emotional and subjective dimensions of the participants' lives and experiences, while "knowledge" includes these but, as the British poverty scholar Peter Beresford (2000) points out, also includes their perspectives, interpretations, meanings, hypotheses, analyses, and theories. The participants were thus treated as citizens with knowledge not only of their own personal experiences but also of *social institutions* and society itself.

The discussion groups were followed by a long process of writing and rewriting three position papers, one on each system, summarizing the knowledge of the group participants. We sent the position papers to the relevant ministries as well as to professionals, academics, and social activists, and invited them to a conference at the university. Each paper was presented by a group participant and then discussed by four people involved in the system in question: a representative of the relevant ministry, a professional, a social activist from a relevant NGO, and an academic.

"So what kind of change did the PAR make?" Shai asked. I said that it made some change in the lives of the three participants who presented the position papers. Preparing for the conference, they revised the papers so as to feel comfortable with their contents and language and to make them their own, without violating the perspectives and experiences of the other participants. Through this process, they gained insights into their own and others' experiences and perspectives and also became aware of the political dimensions and the public roots of private troubles (Mills, 1959). Presenting the papers thus became both an empowering experience and an experience that raised their political awareness of the roots of poverty and the social structures that maintain it. After the conference, all three presenters went on to become social activists.

Shai was disappointed. Personal change isn't enough, he said. He was interested in research that would affect the lives of more than just a few individuals.

The study did this, I told him. It opened opportunities for the participants who attended the conference to gain some social capital. This was the first time these individuals had the chance to meet with policy makers or social practitioners, who were ordinarily out of their reach, and to meet them as equals. They interacted during the coffee breaks with the director of the largest housing company in Israel and with high-ranking officials in the welfare and education services. Some of the participants used this opportunity to get through to these people and to obtain their assistance in handling problems they had with the relevant services.

This, too, was not enough for Shai. He wanted to make changes on a macro level, not only on a personal level.

I had to confess that the position papers did not directly lead to any macro-level changes. They were testimonies of injustice. They named and described in detail various kinds of injustice, from the social workers' attitudes toward people in poverty to the banks' lending policies. The papers received some media publicity and have been incorporated into some of the social work and law courses in Israel. Moreover, some of the recommendations in the papers were adopted. For example, I know of one public school in Israel that made structural changes in the way it treated immigrant pupils from Ethiopia.

I also admitted to Shai that, unfortunately, identifying injustice is only the first step in making macro-level changes. Fighting injustice is a very long haul. To effect changes, you have to lobby, petition, participate in parliamentary committees—and more. Legislation has to be passed and implemented. Our position papers were replete with accounts of injustices that required a macro-level change to correct. At that time, I identified and publicized them. To create macro-level change, researchers must work together with social activists and NGOs.

Shai replied that he never realized it was so complicated. I think that it's quite depressing, he said.

I said, yes, I know what you mean. So as not to feel too depressed or helpless, you have to find things that give you energy and hope. For some people, some of our students, taking part in demonstrations boosts their morale. For me, it's the relationships I develop with the study participants, which are based on resisting Othering. The very fact of their participation in the process, the opportunity it created for them to determine the agenda of an academic conference, the way that the academics, social practitioners, and policy makers responded to their position papers, their phrasing of the issues, the way they stuck to their own opinions—this is what keeps me going. By doing research this way, research has the potential to become part of the democracy and not part of the on-going exclusion of people with direct experience of social problems from the social realm of knowledge.

## Resisting Othering in Interpretation

Although in PAR interpretation is a joint endeavor of the outside and inside researchers, in most genres of qualitative research, interpretation is the sole responsibility of the researcher, and in general, interpretation is not guided by the aim of challenging Othering. I suggest that while interpreting, researchers take an Othering-aware approach, checking their interpretation in light of the existing normative meanings. Interpretation will be based on revealing the social and political infrastructures dimensions that shape various categories as if they were natural, immanent, and essential. This kind of interpretation will point to the ideological (i.e., gendered, racialized, or otherwise biased) base that underlies these definitions.

I remember an article I read whose aim was to make a qualitative analysis of the factors related to the successful transition of young people from residential care to independent living. One major preventing factor identified was the young people's inability to seek help. Based on interviews with the young people, the researcher differentiated between those who asked for help and those who did not, and interpreted it as an evidence of their ability or inability to seek help. Not surprisingly, she found that the ones who did ask for help had better achievements than the ones who did not. I see this interpretation as contributing to Othering because it essentializes the differences between the behavior of two groups of young people, attributing psychological differences to their failure or success.

Nevertheless, the citations given to illustrate this psychological inability suggest a rather different story, namely, a sociological narrative rather than a psychological one. The quotation "I don't ask for help so I don't get it. I don't see anybody that can help me financially, I did it all alone" was interpreted as indication of an inability to seek help. But this interpretation ignores the other possibility—that is, that she did not have "anybody that could help." Another quotation: "Nobody helps me, I help my mother and took a bank loan for this purpose" was also given as an example of the inability to seek help. The researcher did not refer to any differences between the young people who succeeded and the ones who did not succeed with respect to the actual resources they had access to, such as their or their families' material or symbolic capital. A more critical perspective will reveal this interpretation as misleading. It was a translation of a lack of actual support and poverty into psychological terms. The "finding" that the young people who did not manage well in their transition to independent life were characterized by an inability to seek help portrayed these people as Others, psychologically inferior.

A different interpretation, one that will resist Othering, would aim to understand their behavior in the actual context of their lives, the context of transition from the holistic care given by the residential care system to the jungle of life, poverty, stigma, and lack of support. This is also an example of the radical power of direct quotations of research participants in qualitative inquiry—they talk to us, the readers, behind the back of their interpreter, and sometimes they know and reveal more than the researcher knows or wants the readers to know.

## Resisting Othering through Writing

In terms of content, writing against Othering requires presenting the reality that is being written about in as much fullness and complexity as possible. It requires avoiding the oversimplifications of good versus bad and of facile explanations for behavior. It requires that the subjects be seen as both good and bad, weak and strong, and also as people who, at one and the same time, both internalize and struggle against hegemonic social constructions and the negative social stereotypes that are held of them. Writing against Othering also demands that people's behaviors be presented in the contexts of their previous experiences and of the social pressures and power relations, whether material or symbolic, that give rise to those behaviors, and are reflected in them.

There are quite a number of writing strategies that can be useful in resisting Othering, and I suggest only three of them here: narrative, dialogue, and reflexivity.

By *narrative*, I mean a text that has a plot—an event or series of events—and one or more characters situated in time and place (Chase, 2008). The narrative can be told by the protagonist or by the researcher. The focus on the actual facts of the persons' everyday lives enables contextualizing and reveals the protagonists' subjectivity, attitudes, opinions, and theories about their lives (i.e., what I earlier referred to as their knowledge), as well as their history and dreams. With such narratives, there is a chance that even if the persons being written about are different than the writer or the audience, they will not be tainted by Othering. As Laurel Richardson (1990) writes, narrative is a "contextualized story method" that "displays the goals and intentions of human actors; makes individuals, cultures, societies, and historical epochs comprehensible as wholes; humanizes time" (p. 20).

*Dialogue* begins with the conversation or interview. In these encounters, interviewees sometimes say things that surprise or shock us because they diverge from the hegemonic value system (Sands & Krumer-Nevo, 2006). Our instinctive response to such statements is often Othering. An example is the story that Sara, a single mother of three children living in poverty, told me in the framework of an interview. She was on the verge of being evicted from her apartment for non-payment of rent. Despite this threat, she told me that she had used the rent money she received from the welfare agency to buy the children a television and a video player. It is all too easy for researchers, who have never experienced poverty, to interpret such behavior as evidence of poor judgment and irresponsibility—that is, to "Other" her. To avoid such Othering, I suggest that the researcher discusses the matter with the interviewee, inviting her to interpret it and to bring to the forefront her knowledge. This kind of dialogue over "hard" questions is possible only when the interviewee can take these questions as an invitation for self- reflection, and only when she can believe that the interviewer wishes to understand her, not to judge her. When I asked Sara how she understands her decision to buy a TV and video, rather than to pay for her rent, Sara, who had experienced an extremely abusive and deprived childhood, offered a cogent explanation:

> I don't ever in my life want my kids to feel what I felt, *ever*. ... I'll do everything for my children. *Everything*. ... Look here, I could pay my rent four months in advance and have nothing to worry about. But no, I said, I'll buy them a TV, I'll buy her a video, so that they can ... enjoy themselves and not have to feel that they don't have these things.

Sara went on to analyze the social welfare policy, suggesting that the welfare services would never pay for a TV or video, but would still pay her rent even after she bought these things.

Through this dialogue, Sara was able to historicize her behavior—placing it against the background of a personal biography—and to contextualize it—placing her behavior in the context of her relationships with the welfare services. By showing the logic of her behavior, her explanation checked any tendency toward Othering that I, as the researcher, may have had at this critical moment.

Moreover, it is not enough that dialogue be pursued in the interview. It must also be represented in the writing, through extensive use of direct quotation. The use of quotations has the advantage of presenting the interviewee's voice and knowledge directly; furthermore, it enables the reader to audit—that is to confirm, question, or reject—the researcher's interpretations.

By *reflexivity*, I mean the researcher's ability and willingness to observe her or his own responses and to include them in her or his interpretation and writing not for the purpose of confession (Pillow, 2003), rather as a mode of political awareness (Callaway, 1992). The look inward can be directed toward one's self, one's history and position, and/or the writing itself, that is, the "unnoticed authorial and textual workings" (Macbeth, 2001, p. 42). It entails an analytic perspective focused on both cognitive processes and emotional and bodily ones.

Reflexivity became a crucial source of understanding in the case of Michelle, whom I interviewed in the presence of her two small children, the oldest being a four-year-old girl. Michelle talked with great openness about her physical and sexual abuse by her father and brother, her drug addiction, and work in the sex industry, the man who was her lover and pimp and was murdered in jail, her own confinement and rehabilitation in prison, and her subsequent pregnancy and marriage. When I left her home late at night, I wondered to myself what Michelle's story was really about: Deprivation and poverty? Deviation and psychopathology? Or perhaps motherhood as a vehicle for rehabilitation? But what revealed a most important but implicit and unspoken aspect of the interview was the sharp stomach ache that I had when I got home.

Reflecting on it, I understood the stomach ache as a projective identification, arising from the tremendous pain in Michelle's life and the life of her little girl, who listened to our conversation. Only after I felt this pain in my body could I properly analyze the many instances in which my interviewees had referred to pain, mostly to emotional pain, in their interviews and talks. It led me to thinking of what are called poor neighborhoods not as places of violence, deprivation, or neglect, but as "neighborhoods of pain." I was a witness to Michelle's pain. I felt it forcefully for a moment, for a few hours or a day, and, then, after the acute pain had passed, I was left with a sense of responsibility and the strong desire to write, to document, to draw conclusions, and, above all, to share what I learned with others and to imbue them with the same sense of responsibility that I myself felt and still feel.

Such reflexivity becomes "a deconstructive exercise for locating the intersections of author, other, text, and world, and for penetrating the representational exercise itself" (Macbeth, 2001, p. 35).

In including such reflexivity in their writing, researchers create what Tamy Spry calls a "provocative weave of story and theory" (Spry, 2001, p. 713 in Humphreys, 2005).

## A Summary: Back to the Critical Moments

I end this chapter by returning briefly to the Kavkazi community and the as yet unresolved critical moment that I experienced in the face of the boys' view of themselves as strong and worthy of respect and of the girls as weak, gentle, and less worthy of respect than themselves. What I see that I have to do to resist my tendency toward Othering in this instance is to work along the principles I have suggested—that is, to deepen my partnership with the youths, boys and girls both, as well as with the rest of the community; to engage the community in a dialogue that will enable them to historicize and contextualize their attitudes; to present their story with large chunks of narrative and ample quotations; and to deepen my own reflexivity so as to be able to sense and share their feelings and drives. Ultimately, these approaches or strategies will enable writing and interpreting against Othering, creating a disturbing text that will leave the reader sad, uneasy, and unsettled.

The approaches and strategies I suggested here have the power to enable the researcher and reader to experience difference and similarity at the same time and, with this, to gain a sense of solidarity with their subjects. According to the philosopher Richard Rorty (1989),

> Solidarity is not thought of as recognition of a core self, the human essence, in all human beings. Rather, it is thought of as the ability to see more and more traditional differences (of tribe, religion, race, customs, and the like) as unimportant in comparison with similarities with respect to pain and humiliation— the ability to think of people wildly different from ourselves as included in the range of "us." (p. 192)

Solidarity based solely on the principle of similarity denies the psychological and sociological distances between people; solidarity between totally different people is not possible. A sense of connectedness between people who are simultaneously similar and different is what we call solidarity.

## Note

1. This chapter is based on a keynote address given at the 7th International Congress of Qualitative Inquiry, University of Illinois at Urbana-Champaign, May 19, 2011.

## References

Altshuler, M. (1990). *The Jews of the eastern Caucasus*. Jerusalem: Ben-Zvi Institute and The Hebrew University of Jerusalem.

Beresford, P. 2000. Service users' knowledges and social work theory: Conflict or collaboration? *British Journal of Social Work, 30*, 4, 489–503.

Bram, C. (1999). *From the Caucasus to Israel: The immigration of Mountain Jews*. Jerusalem: JDC-Brookdale Institute.

Bram, C. (2000). The recognition of cultural identity as part of the dignity of man. In A. Hareven & C. Bram (Eds.), *The dignity or the subjection of man? The tension regarding the dignity of man in Israel* (pp. 58–75). Tel-Aviv: Hakibutz Hameuchad.

Bram, C. (2005). *Social categorization and visibility: Caucasus immigrants 1989–1996*. Jerusalem: The Hebrew University of Jerusalem.

Callaway, H. (1992). Ethnography and experience: gender implications in fieldwork and texts. In J. Okely & H. Callaway (Eds), *Anthropology and autobiography* (pp. 29–49). New York: Routledge.

Chase, S. E. (2008). Narrative inquiry: Multiple lenses, approaches, voices. In N. K. Denzin & Y. S. Lincoln (Eds.), *Collecting and interpreting qualitative materials* (pp. 57–94). Thousand Oaks, CA: Sage.

Chataway, C. J. 2001. Negotiating the observer-observed relationship: Participatory action research. In D. L. Tolman & M. Brydon-Miller (Eds.), *From subjects to subjectivities: A handbook of interpretative and participatory methods* (pp. 239–255). New York: New York University Press.

Clifford, J. & Marcus, G. E. (Eds.). (1986). *Writing culture: The poetics and the politics of anthropology*. Berkeley: University of California Press.

Cohen, A., & Magor, N. (1982). *Immigrants from the Caucasus in Israel: Absorption difficulties and recommendations for action*. Jerusalem: The Absorption Ministry.

Denzin N. K., & Lincoln, Y. S. (2008). Introduction: Critical methodologies and indigenous inquiry. In N. K. Denzin, Y. S. Lincoln, & L. T. Smith (Eds.), *Critical and indigenous methodologies* (pp. 1–20). Thousand Oaks, CA: Sage.

Fine, M. (1994). Working the hyphens: Reinventing self and Other in qualitative research. In N. K. Denzin & Y. S. Lincoln (Eds.), *Handbook of qualitative research* (pp. 70–82). Thousand Oaks, CA: Sage.

Fine, M. (2006). Critical reflections on epistemology and the production/performance of knowledge. Distinguished Visitors Program. Lecture conducted at The Israeli Center for Qualitative Research of People and Societies, Ben-Gurion University of the Negev, Beersheva, Israel, December 16.

Fine, M. (2007). An epilogue of sorts. In J. Cammarota & M. Fine (Eds.), *Revolutionizing education: Youth participatory action research in motion* (pp. 213–234). New York: Routledge Publishers.

Humphreys, M. (2005). Getting personal: Reflexivity and autoethnographic vignettes. *Qualitative Inquiry, 11*, 6, 840–860.

Jensen, S. Q. (2011). Othering, identity formation and agency. *Qualitative Studies, 2*, 2, 63–78.

Hall, S. (1997). The spectacle of the "Other." In S. Hall (Ed.), *Representations: Cultural representations and signifying practices* (pp.223–279). London: Sage.

Kristeva, J. (1991). *Strangers to ourselves.* New York: Columbia University Press.

Krumer-Nevo, M. (2009). From voice to knowledge: Feminism and participatory action research. *International Journal of Qualitative Studies in Education, 22*, 3, 279–296.

Krumer-Nevo, M. & Barak, A. (2007). Service users and personal social services in Israel: Are we ready to hear what clients want to tell us? *Journal of Social Service Research, 34*, 1, 27–42.

Krumer-Nevo, M., & Benjamin, O. (2010). Critical poverty knowledge: Contesting Othering and social distancing. *Current Sociology, 58*, 5, 693–714.

Krumer-Nevo, M. & Malka, M. (2012). Identity wounds: Multiple identities and intersectional theory in the context of multiculturalism. In R. Josselson & M. Harway (Eds.), *Navigating multiple identities: Race, gender, culture, nationality, and roles.* NewYork: Oxford University Press.

Lather, P. (2007). *Getting lost: feminist efforts toward a double (d) science.* Albany: State University of New York Press.

Levinas, E. (1969). *Totality and infinity: An essay on exteriority* (Lingis, A., Trans.). Pittsburgh: Duquesne University Press.

Lister, R. (2004). *Poverty.* London: Polity Press.

Lykes, M. B.& Coquillon, E. (2007). Participatory and action research and feminisms: Toward transformative praxis. In S. N. Hesse-Biber (Ed.), *Handbook of feminist research: Theory and praxis* (pp. 297–326). Thousand Oaks, CA: Sage.

Macbeth, D. (2001). On "reflexivity" in qualitative research: Two readings, and a third. *Qualitative Inquiry, 7*, 35–68.

Marcus, G. E. & Fischer, M. M. J. (1999). *Anthropology as cultural critique: Experimental moment in the human sciences* (2ⁿᵈ ed.). Chicago: University of Chicago Press.

O'Barr, W. (1994). *Culture and the ad: Exploring otherness in the world of advertising.* Boulder, CO: Westview.

Oakley, A. (1981). Interviewing women: A contradiction in terms. In H. Roberts (Ed.), *Doing feminist research* (pp. 30–61). London: Routledge & Kegan PaPickering, M. (2001) *Stereotyping: The politics of representation.* New York: Palgrave.

Pillow, W. S. (2003). Confession, catharsis, or cure? Rethinking the uses of reflexivity as methodological power in qualitative research. *Qualitative Studies in Education, 16,* 2, 175–196.

Polkinghorne, D. E. (1988). *Narrative knowing and the human sciences.* New York: State University of New York Press.

Reason, P. & Bradbury, H. (2001). Introduction. In P. Reason and H. Bradbury (Eds.), *Handbook of action research: Participative inquiry and practice* (pp. 1–14). London: Sage.

Richardson, L. (1990). *Writing strategies: Researching diverse audiences.* Newbury Park, CA: Sage.

Riggins, S. H. (1997). The rethoric of Othering. In: S. H. Riggins (Ed.). *The language and politics of exclusion: Others in discourse* (pp. 1–30). Thousand Oaks, CA: Sage.

Rorty, R. (1989). *Contingency, irony, and solidarity.* Cambridge: Cambridge University Press.

Sands, R. G. & Krumer-Nevo, M. (2006). Interview shocks and shockwaves. *Qualitative Inquiry, 12,* 5, 950–971.

Schwalbe, M. Godwin, S. Holden, D. Schrock, D. Thompson, S. & Wolkomir, M. (2000). Generic processes in the reproduction of inequality: An interactionist analysis. *Social Forces, 79,* 2, 419–453.

Shumsky, D. (2004). Post-Zionist orientalism? Orientalist discourse and Islamophobia among the Russian-speaking intelligentsia in Israel. *Social Identities, 10,* 83–99.

Smith, D. E. (1987). *The everyday world as problematic: A feminist sociology.* Toronto: University of Toronto.

Smith, D. E. (2005). *Institutional ethnography: A sociology for people.* Lanham, MD: Rowman and Littlefield.

Smith, L. T. (1999). *Decolonizing methodologies: Research and indigenous people.* London: Zed Books.

Spry, T. (2001). Performing autoethnography: An embodied methodological praxis. *Qualitative Inquiry, 7,* 6, 706–732.

St. Pierre, E. & Pillow, W. S. (2000). *Working the ruins: Feminist poststructural research and practice in education.* New York: Routledge.

Yosephov, M. (1991). *The Mountain Jews in Caucasus and in Israel.* Jerusalem: Printiv Printing.

Chapter 9

# Ecoaesthetics

## Critical Arts-Based Research and Environmental Advocacy

Susan Finley

What I call critical arts-based research is a lot like activist art (Finley, 2005, 2011a). It is performative and political and it engages in public criticism. It is resistant to neoconservative and neoliberal discourses that threaten social justice. It explores feelings and relationships through dialogue and increases visibility of diverse community participants. Its performance commands innovative uses of public spaces to address issues of sociopolitical and cultural significance. In critical arts-based research, engagement of community participants makes the personal political (Finley, 2007). Its performance is local, immediate, and particular to communities and constituencies that share a personal stake in the issues addressed.

Critical arts-based research can create the necessary momentum for a profound and revolutionary educational aesthetic that is transformative and productive in terms of ecojustice. This is an arts-based research that is committed to democratic, ethical, and just problem solving to arrive at creative solutions to local ecological problems. My purpose in this chapter is to explore the power

*Qualitative Inquiry and the Politics of Advocacy,* edited by Norman K. Denzin and Michael D. Giardina, 205–220. © 2012 Left Coast Press, Inc. All rights reserved.

of arts-based research as a voice of dissent at the core of a critical, ecoaesthetic pedagogy (Finley, 2011b).

Critical arts-based research holds promise for creating a powerful political voice within the context of a people's pedagogy. Of particular interest are the concepts of space and transformations of relationships between self-and-nature and self-and-others through community-based research efforts using arts. Green art is explored as a potential space for an educational aesthetic that is transformative and productive in terms of ecojustice. These performances of ecoaesthetics demonstrate the types of transformative teaching and learning that are based in social justice and ecological responsibility. The pedagogy and performance of a radical, ethical aesthetic is potentially transformative to education, ecology, and community. It can be the catalyst for deep and meaningful social change.

I believe that with art we can discover a viable antidote to neocapitalistic political influences that impose on social and environmental justice. My hope is that the description of the programmatic implementation of an "ecoaesthetic pedagogy" that follows will fulfill the promise of something seemingly utopian that has actually been put into useful practice.

## Globalization of Greed

"Ecological destruction is a profitable business," writes Greg Palast (2003, p. viii). Deforestation presents an ecological issue that highlights the globalization of greed and opens points of discussion for what is needed in the way of an ecoaesthetics that features critical pedagogy and arts-based research.

Consider the following:

U.S. and European companies long ago perfected the practice of clear cutting and invested in destruction of forests across the world. Current economic globalization complicates the narrative—foreign investment in U.S. timberland, for example, is steadily increasing, and to 2009, forests account for 59 percent of foreign-held U.S. acreage (The Timberland Blog, 2011). During economically bad times in the United States, state and federal funds have been used to support investments of Chinese mill-owners who have taken over U.S. pulp production. The argument for these investments is staked on job creation and sustainment in forestland states such as Maine and Oregon.

In an earlier example of what is now happening in the United States, the U.S. Potlatch Corporation was profoundly implicated in the deforestation of Samoa (Shankman, 1999), where the corporation enticed the government to provide financial incentives and other supports for timber cutting. On realizing less profit than expected, Potlatch pulled out of Samoa, leaving the government in considerable debt. According to Shankman's (1999) historical account, however, even more than corporate, international deforestation, the grand ecological story of Samoa is deforestation for the expansion of agriculture. "Economic, technological, and organizational changes at the village level" are responsible for the eventual demise of the Samoan system of small, geographically dispersed villages, surrounded by forests (p. 169). Historically, smaller tracts of agricultural lands were cultivated around each village and were communally held by kin groups. The forests themselves were foraged for timber, wild plants, and hunting of wild animals. Traditionally, wrote Shankman: "Samoans spoke proudly of their particular forest holdings as having the best forest, the tallest trees, the most beautiful stands, or the best wood for house construction" (p. 169).

As told by Shankman, the traditional Samoan belief that certain tree stands were sacred and could not be cut was successfully debunked by European missionaries who demonstrated by cutting the trees without enduring any supernatural repercussions. Subsequent deforestation for cotton, coconut, and taro plantations usurped the promise of preserving the forests for utilitarian purposes. Through the combined forces of colonization and bad weather, Samoa entered a decades-long period of economic decline, during which Samoans experienced the shift of land from communal resource to commercial commodity. By the mid-20th century, "many Samoans no longer lived immediately adjacent to the forest, and increasingly urban and peri-urban populations were less knowledgeable about particular species … gathering of wild plants and hunting of forest species were less common" (Shankman, 1999, p. 176; and see Cameron, 1962). In this context, land tenure practices shifted from the communal kinship model to individualized land title holdings. "Land formerly held in common by a village now has become the property of families and individuals. The tragedy of the commons is occurring as the forest is privatized in piecemeal fashion" (Shankman, 1999, p. 180). Shankman rests his case for the exploitation of Samoa at the hands of its indigenous people on a troubling argument offered by Garret Hardin (1968), to wit, that when left unregulated, a shared resource will be depleted for immediate gratification of needs by users even when it is not beneficial in the long term to do so. Speaking about Hardin's argument, Ian Angus (2008) objects that it "has been used time and again to justify stealing indigenous people's lands, privatizing health care and other social services, giving corporations 'tradable permits' to pollute the air and water, and much more" (para. 3). The true tragedy of the commons in Samoa has been the story of indigenous people, the dissolution of their communal way of life, and their subjugation to Western economic ideology.

## The True Tragedy of the Commons

To be isolated from natural habitats also separates people from other people. Economic progress as it has been exercised in colonial, capitalistic systems creates divisions of self-from-Other and self-from-the natural world and the senses that perceive it. This growth-and-greed way of constructing the world fosters other perceived dichotomies that are similarly destructive. Among these, nature-versus-culture, ecology-versus-jobs, and art-versus-science dichotomies lead to us-against-them power struggles that determine who controls knowledge production, who dictates land usage, and, ultimately, who constructs patterns of world dominance that play out in wars and struggles between humanity and all else in nature. The practice of this type of ideology, Grande concludes, "promotes 'ego systems of expression' that nurture an exploitative view of culture and history" (2004, p. xvi).

Thomas Berry, speaking in an interview with Derrick Jensen (Jensen & Berry, 2008) sees two dimensions to the transformation of our current, out-of-control social order and movement toward environmental sustainability. The first is to eliminate the artificial dichotomy between "the human community" and the "rest of the world" (p. 41). "There is only one community" says Berry, "and it lives and dies as a unit" (p. 41). Second, says Berry, "It seems clear the mission of our times is to reinvent what it means to be human" (p. 41). Perhaps those dimensions are merely different sides of the same coin. If we can reestablish "the commons" we will, in fact, have transformed Western civilization.

With the legacy of neoconservatism establishing ubiquitous capitalistic growth, humanity's ability to experience and act on empathy is seriously diminished. Until we are one with each other as people and at peace with the world, we cannot attain the levels of respect that are necessary for systemic, ethical ecojustice in support of communities of difference. Without melodrama, it needs to be said that the future of the planet rests on the ability of a place-based pedagogy that can replace world-dominance through capitalism with a new worldview. To reach these heights requires a futuristic pedagogy that is purposeful in preparing a new generation of international, pluralistic leaders who are equipped to take on the kind of tenacious struggle against power elites that will be necessary if we are to enact ethical and just environmentalism.

## The Tragedy of Hegemony

Attitudes about nature and environment in the 21st century reflect the dominant ways of thinking brought about by Christian doctrine and Western Enlightenment. Susan Buckingham (2008, p. 13) delineates four themes about the environment that have evolved from the intertextual merger of Christianity and Enlightenment traditions: (1) dualism, which divides humans from the rest of the natural world; (2) hierarchy, which places humans above the rest of the natural world; (3) utility, which relegates the natural world to be valued only as resources for human progress; and (4) stewardship, which calls on humans to utilize their superior intelligence to care for the natural world and future generations of humanity. Within this context, similar themes have emerged to define human relationships. In a world dominated by capitalism, we are deeply ensconced in a project of human dominance over nature, as well as dominance by humans over people who are seen as Other and who function within a similar pattern of social dualism, hierarchy, utility when nations and individuals are exploited as commodities, and a call to postcolonial stewardship by which wealthy nations search for technological approaches to solving ecological problems. Examples exist as ecocolonialsim, ecotourism, green-design, and similar innovations that impose solutions to environmental problems while preserving the economics of dominance and oppression.

In educational arenas, science has held a monopoly on claims of objective truth. Stanley Aronowitz, among others, argues against the perception of science as a superior way of knowing. Science, Aronowitz claims, is "an ideology, and one that is based on domination of the living world" (Aronowitz, 2011, p. 35). Says Aronowitz, "The scientific community wants us to have faith in them that they will do whatever is right for us. But I don't believe them. I don't have faith in anybody, except people collectively deciding what they want to do with their own lives" (p. 35). In fact, one of the constraints placed on environmentalists seeking to educate the population is the co-option of language to depict the ecological and social crisis we (all of humanity and all else) embody. Neocapitalistic, neocolonial dogma now works to induce an overwhelming malaise that counters desperate calls for public responses to the overwhelming ecological crisis that defines our current existence globally. This is a deliberate effort at deceit and a manipulation of people's faith in the objectivity of science—science is truth.

Let's consider, for example, a smoke-and-mirrors story about language, ecology, and education. In this example, teachers who were included in a project to critically assess commercially produced educational programs about ecology and sustainability showed unbridled enthusiasm for Project Learning Tree curricular units. Project Learning Tree's neatly packaged *Energy and Society* module, for example, includes activity guides for teachers, and its bright, busy, cheery classroom posters reinforce learning concepts. A music compact disc with an energetic beat prepares students for a more kinesthetic learning experience through the *Energy and Me Music and Dance* video. The *Energy and Society* module is available at zero cost to any teacher who wants to use it, and several additional items are available as electronic documents that can be downloaded from the Project Learning Tree website or are available by mail order.

The kit purports to teach children personally responsible energy use and encourages them to think about energy production in the context of their own communities. The collaged poster, for instance, briefly explains cloud types and cites statistics on the likelihood of being struck by lightning—"The National Safety Council reports that an average of 100 Americans are killed by lightning each year," it says, and asks: "What precautions should you take in a thunderstorm?" Materials in the kit include information about the energy generated by a person rollerblading. A description of the energy it takes for an adult giraffe to push food through its four stomachs makes for fascinating reading.

This arts-infused, multidimensional curricular bundle about energy is published by Project Learning Tree, which is a program of the American Forest Foundation, which, in turn, is a nonprofit partner of the U.S. Forest Service. The American Forest Foundation was created by Congress in 1992 and is sustained in part by federal funding and in larger part by donor funds. The purpose of the foundation is to support the National Forest Service's mission to "maintain the nation's forests for future generations," which the foundation does, primarily, by soliciting donor funds from the private sector to be used for educational purposes.

Drawn in by arts-based learning, enjoyable activities, and items to generate personal connections among children and curriculum, the students are prepared for a deeper message. Of equal interest to the depiction of giraffe digestion, but far more disturbing, are the platitudes embedded in the curriculum that soft-peddle the environmental impact of large-scale energy production. For instance, the poster states: "New exploration and production technologies have increased producers' abilities to locate and recover crude oil, and new technologies such as horizontal drilling enable oil producers to drill using fewer wells." Nothing is written about crude being a nonrenewable resource—and no mention is made of the more extensive damage that can be done to reservoir productivity because of the greater exposure to borehole fluids contingent in horizontal drilling.

Similarly, the curriculum states that "water treatment and conservation can help minimize the environmental effects of coal production and consumption," and "safely storing radioactive waste requires that it should be placed in secure container systems." Students are assured that "the government is trying to find an acceptable site" for permanent disposal of those nuclear waste containers. If solar energy seems to be a viable option, learners take heed, "solar energy can be a very expensive way to produce energy in large quantities" and "solar plants require a large amount of open land," a contingency not mentioned with regard to wind turbines or other land-dominating energy sources.

*Energy and Me*, published by Project Learning Tree, with its structure of combined government and private funding, touts a neoliberal, neocapitalistic dogma that ultimately works against any legitimate effort to educate American children to awareness of the ecological peril associated with energy production by corporate powers. Nor does it encourage students to develop critical and creative skills for problem solving in response to ecological crisis, to recognize the importance of their own ingenuity and power of imagination in a search for new ways of understanding their world, or to act from a place of shared responsibility for preserving the world's ecological structures. The curriculum does not inspire the type of social and political leadership that is needed in future generations if we are to reverse the mind-set that rewards human exploitation of all things in nature. Instead, it selectively informs, peddles half-truths as facts, and, at its best, entertains children who, having experienced the unit, now think they know something about environmental science and ecological sustainability.

Follow Project Learning Tree to its roots—or follow the money, and the corporatization and co-option of U.S. education about environmental crises is even clearer. The contributors list on the parent organization's website is enlightening. Included among the various governmental agencies and representative cooperative extension services are a host of invested corporations and foundations that include major corporate donors such as the American Forest & Paper Association, the Potlatch Corporation, and the Weyerhaeuser Company Foundation.

The American Forest & Paper Association, for example, boasts a board of directors comprised of powerful corporation CEOs, chairmen, and presidents of major corporations invested in paper, cardboard, and wood production. No ecological activists, academic environmentalists, or governmental agency representatives are listed as members of the board. Further, the website of American Forest & Paper directs users to policy statements, including as an example, the organization's take on the Environmental Protection Agency's (EPA) proposed rules for industrial emission limits for institutional boilers using fossil fuels. The policy brief takes issue with EPA efforts to limit fossil fuel emissions, declaring them to be "unreasonably burdensome."

Next, American Forest & Paper threatens an already precarious economy with further job loss if the new, stricter emission standards are passed into law, thereby furthering a false dichotomy that pits prospects for work against environmentalism in much the same way as the preservation of spotted owls was made to seem to threaten jobs among lumber workers in the Pacific Northwest region of the United States. The policy brief continues: "Given the jobless nature of the economic recovery, this rulemaking will add excessive burdens at the expense of manufacturing workers. ... For the paper sector only, the additional costs will put over 70,000 jobs at risk in our mills and communities" (2010).

Meanwhile, the Potlatch Corporation—the same Potlatch Corporation that compromised the economy of Samoa—is another organization represented as a major contributor to the U.S. National Forest Foundation. Potlatch, in turn, has its genesis in the Weyerhouser corporate empire, which has created still another nonprofit foundation that is also a major contributor to the U.S. National Forest Foundation. Weyerhouser invented clear cutting. Potlatch, meanwhile, was described by environmentalist Winona LaDuke (1999) as one of the largest clear-cutting operations in existence. She continued to illustrate the complicated interrelationship of U.S. ecology policy, economics, and big money influence. "Federally managed lands are equally problematic," she states:

> President Bill Clinton, early on in his administration, talked about providing economic opportunity for Indian tribes, by

"bringing backlogged Indian timber to market," something Native forest activists have referred to as "equal opportunity clearcutting." Federal officials prioritized logging and cultivation of aspen in the Tamarac National Wildlife Refuge, which spans some 21,000 acres of the reservation. Between 1982 and 1992, 97,970 cords of wood were taken from refuge lands, 83 percent of it "popple" or aspen. The vast majority of the harvest was designated for Potlatch and other paper mills in the region. (p. 128)

These are examples of what Richard Kahn (2010) has described as "life at the edge of the abyss: The dance of global capital and ecological catastrophe" (p. x). Kahn entertains doubts that education can counter the impact of today's globalization, in part because of the co-option of education by establishment powers as well as by environmental education's current technocratic approach to pedagogy.

In part, my own frustration with Project Learning Tree curriculum, in addition to its blatant manipulation of facts, is the use of arts in teaching in a program that has been adapted to capitalistic purposes. Indeed, educators have long recognized the value of teaching people the skills related to arts activities, both because the arts are themselves distinct ways of knowing and being in the world and because of the widely acknowledged realization that arts-infused curriculum has unique potential for engaging students in learning. Yet, in our schools, we face severe financial restrictions that, in effect, prohibit skills education in the arts and we are forced into standards-based instruction that allows no time for learning critical and creative thinking skills.

In his argument that environmental education has been co-opted through corporate domination, Kahn further points out that environmental education is largely ignored in teacher education, such that classroom teachers are not prepared to bring a strong ecopedagogy into teaching and learning settings. As with arts instruction, what little environmental science is taught is done in canned, standardized curricula that encourage social reproduction of a fixed set of values. Although environmental education has more recently been accepted into the academy as a distinct discipline, among K-12 teachers Kahn cites a "deep fracture" between educators who favor "wise use" and conservation education and those educators and their collaborators who seek a radical, ethical ecopedagogy. In liberationist terms, Kahn explains the need to free schools entirely from the conservationist mode and from that position to forge on to academic innovation with regard to ecopedagogy. While presumably agreeing with Kahn on most points, Berry (2010) offers encouragement to find solutions from within the system. He writes:

> Anything Westerners do will be driven by this millennial vision. The belief that someday there will be a communist workers state, and then we can have peace, justice, and abundance. Someday, the riches of the capitalist system will trickle down to bring peace, justice, and abundance to those made poor by this same system. Someday, modern science and technology will create some sort of heaven on earth. Someday, someday, someday. ... When I say the problem is within the Western world, the solution must be there also. You find the solution where the problem is. You can't avoid it. (p. 53)

Perhaps Kahn and Berry would each agree that the primary solution to environmental crisis is to transform what it means to be human, to reinvent relationships between self-and-nature and self-and-others. That is, to address the "tragedy of the commons" calls for the elimination of the dichotomy between humans and nature, and the remedy for the tragedy of hegemony is to redefine what it means to be human by diversifying ways of living beyond capitalistic definitions of being.

## Ecoaesthetics: Critical Arts-Based Research and Social Transformations

I believe we can discover artful and aesthetically grounded solutions to the problems of apathy and ignorance about the environment, while countering dis-education and capitalistic domination, by engaging in critical, arts-based research. Critical arts-based research can open spaces for a profound and revolutionary educational aesthetic that is transformative and productive in terms of ecojustice. Of course, there is no panacea, but a critical approach to social issues through arts can move the projects of environmental awareness and activism forward. These goals call for an arts-based research that is committed to democratic, ethical, and just problem solving to arrive at creative solutions to local ecological problems. Critical arts-based research holds promise for creating a powerful political voice within the context of a people's pedagogy. Of particular interest are the concepts of space and transformations of relationships between self-and-nature and self-and-others through community-based research efforts using arts. The pedagogy and performance of a radical, ethical aesthetic is potentially transformative to education, ecology, and community. It can be the catalyst for deep and meaningful social change. To do so, critical arts-based research should be characterized by:

- performances of useful, local, community service;
- enactments of cultural pluralism through devises such as cacophony, bricolage, collage, and other means for creating open spaces for broad participation;
- demonstrations of passion and joy for humanity in communion with nature;
- resistance to neoconservative research discourses, as well as other hegemonic discourses that establish dualities of self-and-other and self-and-nature;
- embodiment of its pedagogical purposes such as encouraging responsible citizenship in support of social justice, ecojustice, and ecological responsibility; and
- move its participants/readers/viewers to engage in some kind of positive social action. (adapted from Finley, 2011a, p. 447)

Researchers might take various roles in these projects. For instance, they might seek out literal, physical spaces in which people can be brought together to establish dialogue; they might serve as a "transformational intellectual" who identifies hegemonic language and structures that enforce "cultural codes" (Berlin, 2003, p. 121). In all instances, the researcher should keep community participation at the forefront of any project, so as not to slide into a colonialist role of imposing paradigms of knowledge on indigenous peoples or other community residents. With reference to Samoa, Shankman (1999, p. 181) similarly warns against ecological projects that might commercialize the land. His concern is primarily with the potential for local residents to demand cash for their sacrifice of agricultural land for conservation purposes, whereas my concern is more with the potential commodification of conservation sites through the rising interest in ecotourism.

## In Response to the Colonization of the Commons and Corporate Hegemony

How can arts-based research play a role in a utopian effort to form just one community comprised of all of humanity and the natural world? "We must be taught how to be human, through our parents, through our community, through rituals, through interactions with the natural world" says Berry (2010, p. 41). "Because language derives from experience, and ultimately from the natural world, we're in a situation that is hard to present in any kind of known language. All this means is it can be hard to imagine the type of transformation that is necessary" (p. 42). "Postmodern democracy cannot succeed," Denzin (2008) argues, "unless critical qualitative scholars are able to adopt methodologies that transcend the limitations and constraints of a lingering, politically and racially conservative postpositivism" (p. x). Like Denzin, I am endorsing a research approach that expounds a certain ethical perspective that includes social responsibility, caring for others, and respect for arts, nature, and local intellect; that is critical of capitalistic and enlightenment hegemony; and that is reflective even as it is framed in futuristic planning and mapping of humans' relationships with nature.

Gathering information and making meaning in community is one performance of a useful, local, community service. When arts-based researchers open spaces for dialogue and discussion, those spaces are constructed homes for enactments of cultural pluralism and embodiments of responsible citizenship. The processes of making art can draw people into new relationships with themselves, with others who share the experience of art, and with the environment in which art performance (process not product) occurs. Art making can be the source of new relationships with nature. Arts communicate by heightened senses and emotions. Arts-based research can bring together people in communities to explore differences and relationships; it can provide a space within which people can examine and refine the ethics of their shared existence; and it can demonstrate the joy of everyday life.

To renew the commons, arts-based research must take place within a local community and be engaged with the particular ecology of a place. It "does not look at art as a product to be evaluated, but instead as a process intrinsic to the human perspective, and ultimately one that belongs in all aspects of our lives" (Graddy, 2010, Note 1). To eschew the conventions of enlightenment attitudes toward art and community, it will serve us well to recognize, as Graddy does, that "the majority of preindustrial societies do not generally have an independent concept of (or word for) art—even though people in these societies do engage in making and enjoying one or more of the arts and do have words that refer to carving, decorating, being playful, singing, imitating" (Introduction, para. 7–8). Art, Graddy continues, is simply part of most people's lives all over the world, and only in post-industrial society have we separated it into a specialization, a unique occupation, removed from the rest of society. As I have written elsewhere (Finley, 2011b), "through language and imagery that are reflective of the vernacular and everyday ... it is a sensous, embodied pedagogy in which emphasis on sensory experience is encouraged as a way of relating self to local environments" (p. 309). "Art that is incapable of being collected, like the work of ecological artists now blossoming throughout the world, has virtually no value in a capitalist economy," says Daniel Dancer (2001, para. 4). Dancer continues:

> Generally, unless we can process and profit from it, we give such things no real value. So it is with ecological art. Despite our cultural bias toward museum and gallery based art our forms of art that reach back to a time when art was part of everyday life (when everyone was an artist) will continue to thrive. Why? Because such work speaks to the core of who we are as authentic human beings, unplugged from the corporate juggernaut, connected to nature, truly alive. ... It calls us out of our comfortable denial. (para. 6)

To know oneself to be "truly alive" as Dancer says it, recalls a similar statement from environmental artist Andy Goldsworthy in the film *Rivers and Tides* (2001) where he exclaims at his amazement that he, too, is deeply aware that he is *alive*. I think that is the purpose of arts-based research. It reminds us that we are alive.

## References

Angus, I. (2008). The myth of the tragedy of the commons. *MASSLine.* http://www.massline.org/PolitEcon/Misc/MythTragCommons.htm (accessed February 4, 2012).

Aronowitz, S. (2011). Interview conducted at his office in New York, September 10, 1999. In D. Jensen (Ed.), *Truths among us: Conversations on building a new culture* (pp. 35–57). Oakland, CA: PM Press.

Berlin, J. (2003). *Rhetorics, poetics, and cultures: Refiguring college English studies.* Anderson, SC: Parlor Press.

Berry, T. (2010). Thomas Berry: Interview conducted at a hotel in Greensboro, North Carolina, 11.16.00-11.17.00. In D. Jenson (Ed.), *How shall I live my life?: On liberating the earth from civilization* (pp. 37–58). Oakland, CA: PM Press.

Buckingham, S. (2008). Approaching environmental issues In S. Buckingham & M. Turner (Eds.), *Understanding environmental issues* (pp. 11–32). Thousand Oaks, CA: Sage.

Cameron, S. S. (1962). Vegetation and forest resources. In J. W. Fox & K. B. Cumberland (Eds.), *Western Samoa: Land, life, and agriculture in tropical Polynesia* (pp. 63–77). Christchurch, New Zealand: Whitcombe and Tombs.

Dancer, D. (2001). Art in a dangerous time. http://greenmuseum.org/generic_content.php?ct_id=84 (accessed February 3, 2012).

Denzin, N. K. (2008). *Searching for Yellowstone: Race, gender, family, and memory in the postmodern West.* Walnut Creek, CA: Left Coast Press, Inc.

Finley, S. (2005). Arts-based inquiry: Performing revolutionary pedagogy. In N. K. Denzin & Y. S. Lincoln (Eds.), *Handbook of qualitative research*, 3rd ed. (pp. 681–694). Thousand Oaks, CA: Sage.

Finley, S. (2007). Arts-based Inquiry: A community approach to political action. In A. Cole and J. G. Knowles (Eds.), *International handbook of the arts in qualitative research: Perspectives, methodologies, examples, and issues* (pp 71–81). Thousand Oaks, CA: Sage.

Finley, S. (2011a). Critical arts-based inquiry: The pedagogy and performance of a radical ethical aesthetic. In N. K. Denzin & Y. S. Lincoln (Eds.), *Handbook of qualitative research*, 4th ed. (pp. 435–450). Thousand Oaks, CA: Sage.

Finley, S. (2011b). Ecoaesthetics: Green arts at the intersection of education and social transformation. *Cultural Studies↔Critical Methodologies, 11*, 3, 306–313.

Graddy, S. E. (2010). Creative and green: Art, ecology, and community. http://greenmuseum.org/generic_content.php?ct_id=238 (accessed February 3, 2012).

Grande, J. K. (2004). *Art nature dialogues: Interviews with environmental artists.* Albany: State University of New York Press.

Hardin, G. (1968). Tragedy of the commons. *Science, 162*, 1243–1248.

Jensen, D., & Berry, T. (2008). Thomas Berry: Interview conducted at a hotel in Greensboro, North Carolina, 11.16.00-11.17.00. In D. Jensen (Ed.), *How shall I live my life: On liberating the Earth from civilization* (pp. 39–56). Oakland, CA: PM Press.

Kahn, R. (2010). Towards ecopedagogy: Weaving a broad-based pedagogy of liberation for animals, nature, and the oppressed people of the Earth. In A. Darder, M. P. Baltodano, & R. D. Torres (Eds.), *The critical pedagogy reader*, 2nd ed. (pp. xx–xx). London: Routledge.

LaDuke, W. (1999). *All our relations: Native struggles for land and life.* Cambridge, MA: Southend Press.

Palast, G. (2003). Foreword. *How the rich are destroying the Earth.* White River Junction, VT: Chelsea Green Publishing Company.

Shankman, P. (1999). Development, sustainability, and the deforestation of Samoa. *Pacific Studies, 22*, 3/4, 167–188.

The Timberland Blog. (2011). http://thetimberlandblog.blogspot.com/ (accessed February 3, 2012).

## Chapter 10

# The Production of Girl Life

Jean Halley

It's funny I forgot this year.[1] Ash Wednesday is still my mother's
favorite religious day. Like much in the Catholic tradition, it is a
day whose symbolism is deeply rooted in the earth. From ashes
we come, and to ashes we shall return. We were Catholic. For my
grandmother, it would have been unforgivable not to go to Mass
on Ash Wednesday. In fact, both my grandmothers used to go to
Mass every day. In our Irish Catholic family, religion was a place
where women had some power. I guess it had to do with that
earthy thing. Blood and bodily pain were women's domains, both
dirty and awesome, animal and Godlike at once. It was known
that women were especially connected to God.

Men, on the other hand, ran things. While women lived in
the day-to-day simple and mundane rituals of life, men lived in
the *world*. They made things happen. My grandfather was a powerful man. In the family, and outside too, he held respect. He
owned places and things in the world, land and cattle and people's
jobs. He grew wheat and corn, and raised beef. To me, they were

*Qualitative Inquiry and the Politics of Advocacy,* edited by Norman K. Denzin and
Michael D. Giardina, 221–236. © 2012 Left Coast Press, Inc. All rights reserved.

cows, soft and brown, thoughtful creatures with big sad eyes. But to my grandfather, and he knew, they were beef. New calves, yearlings, two year olds ready for slaughter, breed cows were all potential meat. And meat was money—money and power. This was the language of his world.

He taught me things, my grandfather. He showed me how to eat a baked potato, deep yellow with half a cube of butter and lots of salt. From him, I learned that to order steak rare was not ladylike, but medium did a disservice to our ranching family. I ate my steak medium rare to make my grandfather proud. My brother, who was adopted, ate his steak well done, a sure sign that his blood was not the same as ours. My grandfather, although polite to my brother, never quite accepted him. For family, next to business, was everything. And like business, you were born into the family or you were not. Success ran in the blood, preordained.

Yet, I was a girl. And while my blood was his, I could not share his world. When I visited my grandparents, I spent time with my grandmother. She opened her life to me. And for a time, I would rest there.

My grandmother had a rose garden. This I know. When I think of her, I remember a smell both elegant and distant, like a rose. My grandmother was elegant and distant. My grandmother did not hold me. She never touched me. I don't know what her skin felt like—only that she had spots, brown spots, on her hands. And, I know, she disliked the spots intensely. To her, they were no accomplishment of growing old, marks of a life well lived. For her, the spots were dirty, stains that could not be removed. They were like shame.

My grandmother had a rose garden in her backyard. I would follow her there under the pretense of helping. She knew many things about roses. She knew where they should be cut, and when, so as not to hurt the plant. She knew how to make a yard quiet and time stop, so that the roses would grow in abundance. She knew how to gather them and put them together in a bowl so that they were beautiful, so beautiful your breath halted for a second when you saw them. They would fill a room with their rich scent, both elegant and distant. Roses are not like daisies. One has to be careful when picking a rose, with its sharp strong thorns. Roses are not like daisies, overjoyed to be alive, reaching eagerly for the sun. Roses demand a certain awe. Maybe my grandmother loved roses because she saw herself in them. Or maybe it was because they reminded her of her God, who was also awesome, who was also distant. My grandmother lived in very certain spaces. She lived in her rose garden. She lived in her kitchen. And she lived in her church. Hers was a world where women had their place. And men, men had everywhere else. Luckily, women got God. Although it was only because men did not need him. They were in charge anyhow.

My grandmother's God was awesome. His house was at the Catholic Church. And he, like my grandmother, was removed. While always present, he was never familiar. We did not discuss God. To speak of God in daily conversation was something worse than disrespect. Yet, even so, the silence granted God was not unusual. My family was filled with silences. Gaping quiet. Empty places. God existed somewhere there, in that silence.

● ● ●

In this chapter, I explore trauma and its normalizing effects in my own childhood. I also examine the ways that my experience reflects the larger normative culture as described by the radical feminist movement of the 1970s. In my childhood, violence normalized. It worked to gender me as a normative girl. I became quiet, accepting, submissive, disembodied and disassociated from my body, without sexual feeling, and ashamed. Along with violence, trauma saturated my childhood. And the sexual clung to, fed, and burst from my gendered experiences of both. For me, becoming girl meant succumbing to another's sexuality. Being-girl was a matter of no-longer-mattering, in both senses of the word. My girl-experience was that of no-longer-being-embodied. Instead, my form became the surface for the pleasure of another.

● ● ●

My sister Annie and I share a dream-memory, or perhaps merely a dream, or perhaps actually a memory. It is hard to say. The dream-memory happened to each of us when we were three. Or it didn't happen. It is hard to say.

Being three years apart, of course, we were not three at the same time. I was three and staying with my grandparents in Kidron while my mother was giving birth to my sister, Annie. She was three when I was six, and for some reason she was visiting my grandparents in Kidron at three, just like I had done, only this time there was no little sister being born.

## My Grandfather Clarke

Clarke may be the closest thing I can find to a starting point. Everyone else seemed to have a reason that came before them. My father, for example, had Clarke. But Clarke, Clarke, it seems to me, was simply cruel. Clarke was cruelty out of nowhere. Or maybe the cruelty came from the world. Maybe the world rotted Clarke. Maybe the job of living was too much for him and he gave in to killing instead. I don't know.

But he was cruel. No one said it. That was not allowed. Maybe no one even thought it. Except for me.

Clarke was the king. And everyone pretended everything was okay. Everyone pretended not to see. Or maybe, maybe, they were not pretending. Maybe, if one does not see for so long, too long, generations, one loses the capacity to see. Or maybe blindness simply ran in the family. I don't know.

But I do know that something, something, was wrong with Clarke. And Clarke brought wrongness with him. He spread it everywhere.

My father did not tell me stories about Clarke. He just gave me the party line. Clarke he held up as an example of how The Father must be treated. One did not question Clarke. One did not question the father. This never-to-be-questioned status was a birthright, a birthright of the father. Even God said so.

I only heard a few stories about Clarke. I heard them from my mother and my grandmother. Behind the curtain shielding what was from what was real, my grandmother slipped me some truth. My grandmother told me a few stories, a few stories about Clarke.

And the sad thing is that it's over. And yet it's not. My childhood was a horrible place to be. And it is over. It is over, and yet I do not know how to leave it behind. That is the sad thing. I am not sure how to live in this world. I am not sure how to live with what happened. I am not sure that I want to.

I can tell you what I want, what I really want. I want for none of this to have happened. I want a different set of memories. I am not who I want to be.

Will you tell me how to live with this? Can you, can you tell me how to live?

## Out of Nowhere

Here is something I remember. It is a dream or a memory, and it is strange. And it is out of nowhere. And I am so afraid. The word, afraid, cannot cover what I feel. Here is something I remember.

I am small, maybe three years old or so. And I am sitting on a tall wooden chair. It is an adult chair, and I am a small girl. The chair is much too big for me. I want to tell you that they had tied me to the chair. But I am afraid you won't believe me. Even so, I think they did. And everywhere is dark. I can barely see. And suddenly a strange man, although maybe not so strange, in some way I recognize him as the doctor who lived down the street from my grandparents, the doctor who was friends with Clarke, suddenly this man pierces me with a needle. He grips me tightly to hold me still and pierces my arm with a needle. He gives me a shot. And then all is gray. And then all is blank. That is all I remember.

## Men Work

My grandmother said that maybe they were too hard on my father. I wondered who "they" were. It seemed she meant herself and my grandfather, Clarke. Yet I think the "they" was really just Clarke. About this, about Clarke, she only told odds and ends, no complete stories, no full information. She said my grandfather used to beat my father. Maybe it was too much, she said. Maybe. And, she said, my father had terrible allergies to hay. He had spring fever. But not the regular kind. It got so bad his face swelled up, and he almost could not see. And in those days, there weren't all the different allergy medications that we have now.

I myself am a big user of allergy medications. I, like my father, have spring fever. I am particularly allergic to spring in New York City. I guess because it is not my home. But for me now there is no home. So I take the medication and wait for the allergies to pass. My father could only wait. He did not have the medication to take. The best thing for him would have been to stay away from hay. But Clarke did not care about the best thing for him. Like I said, Clarke was cruel. Clarke believed young men should work. Clarke believed young men should work for their father. Clarke believed men did not stop work because of a little allergy. To be a man meant to work and be strong, no matter what. And so, at Clarke's salebarn,[2] surrounded by hay, my father worked his way through sickness, he worked his way through spring.

## The Dream-Memory Happened Like This

Once when I was very small, Clarke did something cruel to me as well. Was this why my grandmother had me stay in her room with her? I don't know. I don't know if it ever happened again. I don't know if anything else happened. I don't know if *it* happened, at all. I don't know. I don't know.

You probably won't believe me. You probably won't believe what I have to say. But I will tell you anyhow. At least one time, Clarke did something cruel to me. It happened like this.

When I was almost three, in May, my sister was born in the hospital in Grand Junction. My father, being the father, could not take care of us. He could not take care of my brother. He could not take care of me. He was the father. So he took my mother's dog to the vet and had the dog put to sleep. That dog was named Tinker, and he was my mother's favorite dog ever. She really loved that dog. But my father being the father could not take care of a dog. He had important things to do. So he killed the dog and he took my brother and me to my grandparents' house. I guess my brother and I were lucky. We were lucky that my grandparents agreed to take us. We were luckier than that poor little dog, Tinker, my mother's favorite dog ever. He was such a good dog, my mother said. And so smart. Well, my father left us at my grandparents' house for two weeks. I don't remember my brother being there. I thought I was there all alone. But my mother says he was there. And my brother does not remember.

My mother remembers looking out her hospital window and watching us drive by. My father, my brother Martin who we called Marty then, and me. Anne, who we called Annie, was in the hospital with my mother. She had just been born. And I guess the dog was already dead. My mother says she watched us drive by from her hospital window. She says she waved to us. Somehow I remember watching her disappear, her face in the window, in the hospital, everything becoming smaller behind us as we drive away. Although maybe I don't really remember, maybe I just think I do.

My mother told me she did not know he was going to take us away. She did not know he was going to kill her dog either. He didn't tell her. He just did these things. That's how it was. He was the father. My mother cried when she told me this story. She cried. And, she said, he could have let you talk to me on the phone. He could have let you say goodbye. When she told me, I cried too. She cried for us and I cried for her, her and her little dog, her little dog, Tinker. My father at this point had already become cruel. He was young, only twenty-nine. He was younger than I am now. Yet it was too late. For him, it was too late. He was already cruel like my grandfather.

My brother, Martin, was the first grandchild to my father's parents. I was the second. We made my father's parents into grandparents. Before us, they were only parents. My grandmother was glad to be a grandmother. And my brother called her Gram. My brother named my grandmother. He named her, Gram. But Clarke did not want to be Grandfather. He named himself with his last name. He named himself Clarke. And so we called them Gram and Clarke.

And my father left us there. My father left us with Gram and Clarke for two weeks. He had important things to do. And my mother had just given birth. Annie had just been born. My mother has a picture from that time, in our family album. It was taken of me at my grandparents' during those two weeks, those two weeks when my father left us there, when Annie had just been born. In the photograph, I am standing alone, in front of what were probably the living room curtains, and I am crying. I am crying and crying. They say I cried the whole time I was there. I cried and cried.

And I didn't remember. Until four years, ago I didn't remember anything of that trip. And then four years ago, I did. It was a dream that I remembered. Or it was a memory. I cannot say.

I already told you that my grandfather was cruel. He was cruel. But beyond that I don't know who he was. I never knew him. I never knew that man. There were strange bits and pieces that burst through the story we lived with from day to day. Like once, when I was talking with my aunts in my grandmother's kitchen, some of my boy cousins came running in from downstairs, downstairs past where The Girls' Room waited, downstairs again to the basketball court that my grandfather had in the basement. My cousins were shouting excitedly that they had found Ku Klux Klan robes in my grandfather's basement. Really, they said, really. They were thrilled with their discovery. The aunts hushed them, hurriedly, moving them back out of the kitchen to silence. Later, when we, some of us cousins, went back to look at their discovery, the robes were gone.

My grandfather gave me shiny new silver dollars when I came to visit. He pulled my hair. He asked, what do you know? Only my grandmother had an answer to that question. She would respond, it takes a big dog to weigh a hundred pounds.

When I visited my grandmother, she would take me shopping in Salida. We would make a day trip in her fancy car. We would drive to Salida. Salida was in Nebraska, just across the Wyoming border. Salida was where my grandmother grew up. She had been a little girl there. Compared to Kidron, Salida was big. It even had a country club. On our shopping trip, our special trip to Salida, my grandmother would buy me a whole new outfit and she would take me out to lunch. Usually we went to eat at the country club. It was a special day, just she and I. And I loved it.

My grandmother would buy me a brand new outfit at the children's store in Salida. The lady at the store knew us. She knew my grandmother, and she was very nice to us. She was very nice in a way that nobody was to my mother when she went shopping. I noticed the difference. It made me feel both good and bad at once. I loved being with my grandmother. I loved being special.

But, nonetheless, the lady's niceness made me ache inside. It made me ache for my mother.

My grandmother liked girl clothes. She liked lacy dresses and shoes with bows and ribbons, clothes that made things clear. In them, everybody knew you were a girl. Everybody knew what was what. Unfortunately, I on the other hand, I did not like girl clothes. I liked clothes that one did not have to keep track of. I liked clothes that took little effort when they were, and when they weren't, on one's body. I did not like ribbons. This was a problem. I hated to disappoint my grandmother.

When we got home from our shopping trip, our day that always went too fast, I would try on my clothes for Clarke. I didn't want to do this. But my grandmother asked me to, so I would. And Clarke would comment. And then it was over. The day, the special shopping day, but also my contact with Clarke was over. This was really the only contact I had with Clarke. Like I told you, I really never knew my grandfather.

And then, four years ago, I remembered a dream. Or a memory. I remembered a dream-memory of what had happened when I was three and staying with my grandparents, when I was staying with my grandparents because my sister, Annie, had just been born and my father, being the father, could not take care of us. I remembered and I didn't. I cannot be sure. I remembered, but not like a photograph. I remembered but I cannot take the memory out of my pocket. I remembered but I cannot show you the memory and say see, here it is. I have nothing real to show, only vagueness. And yet, I remembered. And while you probably will not believe me, I remember nonetheless. I remember now.

I remembered being small and in a room. And the room was actually a little barn or shed that stood in front of Clarke's sale-barn. Other than this memory, I have never been in that shed. But the shed exists. It exists outside of my memory. It is real and can be found in front of what used to be my grandfather's sale-barn, until he sold it years ago. It is still there unless they tore it down. And I was on a chair. It is a tall wooden chair. And I am a small girl. The chair is much too big for me. And there was a table, long and wooden. And men were standing around the table and I was at one end on the chair and the men had funny outfits on with hoods. And I think the doctor was there, the doctor who lived down the street from my grandparents, the doctor who was friends with Clarke. And my grandfather stood at the other end of the table. I think it was my grandfather standing there, holding a kitten. And he killed the kitten with a knife. And they painted the blood around the room. I was too scared to cry, I remember.

## Trauma and Time

My story, as told, mimics the lived experience of trauma circling around and through tone, place, and familial generations. In my experience, trauma cuts through time and reoccurs as a compulsive repetition of the traumatic moment, of the violence. The traumatic experience happens in and is made up of bodies as much as it is held in other spaces, times, and places.

I tell my childhood story much as it was and continues to be experienced by me, almost as though time does not move forward. In contrast, the story I tell of U.S. beef cattle moves chronologically through time, starting with the cows' arrival in North America, moving forward to the industrialization of the meat industry, and a present-day look at the lives of cows, their deaths in slaughterhouses, and what becomes of them once dead. The story from my childhood circles around on itself, with no particular beginning and no real ending. This circling represents, I believe, the experience of trauma as timeless, in the sense of always being there, as fresh and vivid and gripping as the violent, gendered, and sexual acts that birthed the trauma, indeed perhaps more present even than when the violence was experienced.

● ● ●

It was late at night. And we were little girls. My sister even smaller than me. My sister loved that cat. She loved that cat. Really, she had not much else to love. And he woke us up. And he brought us to the garage. I don't remember getting there. Instead, suddenly, in my mind, it is night and we are there, my sister and I, standing side by side.

● ● ●

During violence, the traumatized being often "shuts down," numbs out, or in a sense, leaves, and while away, she stores the violent experience in her being until a safer time to re-experience it, and often, re-experience it again, and again and again. Trauma involves lives caught in the past, and in particular, caught in a past moment of violence, or perhaps, merely the moments of life surrounding violence. The past moment plays over and over again like a broken record. And the traumatized person experiences that moment viscerally as a pain or a smell, a sound or a vision (Caruth, 1996; Herman, 1992). Or, rather, to the extent that the event overwhelmed and overwhelms, one does not (re)experience the traumatic moment but instead circles around the experience compulsively and repetitively.

In remembering how thirty-three years ago, my father gutted my sister's beloved childhood cat in front of us in a drunken rage, I circle around the violence, remembering the events and affect leading up to and following it without ever fully knowing, mastering, moving through and beyond, or releasing the experience. It grips me, and I experience aspects of the event again and again and again, sweeping over me, as though they were actually occurring in the now. Cathy Caruth (1996) writes that "these repetitions are particularly striking because they seem not to be initiated by the individual's own acts but rather appear as the possession of some people by a sort of fate, a series of painful events to which they are subjected, and which seem to be entirely outside their wish or control" (p. 2).

In turn, my father's violence was inextricably connected to his experience and expression of manhood. That night, when he killed my sister's cat and so many other things as well, he shouted at us, or perhaps at someone we could not see, "I am a man! I am a man!"

In my experience of manhood, in my family, being a man meant rupturing the other, bursting through barriers of skin and flesh in violence, all too often sexual. To some extent, I think this reflected manhood in the larger normative culture. Going from boy to man, to being a "real man," meant taking on a never-ending struggle to prove oneself until finally, one did reach the end. And the only end to this was death. For men, real men, there was no stopping during life. Whatever one might want, once obtained, no longer meant much at all. The real thing was always another thing, something else. There was no point of saturation, no stopping, no lasting experience of enough, no money, no cow, no production, no deaths of others, no sex enough. No end to this hunger.

Beef reflects this orientation. The beef industry epitomizes my family's, our culture's desire for, our pressing need for more, and again, more. In sharp contrast to raising cattle, my grandmother grew roses. Her roses contained their meaning in the now. My grandfather's cows were for something else. They were for what they would become—meat. And money.

## Trauma and the Radical Feminist Movement

Now I want to engage my experience and thinking with a broader conversation. The radical feminist movement of the 1970s happened simultaneous to my childhood. This movement brought normalizing gendered violence and trauma to national attention. Radical feminists, a prominent faction of the second-wave feminist movement, argued that girls become girls, in part, through violence and its effects, trauma. Violence normalizes as it produces girlness. Violence/trauma also plays a clear role in the political economic reproduction of gendered power (and the power of humans over other animals). Thus, through violence, gendered power is reproduced.

Radical feminists brought the reality of gendered violence into mainstream consciousness. Suddenly we saw it, and we saw it everywhere: domestic violence, sexual harassment, rape, child sexual abuse, and incest.[3] We recognized violence and trauma at the heart of gendered power, at the heart of normative gender (Halley, 2007).

In 2007, I wrote about this movement: "Radical feminism argued that intimate relationships, and the ways those relationships were lived in the everyday through institutions like the family, were inextricably connected to larger gendered systems of power. Men and boys had power over women and girls." The radical feminists claimed that everyday institutions of our society like the traditional nuclear family played an important role in the oppression of women and girls. And while the radical feminists believed that gendered oppression happened through other forms of power including economic, psychological, and political, violence was the ultimate, bottom line defense. Incest and child sexual abuse exemplified this perfectly.

> Incest was a prime example of male oppression, often enacted through male control over, and abuse of, female bodies. ... Ultimately, radical feminists argued that incest was more than simply a result of the patriarchy; it was a means to re-create the patriarchy. Girls learned to be girls—they became girls— through a socialization process that included male violation of their bodies and selves. (Halley, 2007, p. 134)

About incest, prominent radical feminist psychiatrist and trauma researcher, Judith Lewis Herman, argued, "Female children are regularly subjected to sexual assaults by adult males who are part of their intimate social world." She continued: "The aggressors are not outcasts and strangers; they are neighbors, family friends, uncles, cousins, stepfathers, and fathers. To be sexually exploited by a known and trusted adult is a central and formative experience in the lives of countless women" (1981, p. 7). Herman claimed:

> Father-daughter incest is not only the type of incest most frequently reported but also represents a paradigm of female sexual victimization. The relationship between father and daughter, adult male and female child, is one of the most unequal relationships imaginable. It is no accident that incest occurs most often precisely in the relationship where the female is most powerless. (p. 4)

## Trauma and Its Other (Possible) Effects

The radical feminists presented a worldview where violence/ trauma both produces and reproduces gender and social power. Violence normalizes through reproducing take-for-granted male power. In my experience, this is an adept description of violent effects, albeit perhaps not the full story. In this section, I also want to note that the violence I experienced, and perhaps violence in the larger culture as well, seemed to play multiple roles.

It seemed that my father's out-of-control brutality, springing from his own traumatized history, also pulled apart our world, and did so in a way that opened possibilities. The trauma, and the repetition of that traumatic experience in my everyday life, not only normalized—and built a social order—but also ruptured the order of things, bursting through the zones of confinement to open to something else. In some way, hidden or confined everyday violence and trauma not only reproduced but challenged normalizing power.

I wonder: Outside of my family, like the panic disorders examined by Jackie Orr (2006), how might the crazy, surprising, unexpected nature of violence/trauma pull apart the management of populations, bursting through the seams of the expected, and through trauma opening up the zones that confine? Trauma—like, indeed as, a manifestation of life itself—at times explodes beyond the reach, or perhaps through, power's subsumption of it. Using the example of disease as an example of life itself, Shukin (2009) notes that in the case of animal capital,

> While the balance of power seems, ominously, to be all on the side of capital, it is crucial to also recognize the amplified vulnerability of capitalism in tautological times. Indeed, novel diseases erupting out of the closed loop of animal capital—mad cow disease, avian influenza—are on material sign of how the immanent terrain of market becomes susceptible, paradoxically, to the pandemic potential of "nature." (p. 16)

In my experimental writing, violence/trauma plays diverse roles in the reproduction of life and in the reproduction of normalizing power. In some way, violence seems to move beyond the making of power, in the making of a docile gendered girl population, and challenge it. In my family, violence/trauma—in both its mundane everydayness and in its shocking out-of-the ordinariness—is primarily, but not merely, an instrument of power. In part, this is because violence is also a traumatic response to, rather than merely a result of, discipline and normalization, and perhaps in this, a (traumatized) form of resistance. In my memoir writing, I wonder how—and I write this question around the edges of the story while—these mundane forms of confined violence and its traumatic effects disrupt and challenge normalizing power. If nothing else, it is the trauma in its day-to-day impact on my life that pushed me to face my own history. Really, it left me no choice.

● ● ●

In another place, in another set of memories, clarity might not matter. I mean, really, if all were well, then who cares what happened. If all were well, then what happened, and other such details, are insignificant. But all was not well. All was not well. This much I know. And it is the pain that makes me push the edges of our family truth.

## Notes

1. The first four paragraphs of this chapter are taken from Halley (2000).
2. A salebarn is a place where livestock are auctioned.
3. For an exploration of radical feminist writing on gendered violence, see Brownmiller (1975), Russell (1974, 1986), and Wilson and Connell (1974).

## References

Brownmiller, S. (1975). *Against our will*. New York: Simon and Schuster.

Caruth, C. (1996). *Unclaimed experience: Trauma, narrative, and history*. Baltimore: The Johns Hopkins University Press.

Halley, J. (2000). This I know: An exploration of remembering childhood and knowing now. *Qualitative Inquiry, 6*, 3, 349–358.

Halley, R. (2007). *Boundaries of touch: Parenting and adult-child intimacy* (Urbana: University of Illinois Press.

Herman, J. L. (1981). *Father-daughter incest*. Cambridge, MA: Harvard University Press.

Herman, J. L. (1992). *Trauma and recovery: The aftermath of violence—from domestic abuse to political terror*. New York: BasicBooks.

Orr, J. (2006). *Panic diaries: A genealogy of panic disorder*. Durham, NC: Duke University Press.

Russell, D. E. H. (1974). *The politics of rape: The victim's perspective.* New York: Stein and Day.

Russell, D. E. H. (1986). *The secret trauma: Incest in the lives of girls and women.* New York: Basic Books.

Shukin, N. (2009). *Animal capital: Rendering life in biopolitical times.* Minneapolis: University of Minnesota Press.

Wilson, C. & Connell, N. (Eds.). (1974). *Rape: The first sourcebook for women.* New York: NAL Plume.

Chapter 11

# "I Read the News Today, Oh Boy ..."

## The War on Public Workers[1]

### H. L. (Bud) Goodall, Jr.

Every day I read the news and every day the news I read is worse. American higher education is under siege. It's a war out there. Battle lines have been drawn from sea to shining sea as Republican governors and their legislatures no longer make a secret of their ambition, which is to defund public education, end tenure, and rid the land of the scourge known as the cultural elite.

ALEC, which is the well-funded conservative group responsible for writing template-based legislation to attain those ends, no longer makes a secret of its existence, much less of its funding, which comes directly from wealthy families, such as the notorious Koch brothers, and wealthy corporations, such as many of those whose profits have never been healthier due to two long wars, the Wall Street bailout, and deregulation carried out by the Bush administration.

Tenure is under siege, too. Think of attacks on it as attacks on the supply lines that feed higher education. Without tenure, who in their right mind would choose this line of work? But that, of course, is exactly the point. Without the supply lines, the troops in

*Qualitative Inquiry and the Politics of Advocacy,* edited by Norman K. Denzin and Michael D. Giardina, 237–244. © 2012 Left Coast Press, Inc. All rights reserved.

the field starve. And the hungry easily lose political commitment or are willing to trade it in for the semi-security of annual contracts.

Universities, havens of the so-called cultural elite, are under siege, too from within and without. The big book of shame published this year, Robert Arum and Josipa Roksa's (2011) *Academically Adrift*, argues that students in state universities and colleges aren't learning anything, which only underscores the dogma of right-wing commentators who claim that most professors don't teach, or at least don't teach anything of value, probably because we are too preoccupied with converting students to communism and atheism. In Texas, Governor Rick Perry has introduced a plan to stop funding for higher education in the traditional way and replace it with a voucher system that allows each student—heretofore defined as a consumer—to choose which professors to support with their enrollment.

But wait, it gets better: Faculty bonuses are to replace merit raises, and those bonuses will be based entirely on student evaluations. In Arizona, where I teach, as elsewhere, draconian cuts to higher education budgets—in our case, back to a 1960 level, back when we had 20,000 students instead of today's 74,000 and no real research agenda—means much larger classes, fewer faculty, no new tenure-earning hires, and tuition increases that have almost doubled what it costs to attend our state university, making a college education untenable for a substantial population of our state's poor, minority, and/or immigrant population.

When universities don't have money they have to find it. Guess what? The Koch brothers again. I read in the news just last week, oh boy, that two faculty positions in economics at Florida State University (and others at Clemson University, and still others at other places) were funded by the Koch brothers with the stipulation that they are dedicated to the advocacy of free market capitalism. And the faculty had no real say in who was hired for those positions. As Stanley Fish (2011)—no friend to changing the political world in the classroom—wrote just this week, that decision was, in fact, a textbook violation of academic freedom, as well as an insult to any sense of due process in academic hiring. The cultural elite cry foul! But the economic elite are buying the game.

I could go on.
We all could go on.

. . .

We are fiddling with evaluation metrics while the university burns. We are hiding behind the very traditions that are under attack and we are largely opting out of service in a war whose outcome, if we lose it, will eventually imprison us.

The fact is that after years of doing mostly nothing publicly to combat the growing Republican narrative that demeans our profession, as well as casts cynical doubt on the value of an educated person to a free society, most academics find that we now don't know what to do.

Write letters to the editor?
*Take a look at the public responses.*
Get up a petition for the legislature?
*Uh-huh, go ahead.*
Write a blog?
*Look at mine, read the right-wing trolls who daily attack it, and see if you have the stomach for the fight.*
How about organize a protest?
Or a boycott?
Sure, we can do that, but so far none of the places where that strategy has been tried has produced change. Except in Wisconsin, where it might, but the verdict is still out and a lot of damage has already been done.

Retreat into our offices and wait for the storm to blow over?
I think that is what most of us do. We have been conditioned to do little else. Nor do we have the financial resources to stand up against billionaires and millionaires and state legislatures or even a hoodwinked electorate. We are the cultural elite, not the economic elite. And it takes money, big money, to win a campaign or to counter propaganda.

If you wanted to write a script for a movie or a novel about a right-wing conspiracy to systematically dumb down a populace so that "divide and conquer" fanatical sound bites and mean-spirited slogans, campaigns based on fear and lies and fueled by big moneyed interests whose only real interest is maintaining power through media spectacles, war narratives, and coordinated civic control, you could do no better than what we have right here in River City.

Except no one would believe it.

This truth is not only stranger than fiction; it's a truth that denies the possibility of fiction.

●  ●  ●

We are late to this fight.

Maybe too late.

I don't know.

But what I do know is that we are losing this war. We are losing it in the streets and we are losing it at the ballot box. We are losing it in legislative votes and in congressional action. Even our president, who says he is one of us, is unable or unwilling to stand up for us other than in the most symbolic of ways. Some of us hope that will change if he wins a second term. Some of us doubt it will. And the rest of us?

●  ●  ●

One thing I've noticed while dreaming of a brighter future for higher education is that most of us on the left have lost sight of two important things. First, we have lost sight of a vital historical and cultural truth about labor: *This is class war and our enemy is not ever going to save us or speak up for our rights.* They hate us. Literally hate us. And they use, abuse, and eventually discard what they hate. I wrote a piece for Norman Denzin on this subject and here is the gist of the rich Republican attack on us, an attack based on a very simple premise:

> If we were rich, we would become Republicans. ... We would, if we were wealthy, embrace a rich white man's—or rich white woman's—Republican values. Which is to say we would understand that there is something wrong with people who don't translate the freedoms and liberties, the low taxes and lack of government regulation of this great nation into vast personal wealth. We must be either stupid or lazy. It's really that simple. We only have ourselves to blame.

So why should our enemy support us? Did Caesar free the slaves? Did the bosses take pity on the workers who went on strike? Did our Congress, making claims about the threat posed by the enormity of our national debt, see fit to raise taxes on the rich? Is your college president creating a fund for all the lecturers she or he has laid off?

The second principle we have lost sight of is there are far more of us than there are of them. United we stand, divided we fall. Their strategy—a time-honored first principle of propaganda—is to divide the public from the private, then to subdivide the public into the unionized and the non-unionized, then further divide those who make $41,000 a year as firefighters from those who make $61,000 as assistant professors, and so on. Cast doubt on the patriotism, the loyalty, the honor, and/or the work ethic of those who are in every other way our brothers and sisters in arms, and you slowly but surely divide and conquer.

Finally, we are *not* the cultural elite. We are working-class intellectuals. We don't come from money and we don't have money. The cultural elite was a rhetorical bon bon created and distributed by Wall Street to dangle before status-starved college professors, knowing that we would grab them. But there is a big difference, as Thomas Frank argued years ago, between a cultural elite and an economic elite.

Here's that bon bon. Now swallow it. Meanwhile, the rich get richer, buy elections, cut their own taxes, create subprime mortgages, build hedge funds, manipulate markets, and quietly convince themselves that they are the smart ones as well as the rich ones. Doubt it? Read Karen Ho's (2009) devastating ethnography of Wall Street, *Liquidated*. And the further removed they are from main street, from university drive, from college avenue, the louder they laugh at our expense. I mean, we make really bad choices. It's our own fault.

And what has been our response? So what if we make less than a living wage for many years? We are the cultural elite. We are cool. Smart. Proud of our poverty and proud of how distanced we are from mainstream values and habits. What if once we get a job in one of the most competitive arenas on planet Earth we are paid less and owe more than any of our colleagues in Business, Engineering, or the medical sciences? We are the cultural elite, though. Right?

Oh man, oh woman, what were you thinking when you swallowed that sweet slice of status covering a much deeper cultural sin? Didn't we see it coming? Divide and conquer. Create a category that irks the vast majority of citizens who hated high school, flunked the hard courses in college, and couldn't get into grad school—which is to say, about 75 percent of the voting public—and then get those college professors to parade around in those fancy tenured robes owning that class-based cultural elite rhetoric, I mean, what did we expect? That we would be loved?

Do you love those you don't understand and who you feel have oppressed or made fun of you?

Revenge in a capitalist society is best represented in cold hard cash. It's that Protestant ethic that makes us this way. And with the evangelical zeal of the new "prosperity gospel" that remakes Jesus into the veritable image of conservative Republican values, we end up with a reverse Kenneth Burke: The rich are no longer guilty for being "up" while others are "down"; in fact, it's the opposite. The rich are saved by their prosperity gospel, and everyone else is suspect because, really, we don't seem to be making the right choices for a capitalist America.

How much money do you make? Where do you live? What kind of car do you drive? Where do you vacation? And please, don't tell me you prefer to be relatively poor, or that your values prevent you from seeking wealth and influence. In America, my friend, there are only two right answers to any question regarding money: More is better than less, and sooner is better than later. If you don't know that, then what, really do you know? That is of any value, I mean.

Who knows that lesson better than college presidents? Or overpriced provosts? Or bloated deans? You want something close to a cultural elite, that's where you ought to look. My University president makes $725,000 a year in addition to a generous housing, entertainment, and car allowance. He enjoys unlimited free travel worldwide. And as long as he meets his metrics for enrollment growth (never mind that there is no corresponding faculty growth) and retention, he gets an annual increase somewhere in the neighborhood of a new BMW 7-series. *Which, by the way, he drives.*

His message to the newly minted doctoral class last week was emblematic of his privilege. He said, and I quote: "Stop arguing. Stop it. Just go out there and do something." In other words, fuggedabout politics; make me some money!

And you would be surprised, or maybe not, at how many tenured faculty nodded their heads.

William Deresiewicz, writing in *The Nation* (2011), puts the crisis in higher education this way:

> What we have in academia, in other words, is a microcosm of the American economy as a whole: a self-enriching aristocracy, a swelling and increasingly immiserated proletariat, and a shrinking middle class. The same devil's bargain stabilizes the system: the middle, or at least the upper middle, the tenured professoriate, is allowed to retain its prerogatives—its comfortable compensation packages, its workplace autonomy and its job security—in return for acquiescing to the exploitation of the bottom by the top, and indirectly, the betrayal of the future of the entire enterprise.

So I wasn't surprised to learn from reading the news in May 2011 that according to a new Pew Center/*Chronicle of Higher Education* Study, 69 percent of the college presidents who are supposed to be leading the charge for us are themselves no longer supportive of tenure (Stripling, 2011). More than half say that higher education is heading in the wrong direction. And most of them admit they haven't a clue what to do about it.

That's the bottom line, my friends.

It's the *story* that fuels the revolution.

And we don't yet have one.

## Note

1. The title of this chapter is inspired by "A Day in the Life" from The Beatles' *Sgt. Pepper's Lonely Hearts Club Band.*

## References

Arum, R., & Roksa, J. (2011). *Academically adrift: Limited learning on college campuses.* Chicago: University of Chicago Press.

Deresiewicz, W. (2011). Faulty towers: The crisis in higher education. *The Nation*, May 4. http://www.thenation.com/article/160410/faulty-towers-crisis-higher-ducation?page=full (accessed February 4, 2012).

Fish, S. (2011). Sex, the Koch brothers, and academic freedom. *The New York Times*, May 16.http://opinionator.blogs.nytimes.com/2011/05/16/sex-the-koch-brothers-and-academic-freedom/ (accessed February 4, 2012).

Ho, K. (2009). *Liquidated: An ethnography of Wall Street.* Durham, NC: Duke University Press.

Stripling, J. (2011). Most presidents prefer no tenure for majority of faculty. *The Chronicle of Higher Education*, May 15. http://chronicle.com/article/Most-Presidents-Favor-No/127526/ (accessed February 4, 2012).

# Coda

## Why Faculty Should Join Occupy Movement Protesters on College Campuses[1]

### Henry A. Giroux

In both the United States and many other countries, students are protesting against rising tuition fees, the increasing financial burdens they are forced to assume, and the primacy of market models in shaping higher education while emphasizing private benefits to individuals and the economy. Many students view these policies and for-profit industries as part of an assault on not just the public character of the university but also as an attack on civic society and their future.

For many young people in the Occupy movement, higher education has defaulted on its promise to provide them with both a quality education and the prospects of a dignified future. They resent the growing instrumentalization and accompanying hostility to critical and oppositional ideas within the university. They have watched over the years as the university has lost ground as a place to think, dissent, and develop a culture of questioning, dialogue, and civic enlightenment. They are rethinking what the role of the university should be in a world caught in a nightmarish blend of war, massive economic inequities, and ecological destruction.

---

*Qualitative Inquiry and the Politics of Advocacy,* edited by Norman K. Denzin and Michael D. Giardina, 245–252. © 2012 Left Coast Press, Inc. All rights reserved.

What role should the university play at a time when politics is being emptied out of any connection to a civic literacy, informed judgment, and critical dialogue, further deepening a culture of illiteracy, cruelty, hypermasculinity, and disposability? Young people are not only engaging in a great refusal, they are also arguing for the social benefits and public value of higher education. At the same time, they are deeply resentful that, as conservative politicians defund higher education and cut public spending, they do so to be able to support tax breaks for corporations and the rich and to ensure ample funds for sustaining and expanding the warfare state.

The Occupy protesters view the assault on the programs that emerged out of the New Deal and the Great Society as being undermined as society increasingly returns to a Second Gilded Age, in which youth have to bear the burden of an attack on the welfare state, social provisions, and a huge wealth and income inequality gap. Young people recognize that they have become disposable and that higher education, which always embodied the ideal, though in damaging terms, of a better life, has now become annexed to the military-academic-industrial complex.

What is important about the Occupy protesters' criticism of being saddled with onerous debt, viewed as a suspect generation, subjected to the demands of an audit culture that confuses training with critical education and their growing exclusion from higher education, is that such concerns situate the attack on higher education as part of a broader criticism against the withering away of the public realm, public values, and any viable notion of the public good. To paraphrase William Greider (2011), the protesters have come to recognize in collective fashion that higher education has increasingly come to resemble "an ecological dead zone," where social relevance and engaged scholarship perishes in a polluted, commercial, market-driven environment. The notion of the university as a center of critique and a vital democratic public sphere that cultivates the knowledge, skills, and values necessary for the production of a democratic polity is giving way to a view of the university as a marketing machine essential to the production of identities in which the only obligation of citizenship is to be a consumer.

The Occupy Wall Street protesters reject the propaganda they have been relentlessly fed by a market-driven culture: that markets should take priority over governments; that market values are the best means for ordering society and satisfying human needs; that material interests are more important than social needs; and that self-interest is the driving force of freedom and the organizing principle of society. The protesters refuse a notion of society that embraces a definition of agency in which people are viewed only as commodities, bound together in a Darwinian nightmare that celebrates the logic of greed, unchecked individualism, and a disdain for democratic values.

The old idea of democracy in which the few govern the many through the power of capital and ritualized elections is being replaced with a new understanding of democracy and politics, in which power and resources are shared and economic justice and democratic values work in the interest of social responsibility and the common good. This radical notion of democracy is in the making, unfinished, and open to connecting people, power, resources, and knowledge. And this turn toward a radical understanding of connecting the particular to the general is particularly true of their view of higher education. What the Occupy protesters recognize, as the British educator Simon Dawes (2011) points out, is that, "'the public university' can be read as shorthand for 'not-neoliberal university,' where neoliberal means more than private funding; it means 'not good for democracy'" (para. 20).

All over the country, Occupy movement protesters are setting up camps on college campuses. Not only are they protesting the ways in which universities now resemble corporations—treating faculty as a subaltern class of casualized labor, and defining students largely as customers and clients—they have also recognized that banks and loan corporations, with their army of lobbyists, have declared war on students, killing any legislation that would reduce the cost of schooling, stifling any legislation that would make it affordable for all working- and middle-class students.

Protesters are also raising serious questions about academics. Where are the academics when it comes to protesting the corporatization and militarization of higher education? Why are so many of them complicit with the ideologies and money now used by corporations and the national security state to promote the interest of finance capital and agencies such as the CIA, Defense Department, Pentagon, and other apparatuses of the national security state intent on recruiting students to produce militarized knowledge and create new and ever more sophisticated surveillance systems and weapons of mass destruction? Why do so many academics cling to a notion of disinterested and objective scholarship and publish and make a claim to pedagogy that allegedly decries any relationship to politics, power, or interest in larger social issues? Occupy movement protesters have recognized is that for all intents and purposes, too many academics who make a claim to objectivity, and, in some cases, reject the presence of the military-industrial-academic complex on campus, have become irrelevant to offering any viable defense of the university as a democratic public sphere, or, for that matter, even defending to a broader public the very conditions that make their work possible.

One important question that arises from the Occupy movement's migration to college campuses is: What can academics learn from these young people? One of the things they might learn is that critical and important forms of education and dialogue are taking place outside the university. In those places, issues are being talked about that are often ignored within the halls, disciplines, and classrooms in many universities. Many institutes of higher learning have lost touch with bridging the production of knowledge, research, and teaching with the myriad urgent social issues now facing the larger society, including crushing poverty, environmental degradation, racism, suspension of civil liberties, colonization of the media by corporations, rise of the punishing state, religious fanaticism, corruption of politics by big money, and other concerns.

Since the 1980s, higher education has been increasingly corporatized, militarized, and subjected to market-driven values and managerial relations that treat faculty and students as entrepreneurs and clients, while reducing knowledge to the dictates of an audit culture and pedagogy to a destructive and reductive instrumental rationality. It is hoped that academics might both learn about and be inspired by the current attempts on the part of students to change the conversation about the meaning and purpose of higher education. Academics might be moved and educated by the attempt on the part of many young people today to reclaim higher education as a democratic public sphere, one that not only provides work skills, but also offers a formative culture that prepares students to be critical and active agents in shaping the myriad of economic, social, and political forces that govern their lives.

Students are rejecting a model of education based on narrow forms of measurable utility, capital accumulation, and cost-efficient asset and power-stripping measures; they are rejecting a market-driven model of education that reduces 70 percent of faculty to a subaltern class of part-time workers and treats students as customers and commodities, offering them overcrowded classrooms, skyrocketing tuition rates, and modes of learning that have little to do with enabling them to translate personal troubles into social problems. Universities increasingly have come to resemble malls. Rather than offer students an education in which they can become critical individual and social agents who believe that they have the power to change things, they are largely reduced to passive consumers entertained by the spectacles of big sports, celebrity culture, and the lure of utterly privatized desires.

In many ways, students are offering faculty the possibility of becoming part of a larger conversation, if not a social movement, one that addresses what the role of the university might be in relation to public life in the 21st century. Central to such an inquiry is examining how higher education has been caught in the grip of larger economic and political forces that undermine the social state, social provisions, and democracy itself. The Occupy protesters are arguing that while they might support a limited notion of a market economy, they do not want to live in a market society, a society in which market values become a template for organizing all aspects of social life. They have learned the hard way that beneath this market fundamentalism resides a mode of education and a set of values that contain a secret order of politics that is destructive of democratic social relations, democratic modes of equality, and civic education.

Young people can make clear to faculty that, over the last thirty years, they have been written out of the social contract and are no longer viewed as a symbol of hope, just as they have been written out of the power relations that govern the university. No longer regarded as an important social investment or as a marker for the state of democracy and the moral life of the nation, young people have become the objects of a more direct and damaging assault waged on them on a number of political economic and cultural fronts. They have been deprived of decent scholarships, disrespected in their attempts to gain a quality education, foiled in their attempts to secure a decent job, and denied a voice in the shaping of the institutions that bear down heavily on their daily lives.

Big banks and large financial institutions view them as a drain on the nation's financial coffers and as a liability in making quick financial profits through short-term investments. Young people are now challenging this toxic form of casino capitalism and, in doing so, are changing the national conversation that has focused on deficit reduction and taxing the poor. They are shifting this conversation to important issues, which range from poverty and joblessness to corporate corruption. Put differently, the Occupy protesters are asking big questions, and they are not simply being moralistic. They are also demanding an alternative vision and set of policies to drive American society.

Faculty need to listen to young people in order to try to understand the problems they face and how, as academics, they might be unknowingly complicit in reproducing such problems. They also need to begin a conversation with young people and among other faculty about how they can become a force for democratic change.

Young people need a space on campuses to talk back, talk to one another, engage in respectful dialogue with faculty, and learn how to engage in coalition building. Faculty and administrators can begin to open up the possibility for such spaces by offering the Occupy protesters an opportunity to speak to their classes and create autonomous spaces within the university where they might meet and engage in dialogue with others. They can go even further by joining them in fighting those economic and political forces that are destroying higher education as a social good and as a citadel of rigorous intellectual engagement and civic debate.

Young people no longer recognize themselves in terms preferred by the market, and they no longer believe in an education that ignores critical thinking, dialogue, and those values that engage matters of social responsibility and civic engagement. But students have more to offer than a serious critique of the university and its complicity with a number of antidemocratic forces now shaping the larger society. They are also modeling for faculty new modes of participatory democracy, and exhibiting forms of pedagogy and education that connect learning with social change and knowledge with more democratic modes of self-development and social empowerment. Clearly, academics have a lot to learn from both the ways in which students are changing the conversation about education, important social issues, and democracy, and from what it might mean to imagine a new understanding of politics and a different future.

All of these issues are especially true for those faculty members who believe that scholarship should be disinterested and removed from addressing important social issues. The questions students are raising are important for faculty to rethink: those modes of professionalism, specialism, and social relations that have cut them off from addressing important social issues and the larger society. Professionalism does not have to translate into a flight from moral and intellectual responsibility.

Faculty can also put pressure on their unions to support the Occupy movement, provide them with financial and media resources, and join with them in pushing for educational and political reforms. The Occupy protesters are surely right in arguing that higher education is a vital public sphere that should be at the forefront in addressing important political, economic, and social issues. Faculty should combine their scholarly rigor and knowledge to bridge the gap between the university and everyday life—not to benefit corporate interests or the warfare state, but to benefit existing and future generations of young people who hold the key to whether democracy will survive the current moment in American history.

Too many academics for too long have turned their backs on addressing important social issues, on joining with young people to fight with them for a better future, and on using their knowledge and skills to convince a wider public that higher education is crucial for not only students, but for the common good and the entire society. Joining with students in the Occupy movement is not merely a career choice; it is a choice about what kind of society we all want to live in. The urgency of that question at the current historical moment demands that academics take that question seriously and act as quickly as possible, with passion and conviction.

## Note

1. An earlier version of this chapter was published on *Truthout* (Giroux, 2011).

## References

Dawes, S. (2011). The "public university" as response to funding cuts to UK's higher education. *Truthout*, November 22. http://www.truth-out.org/pub-lic-university-response-funding-cuts-uks-higher-education/1321984014 (accessed February 4, 2012).

Giroux, H. A. (2011). Why faculty should join Occupy Movement protes-tors on college campuses. *Truthout*, December 19. http://www.truth-out.org/why-faculty-should-join-occupy-movement-protesters-college-cam-puses/1324328832 (accessed February 4, 2012).

Greider, W. (2011). The democratic promise of Occupy Wall Street. *The Nation*, December 12. http://www.thenation.com/article/164767/democratic-promise-occupy-wall-street (accessed February 4, 2012).

# Index

# About the Authors

## Editors

**Norman K. Denzin** is Distinguished Professor of Communications, College of Communications Scholar, and Research Professor of Communications, Sociology, and the Humanities at the University of Illinois, Urbana-Champaign. One of the world's foremost authorities on qualitative research and cultural criticism, Denzin is the author or editor of more than two dozen books, including *Performance Ethnography*, *Reading Race*, *Interpretive Ethnography*, *Images of Postmodern Society*, *The Recovering Alcoholic*, *The Alcoholic Self*, and *Flags in the Window*. Most recently, he has completed two-thirds of a trilogy on the American West, *Searching for Yellowstone* (Left Coast Press, 2008) and *Custer on Canvas* (Left Coast Press, 2011). He is the editor of the landmark *Handbook of Qualitative Research* (1ˢᵗ, 2ⁿᵈ, 3ʳᵈ, and 4ᵗʰ editions, Sage, with Yvonna S. Lincoln), and coeditor of the *Handbook of Critical & Indigenous Methodologies* (2008, Sage, with Yvonna S. Lincoln and Linda Tuhiwai Smith). With Michael D. Giardina, he is coeditor of *Contesting Empire/Globalizing Dissent: Cultural Studies after 9/11* (Paradigm, 2006), and a series of books on qualitative inquiry published by Left Coast Press, Inc.: *Qualitative Inquiry and the Conservative Challenge: Confronting Methodological Fundamentalism* (2006), *Ethical Futures in Qualitative Research: Decolonizing the Politics of Knowledge* (2007), *Qualitative Inquiry and the Politics of Evidence* (2008), *Qualitative Research and Social Justice* (2009), *Qualitative Research and Human Rights* (2010), and *Qualitative Inquiry and Global Crises* (2011). He is also the editor of the journal *Qualitative Inquiry* (with Yvonna S. Lincoln), founding editor of *Cultural Studies⇔Critical Methodologies* and *International Review of Qualitative Research*, editor of *Studies in Symbolic Interaction*, and *Cultural Critique* series editor for Peter Lang Publishing. He is the founding president of the International Association for Qualitative Inquiry and director of the International Congress of Qualitative Inquiry.

**Michael D. Giardina** is an assistant professor in the College of Education at Florida State University. He is the author or editor of a dozen books, including most recently *Sport, Spectacle, and NASCAR Nation: Consumption and the Cultural Politics of Neoliberalism* (PalgraveMacmillan, 2011, with Joshua I. Newman) and *Sporting Pedagogies: Performing Culture & Identity in the Global Arena* (Peter Lang, 2005), which received the 2006 Most Outstanding Book award from the North American Society for the Sociology of Sport. In addition to a series of books edited with Norman K. Denzin on qualitative inquiry and interpretive research, Giardina is the editor of *Youth Culture & Sport: Identity, Power, and Politics* (Routledge, 2007, with Michele K. Donnelly) and *Globalizing Cultural Studies: Methodological Interventions in Theory, Method, and Policy* (Peter Lang, 2007, with Cameron McCarthy, Aisha Durham, Laura Engel, Alice Filmer, and Miguel Malagreca). His work has appeared in scholarly journals such as *Qualitative Inquiry, Cultural Studies ⇔ Critical Methodologies, American Behavioral Scientist, Policy Futures in Education,* and *Journal of Sport & Social Issues*. He is associate editor of the *Sociology of Sport Journal,* special issues editor of *Cultural Studies ⇔ Critical Methodologies,* and associate director of the International Congress of Qualitative Inquiry. With Joshua I. Newman, he is completing a book titled *Physical Cultural Studies: Bodies, Spaces, Rhythms* (Peter Lang).

## Contributors

**Tim Barko** is a doctoral student in science education at the University of Florida.

**Kathy Charmaz** is professor of sociology and director of the Faculty Writing Program at Sonoma State University in which she helps faculty with their research and scholarly writing. Dr. Charmaz is the president of the Society for the Study of Symbolic Interaction and has served as chair of the Medical Sociology Section of the American Sociological Association, president of the Pacific Sociological Association, and editor of *Symbolic Interaction*. She has received the Feminist Mentors Award and the George Herbert Mead Award for lifetime achievement from the Society for the Study of Symbolic Interaction.

**John Clarke** is a retired member of the Centre for Educational Research and Evaluation Services in the Faculty of Education, Community, and Leisure at Liverpool John Moores University, United Kingdom.

**Nigel Fielding** is professor of sociology and associate dean of Arts and Human Sciences at the University of Surrey, United Kingdom. He co-directs the CAQDAS Networking Project, which provides training and support in the use of computers in qualitative data analysis. His research interests are in new technologies for social research, and mixed method research design. In research methodology, his books include a study of methodological integration (*Linking Data*, 1986, Sage, with Jane Fielding), an influential book on qualitative software (*Using Computers in Qualitative Research*, 1991, Sage; editor and contributor), and the *Sage Handbook of Online Research Methods* (2008; editor and contributor).

**Susan Finley** is associate professor in the College of Education at Washington State University, Vancouver, where she is the creator and director of Vancouver's At Home At School program. Her interests include educational issues associated with economic poverty and homelessness, diversity, and ways of understanding and being in the world

**Uwe Flick** is professor of qualitative research at the Alice Salomon University of Applied Sciences in Berlin, Germany. He is the author most recently of *An Introduction to Qualitative Research* (4th ed., Sage, 2009), *Qualitative Research in Psychology* (Sage, 2009), *Managing Quality in Qualitative Research* (Sage, 2008), and *Designing Qualitative Research* (Sage, 2008). Dr. Flick has also been a visiting scholar at various universities, including the London School of Economics, Cambridge University, and École des Hautes Études (Paris).

**Henry Giroux** currently holds the Global TV Network Chair Professorship at McMaster University in the English and Cultural Studies Department. In 2002, he was named as one of the top fifty educational thinkers of the modern period in *Fifty Modern Thinkers on Education: From Piaget to the Present.* In 2005, he received an honorary doctorate from Memorial University in Canada. He is on the editorial and advisory boards of numerous national and international scholarly journals and serves as the editor or coeditor of four scholarly book series. His most recent books include: *Youth in a Suspect Society: Democracy or Disposability?* (PalgraveMacmillan, 2009), *Zombie Politics and Culture in the Age of Casino Capitalism* (Routledge, 2011), *On Critical Pedagogy* (Continuum, 2011), and *Education and the Crisis of Public Values* (Peter Lang, 2012). His website can be found at www.henryagiroux.com.

**Bud Goodall** is professor of communication at the Hugh Downs School of Human Communication at Arizona State University, where he has taught since 2004, having served as director of the school from 2004 to 2009. Considered a pioneer in narrative ethnography in the field of communication, he is the author of many books and articles, from *Casing a Promised Land* (Southern Illinois University Press, 1989) to *Counter-Narrative* (Left Coast, 2010), but he is most proud of his ethnographic memoir *A Need to Know: The Clandestine History of a CIA Family* (Left Coast, 2006), wherein his personal quest for the truth about his father was realized. Diagnosed with Stage 4 pancreatic cancer in the spring of 2011, he turned his attention to writing about living with cancer in a blog that is available (along with other works) on his website: http://www.hlgoodall.com.

**Jean Halley** is associate professor of sociology and anthropology at Wagner College, New York. She is the author of *Boundaries of Touch: Parenting and Adult-Child Intimacy* (University of Illinois Press, 2007), and *Seeing White: An Introduction to White Privilege and Race* (Rowman & Littlefield, 2011, with Amy Eshelman and Ramya Mahadevan Vijaya), and editor with Patricia Clough of *The Affective Turn: Theorizing the Social* (Duke University Press, 2007). She is currently completing a book titled *The Parallel Lives of Women and Cows: Meat Markets* (PalgraveMacmillan, forthcoming 2012), which is a mix of memoir and social history of cattle ranching and the U.S. beef industry.

**Mirka Koro-Ljungberg** is associate professor in the School of Human Development and Organizational Studies in Education at the University of Florida. Her work, which focuses on theoretical, methodological, and analytical developments of critical and post-positivist movements in educational research, has appeared in journals such as *Qualitative Inquiry, Qualitative Research in Psychology, Educational Researcher,* and *International Review of Qualitative Research.*

**Michal Krumer-Nevo** is professor and director of the Israeli Center for Qualitative Research of People and Societies at Ben-Gurion University of the Negev. Krumer-Nevo is the author of *Women in Poverty: Gender, Pain, Resistance* (Hakibutz Hameuachad, 2006), the first book in Hebrew to document the experiences and knowledge of women in poverty. She has also published in the areas of poverty, women, youth, and qualitative methodologies in the *Journal of Social Policy, Qualitative Inquiry, Narrative Study of Lives, Qualitative Social Work, Qualitative Studies in Education, Journal of Social Work Education, Current Sociology, Families in Society,* and the *European Journal of Social Work.*

**Luisa Maria-Rosu** is a research associate at I-STEM at the University of Illinois, Urbana-Champaign, where she is involved with the planning and development of the evaluation of iFoundry, a College of Engineering curriculum incubator seeking to transform undergraduate education for engineers.

**Robert Stake** is professor and director of the Center for Instructional Research and Curriculum Evaluation at the University of Illinois, Urbana-Champaign. He is the author of numerous books, including *The Art of Case Study Research* (Sage, 1995) and *Standards-Based and Responsive Evaluation* (Sage, 2004).

**John H. Stanfield, II** is professor of African American and African Diaspora Studies, African Studies, American Studies, International Studies, Philanthropic Studies, and Sociology, and director of the Research Program on Transcultural and Intercultural Philanthropic Studies at Indiana University, Bloomington. He is a consulting faculty member with the Fielding Graduate University School of Human and Organization Development, an honorary faculty member of Unipalmares University in São Paulo Brazil, and a recent Distinguished Fulbright Chair in American Studies and Sociology at the Catholic University in Rio de Janeiro, Brazil. He is author and editor of numerous articles and books on research methods, African American studies, philanthropy, and social theory, including most recently *Black Reflective Sociology* (Left Coast, 2011), *Historical Reflections of Black Reflective Sociology* (Left Coast, 2011), and *Rethinking Race and Ethnicity in Research Methods* (Left Coast, 2011).

**Ian Stronach** is professor of education and director of the Centre for Educational Research and Evaluation Services in the Faculty of Education, Community and Leisure at Liverpool John Moores University, United Kingdom. He was formerly Research Professor at Manchester Metropolitan University and editor of the *British Educational Research Journal*. His most recent book is *Globalizing Education, Educating the Local: How Method Made Us Mad* (Routledge, 2010).